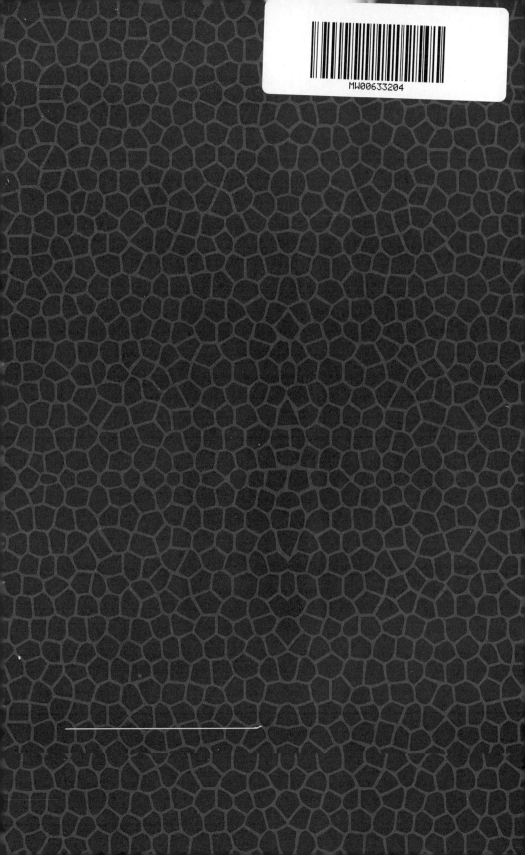

Raising a Community, a Family, and Ourselves

MOSAICA PRESS

RABBI AVRAHAM BOGOPULSKY

Raising a Community, a Family, and Ourselves

Insights from a Rabbi in San Diego

Published by Mosaica Press, Inc.
www.mosaicapress.com
info@mosaicapress.com

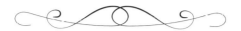

This book is dedicated in loving memory of

גיטל בת עזריאל ברוך ע״ה

Mrs. Kitty Silverman, a"h

נלב״ע ט״ז שבט תש״פ

An *eishes chayil* and the *akeres ha'bayis* of our lives

ת.נ.צ.ב.ה.

By her loving husband and children

RAPHAEL SILVERMAN

LINDA AND JOHN HIRSHLEIFER

PHILIP AND DORIT SILVERMAN

DEBORAH AND MAXWELL BROOKLER

BARBARA AND YITZCHAK FRIEDMAN

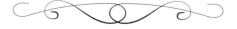

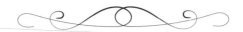

In loving memory

לעילוי נשמת

My dear mother

אמי מורתי **יוכבד** בת **צבי** ז״ל

Anita (Yocheved) Bogopulsky, z"l

נלב״ע י״ז אדר תשע״ז

Who continues to inspire us all!

ת.נ.צ.ב.ה.

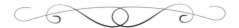

Dedicated by

EDWARD BOGOPULSKY

In honor of his children, grandchildren, and great grandchildren

שיהיו עוסקים בתורה ובמצוות

Dedicated by

TZVI AND PESSI ROSEN

In honor of their children, grandchildren, and great grandchildren

שיהיו עוסקים בתורה ובמצוות

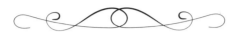

Dedicated by

ROBERT AND CLAIRE SIGAL

In honor of their children and grandchildren

This *sefer* should touch the lives of many *neshamot*,
as does the author and his wife

RABBI AVRAHAM AND REBBETZIN LEAH BOGOPULSKY

who inspire us to live more enriched lives according to Torah values.

In loving memory
לעילוי נשמת אחי הגדול
My beloved brother

ר׳ **יעקב אליעזר** ז״ל בן יבלחט״א ר׳ **יהושע העשל**

Reb Yakov Eliezer Bogopulsky, z"l

נלב״ע כ״ד ניסן תשע״ה
ת.נ.צ.ב.ה.

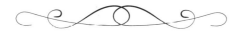

לעילוי נשמת

עטה פייגע בת קלמן ע״ה

Mrs. Edith Wiseman, *a"h*

נלב״ע ה׳ אדר תשס״ט

A woman with great vision

ת.נ.צ.ב.ה.

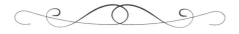

CONTRIBUTORS

Rabbi Zvi and Yehudis Solomon

Norm and Rona Orgel

Marty and Leah Mally

Doris Jaffe

Leopoldo and Marilyn Kahn

Kay Pekin

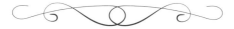

Rabbi Berel Wein

My beloved colleague Rabbi Avraham Bogopulsky has written a book of outstanding importance and relevance. It deals with Jewish life currently—communal, societal, and family. Rabbi Bogopulsky has dedicated a quarter century to the spread of Torah values and knowledge as the rabbi of the congregation in San Diego, California. He is well-known for his scholarship, insights, compassion, and wisdom. There is no doubt in my mind that this is a book that belongs on the shelves of every Jewish home library—to be studied, internalized, and appreciated.

With all best wishes and warmest regards, I remain,

Berel Wein

Rabbi Tzvi H. Weinreb

All of us are frustrated. We face difficulties in our careers, businesses, social lives, and family relationships. We turn to the writings of religious teachers, hoping that they can give us authentic spiritual guidance. Although we find their advice erudite and scholarly, too often it is far removed from our everyday reality. Rarely do we read a book written by someone who is truly familiar with our mundane routines, compassionately empathetic with our daily dilemmas, and yet capable of finding practical, helpful, and inspiring solutions in authentic Jewish sources to our troubling questions. Rabbi Bogopulsky's *Raising a Community, a Family, and Ourselves* fits the bill! It abounds with anecdotes drawn from real life and articulates the questions which really bother us. The reader finds himself saying, "That's exactly what I'm going through!" and is then astounded by Rabbi Bogopulsky's ability to find sources in our tradition—sometimes going back centuries but also quoting from contemporary sages— which address real-life issues. We frequently find ourselves in a wilderness of doubt, confusion, and despair. This book shows us paths out of that wilderness. Congratulations, Rabbi Bogopulsky. Your book is a precious gift to all who seek practical wisdom from the Jewish tradition!

Rabbi Tzvi H. Weinreb

בס"ד

Rabbi Zev Leff   הרב זאב לף

Rabbi of Moshav Matityahu   מרא דאתרא מושב מתתיהו
Rosh HaYeshiva—Yeshiva Gedola Matityahu   ראש הישיבה—ישיבה גדולה מתתיהו

D.N. Modiin 71917   **Tel: 08-976-1138** טל'   **Fax: 08-976-5326** פקס'   ד.נ. מודיעין 71917

Dear Friends,

I have had the honor and pleasure to be hosted by Rabbi and Rebbitzen Bogopulsky in their Kehila in San Diego. I was impressed with their devotion and mesiras nefesh in leading, enlightening and inspiring their community.

Rabbi Bogopulsky gave me the manuscript of the book he is soon to publish. I have read many portions of that manuscript and found it interesting, enlightening, inspiring and entertaining. Rabbi Bogopulsky presents short essays from his rich communal experience and Torah knowledge that convey practical life lessons based on various solid Torah sources. These lessons adress both individual and communal issues.

I am sure that those reading this work will be inspired to apply these lessons into their personal perspectives and conduct.

I commend Rabbi Bogopulsky for a quality presentation and pray that Hashem Yisborach bless him and his family with life, health and the wherewithal to continue to merit his community and the Jewish community at large in his many and varied ways.

Sincerely,
With Torah blessings

Rabbi Zev Leff

Table of Contents

Acknowledgments

הודו לה׳ כי טוב כי לעולם חסדו, הודו לה׳ כי טוב כי לעולם חסדו

*Thank Hashem for He is good, for His kindliness
endures forever.*

THIS *pasuk* is found twice in *Tehillim*, in *perakim* 118 and 136. In *Tehillim* 136, the refrain, "For His kindliness endures forever," is repeated in all twenty-six verses. The *Sefas Emes* explains that we declare that no act of kindliness for which we must thank God is of a temporary nature, lasting merely for a day or a year. The kindliness of Hashem endures forever; we continually reap the benefits of every act of Divine kindliness. *Tehillim* 118 opens and closes with this *pasuk* to emphasize our lifelong obligation once again to continuously thank Hashem. It is precisely because the kindliness of Hashem endures that we are obligated to repeatedly express our thanks.

After completing a second *sefer*, I have come to understand even more profoundly the impact so many people, organizations, and institutions have had on my life. The fact that I have been able to continue learning and writing is a testament to those who gave me the tools, knowledge, time, and encouragement to do so. While many of the people whom I thanked in my first book may or may not be a part of my life today, it is their influence that endures and therefore requires my gratitude and deep appreciation once more.

Cambridge Dictionary defines an "acknowledgment" as a short text at the beginning or end of a book in which the writer names people or other works that have helped in writing the book. The Jewish definition takes it to the next level: *hakaras hatov*—recognizing the good someone did for you. When attempting to thank many individuals for something, inevitably we tend to leave someone out. I fell into this trap while giving *hakaras hatov* and mentioning people and institutions in my first book that was published. A few major key individuals were omitted accidentally. Perhaps one reason I wrote another book was for the opportunity to give credit and thanks to those I missed.

Gratitude is about the present and the past. For this reason alone, I thank Hakadosh Boruch Hu for the past, present, and future of my life, for giving me the strength, health, fortitude, and insights to bring this *sefer* to the world. The publication of a book requires *siyata d'Shmaya*, Heavenly assistance, which I clearly needed and was granted. In my first book I wrote: "An often-asked question is, 'Where do I begin?' I usually suggest starting from the beginning." Unfortunately, I did not heed my own advice and did not begin thanking from the beginning.

We do not take note of all that goes into the making of something. Typically, we only appreciate what we can see, a little behind us and a little in front. Therefore, besides the institutions and individuals, I need to thank the previous generations of grandparents, great-grandparents, and beyond them, for if not for their personal sacrifices for Yiddishkeit, I and anything I have accomplished may not have been possible.

A *rebbi*'s voice and sage advice lingers and grows throughout the lifetime of the recipient. I continue to receive much needed *chizuk* and inspiration from my Rosh Yeshiva, Rabbi Berel Wein and my *rebbi*, Rabbi Leibel Reznick. Their Torah, insights, and *seichel* have woven within me the tools I continue to apply to my learning and work. This is the definition of enduring kindness and the gift of a solid foundation for a lifetime of learning. My everlasting indebtedness goes to my Rosh Yeshiva, Rabbi Wein, who helped guide and shape me for the position of being a pulpit rabbi. I would like to thank my *rebbi*, Rabbi Leibel Reznick, who has guided me and my family for the last thirty-five years. His deep knowledge and insight into Torah and life has truly shaped our family. My appreciation of their greatness only grows over time. Thank you, Rabbi Wein and Rabbi Reznick, for always being there for me.

I mention in the introduction how I came to write a second book and the interaction I experienced with Rabbi Yaacov Haber and Rabbi Doron Kornbluth. It is their vision and insight that led me to create this work. I thank them and their dedicated staff of editors, designers, and support staff, all of whom nurtured this book from its inception. The brilliance of the Mosaica Press team led by Rabbi Yaacov Haber and Rabbi Doron Kornbluth has given me the confidence to publish a second book. Their personal care and touch are only matched by their kindness, piety, and humility. I am filled with gratitude to everyone on the talented Mosaica team.

When you have the best, you stick with it. A tremendous *hakaras hatov* goes to Mrs. Elaine Lepow, who, despite her personal challenges and responsibilities, never fails to help me shape and perfect my weekly Torah messages. No matter how busy, late, or close to Shabbos it is, she always makes time to edit my work. Her dedication and encouragement are unmatched by anyone. The care, dedication, and concern for detail is evident in her editing abilities. I also benefited greatly from having a second editor (again) edit the entire book. Rabbi Eliyahu Friedman's talents were seen in editing my first book, and I again turned to him to massage the flow and convey my message to any reader from any background. Thank you, Elaine and Eliyahu, for your time, patience, and clarity. May you go from strength to strength.

From the teacher who taught me the *aleph-beis*, providing the foundation for all future learning, to the institutions and organizations responsible for guiding, nurturing, and teaching me, my gratitude knows no bounds.

Each institution I learned in, from Etz Chaim Yeshiva in Boro Park to my high school experiences in MTA and onto Yeshiva Neveh Zion in Israel, set the stage for the next level of learning. My years in Yeshiva Shaarei Torah in Monsey, first as a *bachur* and then as an *avreich*, set me on my course for life. I grew and gained from my work experiences from the Talmud Torah level, to day school *rebbi* in Binghamton, to becoming assistant rabbi in Charleston, South Carolina, at BSBI. The *rebbeim*—from yeshiva in Eretz Yisrael to Yeshiva Shaarei Torah in Monsey—gave me *chizuk* and showed me the beauty of Torah. I grew and gained from all these wonderful communities, where I developed skills in teaching Torah in Hebrew school, day school, and at the pulpit.

I was remiss once but not again. Two other institutions and people had a direct effect on who I am today. A special thank you to my uncle and aunt, Rabbi Aharon (Eric) and Libby Ziegler for providing me with a nurturing enrichment component throughout my youth, together with my Uncle David and Aunt Sonja, and all of my cousins, who supplemented a great deal of my Jewish education. My early childhood years in Agudas Achim, the shul I grew up in, had a strong influence on me. My synagogue skills were developed and learned during those years with my older cousins in how to daven, *lein*, and run a shul.

The second major influence came over a ten-year span from the end of my teen years through marriage with two children. This was the precious time I spent my summers at Camp Avraham Chaim Heller. My growth was impacted by several families and it is difficult to describe and explain how they and the supporting cast of the entire staff influenced my life. In particular, it was the mentoring of Rabbi Gershon Kramer and Rabbi Yaakov Bienenfeld and their spouses who taught me how to be a leader and influencer of people. They instilled within me the necessary lessons from which I continue to draw from to this very day. Thank you, Gershon and Miriam, and Yaakov and Feigy, for being great role models for me and my family.

The last quarter-century that I served as Rabbi of Beth Jacob, San Diego, California, has given me the opportunity to nurture and grow this beautiful Jewish community. This continues to be a genuine labor of love even with its accompanying challenges. I feel deeply privileged to have been given the opportunity to encourage and guide so many individuals and families to grow, becoming vibrant and dedicated members of our Jewish community. The families of the shul are exactly that: family. We continue to see generation after generation grow in Torah and *yiras Shamayim*. The members of my shul, friends, and family have supported me in this endeavor, and many others have contributed to the spiritual growth of our community; each one of you should live and be well. Thank you, Beth Jacob and the San Diego Jewish community, and thank you for your positive feedback, support, and encouragement of my weekly articles.

To my in-laws, R' Tzvi and Pessi Rosen, and to my father, Mr. Edward Bogopulsky, along with my mother, *a"h*, thank you for your unconditional love and support, which is a true reflection of your essence. I cannot think of any decision I made that they not only agreed to but encouraged as well. Their financial and emotional support made this project come to fruition. It is only after the passing of my mother, Anita, Yocheved bas Tzvi, that I came to utterly understand the enduring kindness she showered upon me. It will permeate within me for the rest of my life. Despite her physical absence, she continues to give and give. Thank you. They should continue to be blessed with future generations of grandchildren and great-grandchildren being *ovdei Hashem*. Hashem should bless them *u'mi'kol tuv l'olam al yechasreinu*.

To my children, Yehudis and Yaacov Kaplan, Yisrael and Malka Bogopulsky, Dovid and Malkie Bogopulsky, Hadassa and Yirmiyahu Burg, Aryeh Leib Bogopulsky, and grandchildren, Zevi, Raizy, Miri, and Yosef Kaplan, Kayla, Rella, and Gavi Bogopulsky, Ayala and Yocheved Bogopulsky, Yocheved Chava Burg, you are the reasons that Ima and I keep on pushing. The *zechus* of this *sefer* should give you all *siyata d'Shmaya* to grow in Torah and *yiras Shamayim* and to raise children and future *doros* of *bnei* and *bnos Torah*.

To the *akeres habayis*, my dear wife Leah, thank you for all your care and support. It is your drive and focus that shapes our family and me. Your investment in our family gives you more than half of the dividends that stem from this *limud haTorah*. With all that goes on, you are the sounding board of all my thoughts, helping me to shape the ideas and messages of Torah. The time and effort I spent on my learning and writing has also been your time and effort. The rewards I receive are your rewards. We all learned, and we all continue to learn from you. Thank you for who you are and for all you do.

Finally, I receive a *sipuk ha'nefesh*, a satisfaction of writing and conveying my world observations through a Torah lens. I hope you enjoy reading the lessons, parables, and words of Torah. My goal was to make you, the reader, feel the message was intended for you, and not "the other guy." The ultimate purpose is not just to read it, but rather to be inspired and live the lessons that should make us all better Jews to shine as God's chosen people to the world. My hope and prayer are that you, the reader, will draw satisfaction and spiritual nourishment through reading and learning from this *sefer* as much as I gained while writing it. Amen!

Introduction

AFTER writing and publishing my first book, *Developing a Torah Personality*, I had a feeling of satisfaction and accomplishment. The burning desire or great urge to undertake another book was the furthest thing from my mind. There was a purpose and a goal in writing and publishing my writings, and that purpose was fulfilled and completed.

Of course, as I continued writing my weekly messages connected to the *parashah* of the week, people from all over would ask, "So, when is the next book coming out?" My mind was made up: I had done it once and that was enough. For many reasons, it was not something I contemplated doing again…

All it took was a visit, an email, and a meeting for me to decide to go ahead and attempt to publish a second book.

The meeting came as a result of Doron Kornbluth visiting San Diego for a speaking engagement in another part of town, but I would not let Doron decline my hospitality. It was toward the end of 2018 when that visit occurred. Then, only a few weeks later, on January 22, 2019, I read one of the dozens of emails I receive on Torah subjects ranging from *aleph* to *tav*. This particular email was a weekly *dvar Torah* sent out to thousands of people directly by the author, Rabbi Yehoshua Alt.

Rabbi Alt merited to learn under the tutelage of Rabbi Mordechai Friedlander, *zt"l*, for close to five years. He received *semichah* from Rabbi Zalman Nechemia Goldberg, *zt"l*. Rabbi Alt has written on numerous topics for various websites and publications. The Torah piece for that

1

week was entitled "Writing" and focused on giving incredible sources and everlasting impressions on the importance and benefits to writing. With the permission of Rabbi Alt, below are a few.

The Piaseczna Rebbe, Rav Kalonymus Kalman Shapira, *zt"l* (1889–1943), who was killed in the Holocaust, invested efforts into writing whenever he could in the Warsaw ghetto. When asked why he was doing this, by those who reasoned his writings would not survive the destruction of the Holocaust, he responded, "I will do my part and write." When it became apparent to the Rebbe that the end of the ghetto, and all its inhabitants, was near, he buried his writings in a container. Eventually, these writings were found by a worker while laying a foundation for a new building in Warsaw. He gave it to the institute of Jewish History in Warsaw. The *sefer Aish Kodesh*, on "חשיבת הכתבים—the importance of writings," brings the following: The *Sefer Chassidim* writes that if Hashem reveals something to a person and he does not write it, it is as if he has stolen from Him. In the *Hagahos Bris Olam* from the *Chida* to the *Sefer Chassidim*, it is brought from the *Lev Aryeh* that in the time of the Beis Hamikdash, when one brought a *korban*, it would atone for him. And when one writes in a *sefer* a *chiddush* in what he is learning, this writing is in place of a *korban*. An allusion to this is זבח ומנחה לא חפצת...אז אמרתי הנה באתי במגילת ספר כתוב עלי"—Sacrifice and meal offering You did not desire...I have come with the scroll of the book..." (*Tehillim* 40:7–8).

The Mishnah in *Pirkei Avos* (1:6) states: "וקנה לך חבר—Acquire a friend for yourself." Another interpretation is that one should make his pen his friend, as קנה is also a quill. Through the power of the pen, much Torah can be written.

The Gemara in *Bava Basra* 10b says, "Fortunate is the one who comes to the next world, ותלמודו בידו—and his learning is in his hand." The simple meaning is that he remembers what he learned. The *Maharsha* interprets תלמודו בידו as referring to the original insights and explanations a Torah scholar commits to writing; that is תלמודו בידו—Torah that was penned by his hand. Thus, fortunate is the scholar who records his Torah thoughts because his primary learning occurs when he composes those works. Writing something down makes a far more powerful impression,

and this can help one remember it. This is hinted to in "כתב זאת זכרון"
(*Shemos* 17:14), from which we learn that writing something down
helps a person to remember it (see *Kav Hayashar*, chapter 55). For this
reason, Torah scholars are called סופרים, scribes.

Writing notes is so significant that one can have his Torah last even
after he dies. In this manner, we can understand "כתב זאת זכרון בספר" as
meaning, "Write a *sefer* so that it lives beyond you."

In the introduction to *Chovos Halevavos*, the author articulates the
personal hindrances to writing. One may feel he is unworthy of putting out a *sefer*. When Rabbeinu Bachya considered writing the *Chovos
Halevavos*, he felt that a man like himself was unworthy of authoring
such a work. He thought his powers were too limited to systemize the
material, the subject was too difficult, his knowledge too limited, and
his mind too weak to grasp the ideas. Furthermore, he did not possess
an elegant style in Arabic, in which the book would have to be written,
as that was the language best understood by the majority of his con-
temporaries. He then decided to drop his plans. After time, he began
to suspect that he had taken the easy way out; that he had been lazy,
looking for peace and quiet. He told himself that if every person who
intended to perform a good act or teach what is right and virtuous
would keep silent and stand still until he felt perfectly qualified, not
a word would have been spoken by any man since the prophets whom
Hashem had chosen as His messengers and strengthened with His
support. If every person who wanted to perfect himself with all the
best qualities—and was unable to attain them all—would then forsake
those qualities he had managed to attain, all men would be empty of
virtue and deficient in what is admirable. He saw fit to force himself
to assume the heavy burden of writing this *sefer*, to explain the subject
with whatever language he could muster.

Here are some other comments on this topic: Upon the publication of
his *sefer* on *shemiras ha'lashon*, the author was asked whether he should
have refrained from writing it because "מוטב שיהיו שוגגין ואל יהיו מזידין"—it
is preferable that they be unintentional violators and not be deliberate
ones." The Chafetz Chaim replied that if even one reader would change
his behavior as a result of his work, it would be worth all the time and

effort he had put into it. When one puts out a *sefer*, he should think the same. And that applies even if the author is the only one who changes as a result of the *sefer*.

Rabbi Aharon Leib Shteinman, *zt"l*, once remarked that even if those learning from a *sefer* will not benefit, it is nevertheless important for the author to publish it. His Torah thoughts will be organized and developed to the best of his ability. He therefore encouraged writing *sefarim*, "עשות ספרים הרבה—Make many books."

Rabbi Eliezer Papo, in his *sefer Pele Yoetz*, lauds those who are "מלקט—compile teachings." If not for them, Torah would be forgotten from us, especially in our generation where there are so many טרדות, responsibilities, and time does not allow us to learn with such diligence like the Rishonim. In every generation we need such people like the *Rambam*, *Tur*, the *Beis Yosef*, and the like, who were our eyes. Any Torah scholar upon whom Hashem bestows knowledge, and the ability to write many *sefarim*, should try to benefit the public in matters that are needed. As Chazal say in *Bava Basra* 145b: "הכל צריכין למרי חטיא—all are needful for the one who has gathered many teachings." Those who gather teachings (in the various aspects of Torah, not just halachah) are doing the biggest kindness, because it is a kindness of the soul. Those who do this are bringing merit to the public.

How should a *sefer* be printed? In the introduction to his responsa, Rabbi Akiva Eiger requested that his Torah be printed on beautiful paper with black ink and attractive letters. The reader is impressed, his mind at ease, and concentration is aroused from learning from a *sefer* in which the print is appealing. The reverse—if the print is unclear—has the opposite effect.

The last piece of the puzzle came on Friday 17 Adar 5779, the yahrzeit of my mother, Yocheved bas Tzvi, *a"h*. I went to Israel for the yahrzeit, and the opportunity to meet with the Mosaica team led by Rabbi Haber came about on that very day. It was at that meeting that Doron set up for me to meet with him and Rabbi Haber that the decision was made to go forward in producing this work that you are about to read.

Chapter I

VILLAGE
Framing the Glass

IN the course of life, we connect with many people. Some people we meet remain acquaintances while other individuals we meet become our friends. The friendships we make differ, depending upon the time in our life in which each of the friendships were formed. We have friends from grade school, high school, camp, college, and yeshiva or seminary. Typically, those friendships were made when we were single. Another set of friends are made in the workplace, most often post-college. Usually, the later stages of acquiring friends occur after we are married; those friends sometimes come about through our spouses.

I still maintain a friendship with the "guys" from high school. Despite having gone our different ways, we can still sit down for hours and reminisce about the good old days. Unfortunately, one friend from my yeshiva days has been seriously ill, fighting cancer on and off during the past number of years. I spoke to him a few days ago. We had not spoken in about three years; at that time, he was battling his third round of cancer. Prior to that, I had not spoken to him for at least ten years. On this most recent call, he said, "Thank you for calling…you're a good friend."

At that point, I pondered: What is the difference between a friend, a good friend, a great friend, and a best friend? It seemed that if I was close enough, I would have flown cross-country to be there with him. I believe, however, that such an act is reserved for a best friend. I had not spoken to him in such a long time and truly called only because he was sick.

My definitions of these different types of friends are as follows:

A friend is someone you meet and enjoy talking to, but do not have any deep connection to.

A good friend is someone with whom there is mutual caring toward one another and who remembers you in time of need.

A great friend is someone with whom you are frequently in touch and maintain close contact.

A best friend is the person who is truly close and with whom there is a mutual bond that is so strong that, regardless of the situation, in time of need, either individual will basically do anything for the other person, no matter the distance, time of day, or personal cost.

The Hebrew word for friend is *chaver*. The root of the word *chaver* means to "connect" or "join together." Friendship creates bonds that connect and join people as one. One of Yaakov Avinu's grandsons was named Chever. It is interesting to note that in the listing of the seventy souls that went down to Egypt, only four of them were great-grandsons: two from Yehudah and two from Asher. *Bereishis* (46:12) mentions the sons of Yehudah, one of whom, Peretz, had Chetzron and Chamul. Later (46:17), the Torah lists the sons of Asher, one of whom was Beriah, who, in turn, had Chever and Malkiel.

Rav Avraham Eliyahu Mokotow, in his *Sefer Haparshios*, explains the names of two of Yehudah's grandsons, Chetzron and Chamul. Yehudah, in his old age, called one grandson Chetzron, similar to the word *chisaron*, meaning "lacking" or "missing." This was to replenish what was missing due to the death of his son Er. The other grandson, Chamul, which means "spared" or "saved," was so named because Hashem had compassion upon Yehudah by blessing him with Chamul to replace his son Onan. Perhaps, as a sign of consolation, Yehudah received two of his grandsons who were the fourth generation from Yaakov. But why were the grandchildren of Asher mentioned?

The *Midrash Tzror Hamor* explains that these names were a reminder of Yaakov's blessing found later in *Parashas Vayechi*. In *Bereishis* 49:20, the Torah states: "מאשר שמנה לחמו והוא יתן מעדני מלך—From Asher shall come the richest foods; he shall provide the king's delights." The land of Asher was superior and would produce delicious food that would be brought to the kings. Therefore, his grandchildren were named Chever (Friend) and Malkiel (God the King) because they were friends to the kings.

The *Midrash Seichel Tov* explains the uniqueness of the name Chever from a verse in *Tehillim* (119:63). David HaMelech states: "חבר אני לכל אשר יראוך ולשמרי פקודיך—I am a companion to all who fear You, and to those who preserve Your precepts." The *Ibn Ezra* speaks of David HaMelech, who would seek out a companion and a friend who feared the negative commandments. David would associate with someone afraid to transgress the *mitzvos lo saaseh*, the negative mitzvos. On the other hand, the *Radak*, Rav David Kimchi, explains that David HaMelech would extend his friendship to those who hate the wicked, but he *loved* those who fear Hashem and keep His mitzvos. David says: "I love those who fear Hashem and fulfill His commandments...I want to be close to them and become their friend and companion" (ibid.)

Perhaps with this explanation we can understand the teachings of two students, Yehoshua Ben Perachya and Nitai Ha'Arbeili, whose teachings are juxtaposed to one another in *Pirkei Avos* (1:6–7). Yehoshua Ben Perachya says, "Acquire a friend for yourself," and Nitai Ha'Arbeili follows by stating, "Distance yourself from a bad neighbor."

The definition of a good neighbor is someone who is worthy of becoming your friend. These are individuals who fear God and are concerned about violating a negative commandment and also have the proper desire to fulfill the positive commandments. When looking for a place to live, what type of qualities are you seeking in a neighbor? The most important value to find is that the person be a "*chaver*," who seeks out Hashem in the best possible manner.

I would suggest that as the *b'nei Yaakov* were moving into the new neighborhood of Mitzrayim, they needed to be reminded of the value of acquiring a *chaver tov*, a "good friend," who ultimately would be a suitable neighbor as well.

In our lives, we have many different kinds of "neighbors and friends." Wherever we travel, whether on a vacation, a short trip, or relocating to a new home, we should seek out a *chaver*, a friend. Although a friend, a good friend, or even a best friend, is usually determined over time, as the friendship becomes cemented, let's make sure we follow the counsel of our Sages in making the right choice of friends. After all, our lives will largely be determined by who we surround ourselves with.

"À la carte" is a French phrase, which means "according to the menu." When a restaurant offers separately priced items, you can describe its menu as *à la carte*. The literal meaning of the French phrase is "by the card." The opposite of *à la carte* is a "*table d'hôte*," which is a "meal served at a fixed price." Industries have also adopted the phrase to mean a sales model where clients can buy individual parts rather than the whole package at once.

I have often wondered (but have not been curious enough to ask) whether people would prefer to pay a one-price full membership for their shul dues and benefits or would prefer to pay *à la carte*—per person, per event. I surmise that the most common answer would be, "We want to take full benefits but only pay the *à la carte* cost." There are organizations that do not charge for membership but surely make up the difference by charging a hefty price per event.

In my opinion, the "*à la carte*" system is not a Jewish concept when it comes to shuls, schools, and other religious organizations. Becoming a member of a community makes a statement of belonging to and supporting that community.

Membership implies that we may not agree with every policy or decision, but these disagreements should not take away from our support of the institution. Being a member of an organization such as a shul or a school is a privilege that is part of our communal responsibility.

Transitioning from old-school to new-school is easier said than done. As people grow older, the ability to adapt to constantly evolving technological developments in our fast-paced world becomes increasingly more difficult.

I am no exception to this situation. As I get older and technology advances, I find myself slipping behind, losing awareness of new apps and electronic conveniences that life offers. I only use a fraction of the functions my smartphone is capable of. Either I have lost interest in pursuing further into the cloud, or I am just getting older and losing the mental capacity for learning new technology. I am comfortable with certain advances I've adapted to but am now beginning to become reluctant to learn how to make use of even newer functions.

The truth is that many of the advances in technology have eroded the element of personal touch and human-to-human interaction. We barely need to see anyone face-to-face anymore because we can communicate instantaneously at any time, any place in the world, by pushing or stroking a few keys. There are fewer toll road collectors, thanks to E-ZPass and electronic toll roads; these innovations track every vehicle, allowing users to pay online. Then there is online banking. I do a limited amount of banking online, but I am old enough to still prefer walking into the bank and speaking with a teller or my personal banker. Certainly, online banking saves considerable physical time, but unfortunately, we lose out on the time spent on human connection.

On the subject of banking, another lost procedure is the counting of money. Today, whether it's a deposit or a withdrawal of money, a machine counts all the bills. No longer does the teller count out the money in front of you when you withdraw money. In fact, I am so old-school, I ask the teller to count out the money, even though it came out of the automated machine and, afterward, went through the counter. There is something definitive about counting out bills one by one. An impression is made as the money adds up to the sum, and it is interesting to observe the different methods tellers use for counting out the money.

Interestingly, we see the value of counting from the fact that the fourth book of the Torah is called *Sefer Hapekudim*, the "Book of

Numbers," in which Hashem displays His love for His children through conducting a census.

He counts and loves each and every one of us. Should we not take the hint and try to feel that way about each other?

Every so often, I meet someone returning from a trip who gives me regards from someone he met who knows me. I, of course, inquire where and when he met that individual and under what circumstances the conversation took place. I often send regards to someone in the same manner. I have taken this one step further and have requested, especially if someone is going to Israel, "If you meet anybody that I know, please send my best regards," as if I intentionally was giving specific regards to them! I am not sure how many people received my well-wishes, but upon occasion, if a person did receive my regards and felt good because I had expressed interest in his or her life, it would also make me feel good.

A few days ago, I overheard a conversation (I was not eavesdropping!) between two people who had friends in common. The local person said, "Please send regards to so-and-so from me when you see them." When I heard this, I was a bit bothered, and so I started to rethink my entire approach to "sending regards" or "saying hi" to someone on my behalf.

Let's be realistic, with instant communication as we know it today, it is so easy to say hello to someone without an intermediary. In fact, I was thinking that sending someone regards today just might be somewhat of an insult. We are not living two hundred years ago when just hearing from someone meant a great deal. In today's day and age, it is so simple to send a text, make a free WhatsApp call, or write an email to someone across the globe in seconds. If I truly cared to say hello, then perhaps I should do it myself rather than pass it on through an agent.

There is a halachah in Jewish law found in *Shulchan Aruch* (*Orach Chaim* 225:1) that states:

- Someone who has not seen a dear friend and is happy to see him, after a period of thirty days, recites the *berachah* "She'hechiyanu."

- If a period of over twelve months has transpired since seeing the friend, he recites the *berachah* "*Mechayeh Ha'meisim*" (Who revives the dead).
- But if a person received a letter within that time frame or was told about his well-being, then the blessing is not recited.

Many authorities rule that today, because there is so much cross-communication, it is a rarity to recite *Mechayeh Ha'meisim*. Perhaps, while reciting the *berachah* of *Mechayeh Ha'meisim* during the *Amidah*, we could think about a distant friend in order to fulfill this precept. After learning this, I reverted to the old principle that even sending or receiving regards has value, as we see it is noted vis-à-vis the *berachah*. We, nevertheless, need to understand the distinction between hearing and receiving news about someone and the joy of actually seeing that individual in person.

This idea is highlighted in *Yeshayahu* (52:8). The *Navi* states: "קול צפיך נשאו קול יחדו ירננו כי עין בעין יראו בשוב ה' ציון—The voice of your watchmen, they raised a voice, together they shall sing, for eye to eye they shall see when the Lord returns to Zion." The prophet, through *ruach ha'kodesh* (Divine spirit), paints a picture for us explaining how God is going to return to Tzion in the future.

The Yadvana Rav, in his *sefer Shaar Bas Rabim*, gives a parable:

> Behold! A man has only one son who is incredible in every possible way. The father will look and see in the eyes of his son that which he is lacking and pray on his behalf in order to make sure he has everything and is complete. The son is also constantly looking through the eyes of the father to understand that which he wants and what he needs. When it appears that the son is looking to do good and to help his father, the mercy of the father upon the child is aroused. But if the father becomes angry with the son and, as a result, separates and distances himself from his son, then it would not be possible to say they saw into each other's eyes to know what their needs are—because they are far apart. As a result, if the son wanted something from the father, he would need to shout in a loud voice. If the father

wanted to daven for his son, he would need to go into his son's empty room, the place where he would always see his son, and be aroused to pray for mercy on his behalf and lament to how desolate is this room now that his son is no longer here.

The Yadvana Rav is simply using the analogy of how the father and the son—Hashem and His children, the Jewish People—parted ways. For a long time, we, the children, have had to raise our voices whenever we needed something from Hashem. After Hashem hears our pleas and cries, He searches out the rooms that His children have occupied over the centuries of exile in order to have compassion and to show mercy on them. Yeshayahu HaNavi prophesizes the word of Hashem that, in the future times of Mashiach, we will no longer have to call out but rather will see each other eye to eye.

In times of Mashiach, it will not be necessary to send regards and actively make that effort to connect from one to another. Rather, we will all be together. On a deeper level, in times of Mashiach, which will be a time of peace and complete unity among Klal Yisrael, the Jewish People will see eye to eye with each other and will live in peace and harmony. With friends, we understand that there is a greater and deeper relationship when people are closer together. Conversely, when friends are apart, the relationship requires reaching out and connecting: sending regards, calling, texting, etc. There is, however, nothing better than seeing someone you feel close to in person.

It is difficult to keep up with the speed of technology. Today's newest gadget, application, or program is in tomorrow's recycle bin. As I explained above, I personally try to keep up with the techies, but as I get older, I fall behind more and more. By the time I finish writing this commentary, it will be old-school material. I am always torn in my thinking as to whether I should work to keep up with the younger generation, more up-to-date with the constantly changing technology, or give up and live contentedly in the old world which, in many cases, can be a much safer route. The newest techie devices often may not be proper or appropriate. I personally have set boundaries on different means of communication such as texting, email, Twitter, and Facebook. Furthermore, I think everyone should have a well thought-out line in the sand.

One application that I have become intrigued with is WhatsApp. One of the major features in which WhatsApp has an advantage over traditional texting is the ability to create a group chat that everyone can see, read, and reply to simultaneously. Every individual can make his own direct WhatsApp to one user in a group or to one hundred users in a group. Within my family circles there are a few WhatsApp groups: one with my immediate family, another that is expanded to cousins, and a third to a larger group that includes family in Israel. When I was a young boy, most of my cousins lived within a half-mile of each other. Our families made a concentrated effort to get together on special occasions with the other cousins who lived a car ride away. There was no need to call someone up and schmooze because we saw each other all the time. Now, a generation or two later, families have spread out to different cities and even different countries. There are, of course, cheaper phone plans today, allowing families and friends to "reach out and touch someone" or to connect on Facebook or Skype, but those connections tend to be only one-on-one. WhatsApp makes us feel as though we are all sitting around in the same room talking to each other; everyone feels as if they see and hear what is being communicated. I have been communicating to nieces and nephews of whose lives, if not for this application, I would probably not know anything about. WhatsApp has brought a new kind of family bonding that I believe has not existed for a long time. Regardless of the thousands of miles that may separate families, this application effectively brings everyone together; how much more so with Zoom today. While we need to be very guarded about technology, it has its advantages as well!

There are certain things Hashem puts into the world specifically to bring people together. Through certain mitzvos, God helps the Jewish People to bond together. This bonding ranges from the level of immediate family members to national issues and events, particularly those that directly affect the Jewish People. One of the mitzvos that bind us together is that of the half-shekel.

The contribution of a half-shekel was used for census counting and to cover the costs of communal sacrifices. By the time King Yehoash assumed the crown, the first Beis Hamikdash was approximately 150 years old and in need of some repairs. The king told the Kohanim that any money that came in from the annual half-shekel, any self-valuation of a person, or any donation that a man brought in as a result of an uplifted heart should go toward repairing the Beis Hamikdash. The term used for repairing the Beis Hamikdash is *"bedek haBayis."* Years had passed and unfortunately the repairs that the Kohanim were supposed to take care of never happened. The *Radak* explains that the Kohanim were waiting with the intention of not beginning the work until they collected enough money to complete the entire job of fixing all the cracks and deepening crevices of the walls. The king suspected that they were keeping or stealing money as the donations came in, and eventually, he instructed the Kohanim to repair things as soon as the money arrived. The Kohanim were insulted, and a new system of collection was put into place.

Eventually, the repairs were finished and the project of *bedek haBayis* was completed. The Beis Hamikdash is the house that the Jewish People come to that makes us into one large family. The shekel was the mechanism for creating a bond, forming a common goal and purpose for the Jewish People. The shekel directly created a bond because everyone gave the same half-shekel, demonstrating equality. Just as a family should conduct itself to foster the atmosphere that all the children be treated equally, so too the mitzvah of the half-shekel fostered this sense as a national family. Furthermore, the physical purpose of the shekel being used to fix the walls of the house is similar to the bonds being created when brothers, sisters, cousins, aunts, uncles, parents, and grandparents do things to come together.

Communication and relationship-building promotes bonding within the home. The Torah reading of the half-shekel should be a reminder for us to attempt to do things that will create stronger and more meaningful relationships with individuals with whom we would otherwise lose touch.

The food industry is probably the largest industry in the world. Numerous auxiliary businesses and hundreds of workers are involved in the preparation and distribution of meat from the time an animal is processed until it reaches your mouth. Industrial chefs in the ever-expanding food industry create new recipes and food preparation ideas, introducing new foods and products to this worldwide marketplace.

While modern medical and nutritional research continuously expound upon the importance of eating healthy, beneficial foods, halachah affords us a loftier approach to food intake, often through restrictions.

Some examples:

- On Sukkos we can eat what we want (or what we should), but we cannot eat *wherever* we want.
- On Pesach we can eat wherever we want, but we cannot eat *whatever* we want.
- On Pesach we are strictly governed by the laws of *kashrus*.
- On Shavuos we can eat where and what we want, but we practice other customs and eat dairy and then meat, specifically in that order.

There are also curious conventions that develop over time concerning how we eat. At a typical Shabbos *kiddush*, people look forward to taking a bit of white fish or a sliver of herring with onion to layer onto their crackers. Children are seen mushing tuna or egg salad between two crackers, and then, of course, there are the now-famous Oreo-style cookies where everyone secretly pulls the cookies apart to lick the cream. I find it intriguing to observe how people need to combine an item with a cracker rather than taking a bite of tuna and then eating the cracker separately. There is something special and unique about putting and eating foods together.

The modern concept of a sandwich, using slices of bread (as found within the Western world) can be traced back to eighteenth-century Europe. However, the use of some kind of bread or bread-like substance placed under some other food, or used to scoop up and wrap some other type of food, long predates the eighteenth century, and is found in numerous much older cultures worldwide.

The first written usage of the English word "sandwich" appeared in Edward Gibbon's journal, in longhand, referring to "bits of cold meat" as a "Sandwich." It was named after John Montagu, the fourth Earl of Sandwich, an eighteenth-century English aristocrat. It is said that he ordered his valet to bring him meat tucked between two pieces of bread. Others, observing this new food combination, began ordering "the same as Sandwich!" It is commonly said that Lord Sandwich was fond of this form of food because it allowed him to continue playing cards, particularly Cribbage, while eating, without using a fork, and without getting his cards greasy from eating meat with his bare hands (Wikipedia).

On the Seder night we recall Hillel the Elder making a sandwich of meat, from the *korban Pesach*, and *maror* by placing these items between two pieces of matzah as a reminder of the Beis Hamikdash, the Holy Temple in Jerusalem. At the Seder there are a few references to Temple times. How does the sandwich of Hillel the Elder cause us to remember the Beis Hamikdash?

The night of the Seder is filled with references to the joining together of the Jewish People. At the very beginning of the Seder, we invite the hungry and poor to the meal, and even prior to the Seder we make sure everyone has the ability to fulfill the mitzvos of the night. We read of great rabbis joining together for a Seder and discussing the four sons, who are representative of all different types of Jews, coming together for the family Seder. The night the Jews left Egypt, every family huddled together in their homes and demonstrated a sense of unity. During the period when the Beis Hamikdash stood there was no greater time of peace in the world. Peace can only come about through unity, through openly and intentionally supporting each other and working to respect each other. The symbolism of *korech*, the sandwich, is to teach and repeatedly remind us that if we come together we will reach the level necessary to once again have a Beis Hamikdash. Hillel's sandwich alludes to a lesson that teaches us the importance of Jews coming together. It is worthy to mention that the root letters of "*korech*" are *chaf-reish-chaf*, which can also be read as "*krach*," meaning a city in which people live together and are not dispersed by distance.

The Torah often discusses the unity and togetherness of the Jewish People. One famous example is in *Vayikra* (16:17), where the Torah states: "וכל אדם לא יהיה באהל מועד בבאו לכפר בקדש עד צאתו וכפר בעדו ובעד ביתו ובעד כל קהל ישראל—And there shall be no man in the tent of meeting when he [the Kohen Gadol] goes in to make atonement in the holy place until he comes out, and made atonement for himself, and for his household, and for all the assembly of Israel." Rabbi Moshe Teitelbaum explains the need for the Kohen Gadol to atone for everyone's sins. If someone became impure due to a sin and lacked atonement, they could not come to the Beis Hamikdash. In order to allow everyone to come, the Kohen Gadol cleared their slates of sin, so that all of Klal Yisrael were completely atoned, thereby allowing the entire Jewish People to come and gather together before Hashem and for us, in turn, to behold the Shechinah (Hashem's presence). It was the act of the Kohen Gadol that brought togetherness, unity, and the feeling of equality among the Jewish People.

Foods have a certain taste and flavor when eaten independently, yet often taste quite different—and are even enhanced—when eaten together. The Jewish People could have done *teshuvah* on their own leading up to the day of Yom Kippur, but they would have run the risk of someone being left out. The Kohen Gadol, acting on everyone else's behalf, guaranteed their atonement, opening the path for the Jewish People to come together to be "sandwiched" in an attempt to seek out Hashem.

The Torah depicts the Jewish People at Har Sinai as "like one man with one heart." The Jewish People are great and individually worthy and precious; but when we join together—when we "sandwich" ourselves, each of us with each other—we are a People, an example of all that is good in the world.

An essential trait for any "living" language is that expressions, usage, and definitions of words evolve over time. Dictionaries and thesauruses give multiple explanations and substitutions for words, phrases, idioms, and jargons that are used to express context and situations. Sometimes the use of words acquires different meanings as we progress through our lives. For example, as a teenager, if I heard or shouted the words "home run," it literally meant just that—someone had rounded all four bases during a game. But in the colloquial sense of the word, when someone says that he or she "hit a home run," it might mean he did a fantastic job.

I recently encountered one of those words that I enjoyed when I was in grade school but have come to despise in my adult life. I had purchased a new piece of exercise equipment through Amazon, complete with free delivery. Not fully appreciating the value of it coming assembled, I thought that I would be able to easily put it together. Unfortunately, my memory did not serve me well. The last time I bought a new barbecue grill, I bought the floor model that was ready to go because at that time I did remember the previous experience of buying a grill out of the box—which required assembly. At the time of ordering that grill, I was too cheap to spend the extra twenty-five dollars on assembly. Furthermore, the advertisement on the box stated: "Assemble in minutes." Little did I know that it would take me 240 minutes to get the grill assembled. Therefore, when I had the opportunity to buy it preassembled, I grabbed it. Now fast-forward to the new machine. Thanks to my memory lapse and my enthusiastically naive attitude that I could put together the elliptical, I never thought of paying extra to have it assembled. After one week of having a huge box in our kitchen, I gave up on the thought of assembling it myself and called Amazon to take it back. The company offered to send someone to assemble it at about half the cost of the machine itself. Amazon offers a home service that will come to assemble your purchase through them at about a fifth of the purchase price. Ultimately, I hired a local person for the same Amazon price to assemble it for me.

I now cringe when I hear the word "assemble," but this was not always the case. In my youth I got excited when I heard the word "assembly" because that meant more time outside the classroom. I am not sure if the word assembly is used today in elementary or high school, but back in the day, I looked forward to any time there would be an assembly, preferably during a secular class. As a young boy, I did not fully appreciate the experience of the assembly. I simply enjoyed getting out of class and attending a gathering where we could relax and not need to take notes. There was no requirement to pay attention, and we were not held accountable for the purpose of the gathering. My euphoria at having an assembly was the typical reaction—and immaturity—of a youngster.

Neither my peers nor I appreciated the purpose and benefit to the concept of "assembly" and its implications. The fact that the entire school (from the youngest kindergarteners to the really big eighth-graders!) all attended the same event was a statement all its own. The unity and purpose as a solid body coming together was the unsung victory of the cause under which we came to unify. There was an incredible silent message felt by the participants of the assembly.

Unfortunately, our society, including our Jewish community, is lacking this powerful message. Do people understand or even really appreciate the value of an assembly? The secret of the Jewish People's success was the "assembly"—the meeting of the whole—that we read in the story of leaving Mitzrayim.

The Torah states in *Shemos* (10:9): "ויאמר משה בנערינו ובזקנינו נלך בבנינו ובבנותינו בצאננו ובבקרנו נלך כי חג ה' לנו—'Young and old alike we will go,' replied Moses. 'We will go with our sons and our daughters, with our sheep and our cattle. It is a festival to God for *all* of us.'" In the previous verse, Pharaoh, after being menaced by the plagues and second-guessed by his advisors, gives in slightly by almost allowing the Jews to leave Egypt, but catches himself. Instead of allowing the Jews to completely leave he asks Moshe and Aharon, "*Mi va'mi ha'holchim*—But exactly who will be going?" Pharaoh is reluctant to send *all* the Jews away, while Moshe and Aharon recognize the importance of *everyone* leaving together!

Rav Moshe Elyakim Hopshtein (1757–1828), the second Kozhnitzer Rebbe and son of the *Avodas Yisrael*, explains the concept of the young and old in the *pasuk*. He does not learn that Moshe was stating, "with our young," but rather, "like in our youth...in our old age we will go." The measure a person reaches in behavior and activity during youth will determine and be a foreteller for the same enthusiasm in later years.

The Jewish People will always "go" with zest and zeal, always climbing higher and higher. There is a great advantage that old age often brings to society, carrying within it the blessings from life's experiences. Life is compared to wine; wine will be better with age only if the wine in its youth was good. If the wine was bad to begin with, as it ages, it will turn into bitter vinegar. The later years are connected to and draw from the younger years—like the flame of a candle.

A community that abandons its young is compared to an old age home, and a community that forces its seniors into the corners of the room turns those corners into an orphanage! Fortunate are the young whose wisdom of its elders are like a candle at their feet, and fortunate are the elders that the flame of the young strengthens them.

In general, there is a great deal of enthusiasm about Judaism among children. Unfortunately, at times, the parents of those children (who themselves were once enthusiastic about Judaism) feel a sense of slavery to the rigors of a religious Orthodox lifestyle. The parents' wine was at one point very fine, but if it was not properly stored, it may have turned sour. We, the older generation, parents and grandparents, must remain vigilant in our attitude toward our excitement of Torah and Yiddishkeit. Devoid of this vigilance, there will no longer be a younger generation from whom our future will thrive and grow.

I typically do not quote non-Jewish sources, but the words of Harry Chapin's "Cat's in the Cradle" speak directly to this issue. If I can take the liberty to modify the refrain to be "When are you going to do the things you sent me to yeshiva/school for, Dad?" "I don't know when, but we'll get together then. You know we'll do it then." "However, as we all should know, 'then' will never come back again, Dad. You know it will never come back 'then.'" We need everyone on this journey of life to live and flourish through the day-to-day, week-to-week challenges of a full, rigorous, religious, observant Jewish life. We need the commitment of both the young and the old in order for us, the Jewish People, to go forward just as we did when we left Mitzrayim. Moshe Rabbeinu responded to Pharaoh, "Let my people [with the young and the old] go!"

A community needs everyone—young and old!

Throughout the course of our lives, we will meet those who lead and those who follow, those who are loners and those who need to be with others. We surely appreciate an individualistic approach to life; however, those who choose to live and work apart from others often lose out on the advantages of connecting with people. A person gains professionally when he has the opportunity to ask questions of colleagues, not exist alone on an island bereft of the experience of sharing information and expertise. An attorney who works for a law firm will have access to sharing ideas and information with other legal minds in order to discuss complex or difficult cases. Alternatively, someone who works for himself may limit his access to what could be critical information.

There is a Talmudical method of learning called "*klal and prat*," which means, "the general and the specific." The intention here is not to delve into the particulars of this Talmudic analysis, but rather to borrow the terminology to more clearly describe two aspects of the role a Jew has within the community. Every Jew has personal and communal responsibilities, and at times these obligations conflict. In most cases, the communal obligation overrides the personal one. There are clear situations in which halachah determines what takes precedence, the personal or communal.

Life situations are not always black and white. There are abstract or theoretical quandaries in which we find ourselves on a regular basis: what to do or what not to do vis-à-vis my needs and those of the greater community. Often, *derech eretz* will guide us in certain spheres. A few illustrations will make this message clear:

- I am sitting at my table on Friday night, exhausted from a long week. There is a *shalom zachor* in the community and I am thinking of reasons why I should not or do not have to go. Even though I may have good reason not to go, I need to put my own agenda aside to attend a communal *simchah*.
- There is a *simchah* in shul. A family sponsors an open-invitation lunch, inviting the entire community to join them in their particular celebration. Too often, people display the audacity to

just eat and leave when it suits them, paying no regard to the fact that the meal has not concluded. It is rude to eat and run. Imagine how you would feel if you invited guests to your home for a Shabbos meal, and as soon as they finish eating they got up and left: no goodbye, good Shabbos, thank you, or mazel tov.

- Sometimes a shul holds particular communal gatherings, such as *shalosh seudos*, that require everyone's participation in order for it to be successful. In this case, it would be a lack of *derech eretz* for someone to leave to go learn in the *beis midrash* just when a young man gets up to speak.

The point is that every individual (the *prat*) needs to put aside his or her own desires for the betterment of the *klal* and join the *tzibbur* in whatever it is doing. "*B'rov am hadras Melech*—With a multitude of people there lies greater honor to the King." This *pasuk* from *Mishlei* (14:28) is the "positive command."

The flip side, or negative command, is "*Al tifrosh min ha'tzibbur*—Do not separate from the community" (*Pirkei Avos* 2:5).

Rabbeinu Bachya explains the importance and significance of "*B'rov am hadras Melech*" in the context of the "King" referring to Hashem. A king's greatness comes from the fact that there are a multitude of people supporting him. The king has assumed rulership over all sectors of his society. If his support falters, then he becomes susceptible to the whim of the individuals, and his kingship is threatened. He can be transformed into a figurehead or a ruler who needs to apply force to justify his rule over the people. Lacking honor, he is viewed as unworthy to rule. When subjects of a land honor their leader, he is truly the king.

When we say God is One, it does not only refer to Hashem but also incorporates the Jewish People supporting the King and being there with Him as one. Each individual needs to put aside his or her own individuality for the sake of doing what is in the best interest of the *klal*—the community.

This principle extends to our family and other close relationships that we must nurture. Life is not about *me*; it is about *us*. The "I" must be set aside, ready to join the group, ready to give of oneself for the betterment of the whole—the *klal*. This is the lesson Chazal is teaching us regarding how to lead by example for our peers and our children.

In the long run, an individual will benefit more from being part of the *tzibbur* than acting on his own as the *yachid*, individual. By participating with the *klal* we each contribute to the power of the whole, giving recognition and proper respect to our King.

During my many years in San Diego, I have witnessed hundreds of visitors who have come through the doors of our shul, Beth Jacob. Some visit for just a brief time while others choose to stay longer. There is the person who drops in to catch a *Minchah* and those who flee the cold weather, enjoying our community for a few months. The duration of a person's stay does not necessarily correlate with the impact on the community; sometimes those who pass through only briefly leave a lasting impression on the community. I try to get to know our visitors a bit—some more, some less. For many years we had a group of guests dubbed the "Snowbirds," a group of older retired or semi-retired couples who joined us for a few weeks to two months.

Not too long ago, Mr. Manny Mittelman, *z"l*, left this world after ninety-four years, leaving over one hundred direct descendants who were born after he and his beloved wife of seventy years, Bessie, survived the Holocaust. I watched his funeral from Eretz Yisrael, where I was at the time, and was moved deeply by the ninety minutes of eulogies that were so aptly delivered by current and past communal leaders from the Detroit community in which he lived. This was a service I recommend listening to. I will add an insight into who he was based upon the funeral itself.

Viewing the funeral, I paid attention to both the eulogies and to the people who delivered them. Mr. Mittelman was involved in all aspects of the Detroit Jewish community. He was associated with every type of Jew across the spectrum of the Orthodox world. He was a part of shuls, schools, *kollelim*, from the left to the right, from modern to Chassidic and everything in between. The eulogizers were from every camp within the Jewish world. The same could be said within his own family of children, grandchildren, great-grandchildren, and great-great-grandchildren, as they all grew up in his house and are all religious, observant Jews representing all kinds of stripes and colors. His own children, from Chassidic to modern, make up an incredible microcosm of the Jewish People. He accomplished all of this with the help, support, love and encouragement of his life partner, Mrs. Bessie Mittelman, who should live and be well, who contributed actively and meaningfully to the shared life they built together.

Throughout the eulogies, the video camera remained stationary, focusing on the podium from where the rabbis and family members spoke. I am sure that had the camera been rotated, scanning the overflowing crowd of people in attendance, we would have seen a similar image of members of the entire Jewish community from one spectrum to the other. Mr. Mittelman had the uncanny ability to not only relate to everyone but to bring all factions together for one primary purpose: the honor of the Ribbono Shel Olam, the Creator of the World. This ability was not limited to religious differences; it included people of all ages, from those who were older than he to young children. I have an eternally memorable picture of my own grandson reading to him from a siddur. He taught wisdom through the pearls of Torah that would spew from his lips; he demonstrated how to live as a Jew by being a role model for everyone, always displaying his *yiras Shamayim* and *ahavas Yisrael*.

Manny Mittelman's ability to bring Jews together is consistent with the purpose and goals that Moshe aspired to in the desert with the Jewish People, particularly regarding the service and role of the *Mishkan*, as it states in *Shemos* 35:1: ויקהל משה את כל עדת בני ישראל ויאמר אלהם אלה הדברים אשר צוה ה' לעשת אתם. The Sochatchover Rebbe says that the introduction to the *Mishkan* is the understanding of "*Vayakhel*" and the idea of gathering together. The Jewish People stood at Har Sinai, gathered together as *ish echad*—like "one man":

- Up until the time of the *Mishkan*, independent, private altars known as *bamos* were permitted. Anyone could bring a sacrifice at any time or place.

- Once the Mishkan was erected, the private *bamos* were forbidden. Everyone was required to bring their sacrifices to the *Mishkan*. The existence of the Mishkan brought everyone together; it rallied all to one place.

But this was regarding the building of the *Mishkan* prior to the sin of the *Eigel HaZahav*, the Golden Calf. The *Shem MiShmuel* explains that after the sin of the Golden Calf, the only way to build the *Mishkan* was through the power of togetherness, by bringing Klal Yisrael together as one. Before the sin it was possible to build even with the strength of one part, even with the effort of one single individual. The midrash states in *Parashas Terumah*: "Hashem said to Moshe that even one Jew is able to build the *Mishkan*." The verse states: "Any man who gives from his heart" can build the *Mishkan*. Therefore, in *Parashas Terumah*, which is prior to the *Eigel HaZahav*, there is no mention of "*Vayakhel*."

The word "*Vayakhel*"—referring to when Moshe gathered the nation—is identical to Mitzvah #612, which is "*Hakhel*." Once every seven years, on Chol Hamoed Sukkos, the king of Israel would gather Klal Yisrael—all of the men, women, and children—and read selections from the Torah. The mitzvah of *Hakhel* was all-inclusive. There were no distinctions between one Jew and another. The mitzvah reestablished a certain togetherness of Am Yisrael and acceptance toward one another. This was the unique ability, the rare quality that Mr. Mittelman possessed, and demonstrated throughout his life.

This is what we should all be aiming for—building warm, accepting, and vibrant communities.

One Shabbos I experienced the ironic situation of two

events coinciding thousands of miles apart. My son's Litvishe yeshiva in Israel chartered a plane that flew the entire student body and administration to Mezhibuzh in the Ukraine in order to spend Shabbos at the burial site of the founder of Chassidus, Rabbi Yisrael ben Eliezer, more commonly known as the *Besh"t* or the Baal Shem Tov. While in Mezhibuzh, they also visited the gravesite of Rabbi Levi Yitzchak of Berditchov. Both the Baal Shem Tov and Rav Levi Yitzchak of Berditchov were icons of the Chassidic world and movement. The Lithuanian-style yeshiva received an infusion of fervor, drawing powerful energy from the aura of the Chassidic masters, hundreds of years since their passing.

That very same Shabbos, thousands of miles away in San Diego, my wife and I hosted a Belzer Chassid from Boro Park for Shabbos, who was stranded here while on a business trip. The Chassid dressed in full regalia—*bekeshe* with *shtreimel*—celebrated, experienced, and received an infusion of some Litvishe Judaism.

While a student, I primarily studied in Lithuanian-style yeshivos that adhere to the emphasis of textually based learning. This style of learning contrasts with the Chassidic emphasis on singing, dancing, and eating in the service of Hashem.

A bit of background: The Chassidic movement was founded a little over three hundred years ago, circa 1700, by the Baal Shem Tov. The Lithuanian leadership at the time took exception to this newly-founded manner of *avodas Hashem* (service to God) and vehemently opposed it, hence becoming known as the Misnagdim, literally, "the ones against." The separation between these two groups remained steadfast for about two hundred years. After the Holocaust, which had largely decimated both the Lithuanian and the Chassidic worlds, the feelings of difference became less threatening, and the acknowledgement of each movement took hold. While each group was rebuilding independently, by the early 1970s, the groups had merged in certain areas of Jewish life. Orthodox Jewish leadership was shared between the Lithuanian Roshei Yeshiva and the Grand Rabbis of the various sects of Chassidim. Chassidim began enrolling in some Litvishe yeshivos, while many Litvish or *yeshivish* individuals began to adopt certain customs and practices from the Chassidim.

Two differences stood out during the visit of the Belzer Chassid: one regarding food, the other regarding prayer. He did not know where he would end up for Shabbos and had brought food in case he would end up staying in a hotel room by himself over Shabbos. Through an old SEED *bachur*, he connected to me, and we hosted him for Shabbos, along with all his *heimishe* food. The loose meaning of *heimish* is "from the home," but its intended meaning in this case was food that would be acceptable to certain standards of *kashrus*.

The following may seem odd, but our guest chose to eat his own food and this did not bother us one iota. On the contrary, I wanted him to feel at home, and whatever it takes to make a guest feel welcome is certainly worth that effort. The fact that he ate food with the specific *hechsherim* that he adheres to did not bother me. We shared beautiful Shabbos meals together, albeit with different foods. The *kuntz*, the trick, is to find the commonalities and not the differences. We became good friends over Shabbos through demonstration of genuine respect and admiration for each person's right to his or her standards. Such overt respect builds deep appreciation for mutual understanding and friendship.

The other difference was that many Chassidic dialects pronounce the Hebrew vowel "*oo*" as "*ee*," hence the word "*hu*" is pronounced as "*hee*." Even though "*hu*" in Hebrew (הוא) means "he" and the word "*he*" in Hebrew (היא) means "she," it is still an acceptable pronunciation. In fact, Jews throughout the world have different pronunciations, yet all such variances are acceptable for the constituents of that group. There are accepted pronunciations in the Sephardic world, yet the Teimanim (Yemenites) have their own variances. These differences are fueled through the local influence and traditions that were maintained and held on to throughout the exile. While we are aware that *krias haTorah* should be heard within each group's custom and dialect, an Ashkenazic non-Chassid will fulfill his obligation even when hearing a different-sounding word. In *Sefer Vayikra* we are challenged by the many times the words הוא and היא are used, particularly when reading about the sacrifices.

The Jewish People have endured a long *galus* and have developed in many different yet complimentary ways. Whether Sephardim, Ashkenazim, Chassidim, or other variations, we are a part of each other for better or for worse. As far as Chassidim and Misnagdim are concerned, I think in today's world there is a little Misnagid or Litvak in every Chassid and a little Chassid in every Litvak. *Am Yisrael Chai!*

Community is central to Judaism.

What is the center of the community?

The shul.

I was born and raised in Boro Park, a neighborhood in Brooklyn, New York. My family lived within a few blocks of two sets of aunts, uncles, and cousins. My mother, a"h, has a brother, Rabbi Ziegler, who was the rabbi of a small shul where we all davened. All my cousins and I learned how to daven and lead the prayers for Shabbos morning at that shul. My cousin Duvy and I are the same age. We started at the lower end of the ladder by concluding the davening on Friday night and Shabbos morning with *Yigdal* and *Adon Olam*, later graduating to *Ein K'Elokeinu*, then to *Pesukei D'Zimra*, and ultimately—after bar mitzvah—to *Shacharis* and *Mussaf*. The opportunity we had was not wasted as we all learned the skills involved in conducting services, from being the *gabbai* to giving *divrei Torah*, and even learning how to run a shul. Some of my cousins became pulpit rabbis, but even those who did not are fully capable of doing so.

I spent every Shabbos afternoon at the house of my cousin (the rabbi's son). We played board games for hours and reviewed some of what we had learned during the week with his father, my Uncle Eric. *Shalosh seudos* was spent with my Aunt Libby, enjoying her amazing deviled eggs. From there we went to shul, and after Havdalah, as my uncle, the rabbi, was conducting "shul business," he instructed and encouraged us to clean and tidy up the shul. My uncle gave us twenty-five cents per week to put all the *Chumashim* and siddurim back onto their respective shelves. At the time, someone may have accused my uncle of violating child-labor laws. For me, looking back at that small investment in demonstrating the *kedushas beis ha'k'nesses*, the holiness of respecting and maintaining the shul, became a part of my inner self, and it was an invaluable lesson. When someone takes care of something, he ultimately shows respect for it and its environs. The lessons of tidying up a shul have remained with me for life: caring for a shul has been instilled deep inside of me. Therefore, upon entering or exiting a shul, I am drawn to putting chairs back in their places, throwing out the papers and tissues, and organizing the *sefarim*. Even today, I automatically tidy up, foregoing the twenty-five cents that I rightfully earned. This practice of caring for the shul and its property strengthened me in areas of *kavod beis ha'k'nesses*, honor and respect to a shul. To this I owe a debt of gratitude and *hakaras hatov* to my Uncle Eric—Rabbi Ziegler—my Aunt Libby, and my cousin Duvy. They gave me that framework during those early, formative years. I always wondered where my uncle had identified this essential practice, especially for young children. I came upon the answer, which is found in a piece related to the *Mishkan*.

The Torah states in *Shemos* (39:43): "וירא משה את כל המלאכה והנה עשו אתה כאשר צוה ה' כן עשו ויברך אתם משה—When Moshe saw that all the work had been done exactly as God had ordered, he blessed all the workers." *Rashi* explains that Moshe said to them, "יהי רצון שתשרה שכינה במעשה ידיכם—May it be His will that the Divine Presence [Shechinah] abide in the work of your hands, ויהי נעם ה' אלוקינו עלינו, ומעשה ידינו כוננהו—and let the graciousness of Hashem be upon us and the work of your hands."

> The Maharsham, in his sefer Techeiles Mordechai, explains the double usage of "the work had been done," based upon the Alshich's commentary on the verse "V'asu li mikdash," at the beginning of Parashas Terumah, which explains that in addition to the actual building of the Mishkan itself, there is an additional component of building our relationship with Hashem. The verse, "Make me a sanctuary so that I can dwell in it," is, in actuality, two parts: the first half refers to the physical building, while the last words refer to a place for Hashem to reside within each of us. Thus, in addition to the work that was done to build the physical structure, the spiritual structure was also constructed within each individual. Based upon these two components, Moshe blessed the people. "U'maaseh yadeinu konenah aleinu" is the physical building, while "u'maaseh yadeinu koneneihu" is the completion of the individual. The Midrash Tanchuma (Nasso 29) understands the Shechinah of Hashem as resting within those whose handiwork was and continues to be a part of the Mishkan. Today's Mishkan is

represented in every community shul. Moshe blessed the people
for Olam Hazeh when the Jews of the desert built the Mishkan.
HaKadosh Baruch Hu will bless us with Olam Haba when the
upkeep of the Mishkan, or shul, is maintained.

The book of *Shemos* ends with the completion of the *Mishkan's* building. At the conclusion of each *sefer* we call out the words "*Chazak chazak
v'nischazek*—Be strong, be strong, and be strengthened." With the accomplishment of building the *Mishkan*, the Jews became stronger, forti-
fying their identity and connection to Hashem. When one takes out time
and puts forth effort to build something, he cherishes it. Subsequent to
the construction comes the upkeep and maintenance, whether it was
for the *Mishkan*, Beis Hamikdash, or for every *beis k'nesses* in today's
day and age. The ongoing commitment to maintain and beautify the
Mishkan strengthens those who do the work, so they may grow in their
attachment to the Occupant of the *Mishkan*, namely God.

Our *Mishkan*—our shuls—stand as the place in which Hashem
resides. We can strengthen the physical building by donating to fix,
repair, and maintain the physical structure, and by keeping it clean.
We strengthen our commitment through those acts. Second, the more
involved we are in what goes on at shul and community events, the
better. In doing so, we strengthen ourselves and form an ever-deeper
love and commitment to Hashem. If we all participate in both aspects,
each of us will "*chazak*"—strengthen—ourselves so that collectively
we, as a community, will reach the level of "*v'nischazek*," and we will all
come to be strengthened by each other's involvement.

I have visited and prayed at many different shuls throughout my
life. As a pulpit rabbi, I have become acutely aware when I feel comfortable and made to feel like a member of minyanim in some places while
in other places left alone, feeling like a stranger and outsider. There is
such a variety:

- There is a shul that I visit approximately once a year for a few
  days at a time. I do not want to speak disparagingly about the

members or about the shul because it did offer me a place to daven that was close by. Nevertheless, over the few years that I have shown up, only two men greeted and befriended me. I was always made to feel welcome but never made to feel comfortable.

- To the opposite extreme, I found the most welcoming and warm minyan in the last place you would imagine! There is a little congregation at the *vasikin* (early morning) minyan at the Kotel. This group is comprised of Litvish and Chassidic Jews. It is organized by a fellow who runs the minyan and coordinates the logistics, timing, and the welcome to any and all people. As I arrived each morning, he ran to fetch for me, and the others who came with me, chairs and a *shtender* (lectern). At the end of davening, they serve *schnapps* and cake if there is a yahrzeit or sponsor. The atmosphere is completely friendly—its welcome and warmth connected me to a sense of home.

When a person travels for business, or even pleasure, there is a sense of nervousness and fear of being out of his or her element and familiar surroundings. I once learned that a traveler is considered like a poor person. I could not find the source for it, but the rationale is consistent—a traveler does not have his own place to sleep, a place to establish his own meals, and this can make him feel desperate. With some poetic license, I will take the leap from a traveler considered being poor and connect it to the Gemara in *Nedarim* 64b: "*Arba'ah chashuvin k'meis: ani, metzora, suma, u'mi she'ein lo banim*—There are four categories of individuals who are considered dead: one who is poor, a leper, blind, or childless." Since a poor person is considered dead, the traveler—who is considered poor—would share the notion of being considered like dead. Therefore, helping a traveler is akin to saving his life. A stranger or a traveler gains strength and security knowing they are welcome.

If you think being hospitable is just a nice thing to do, you are mistaken! In this context, being hospitable and making people feel comfortable and secure is a mitzvah of returning their lost sense of being. The traveler is at a loss; perhaps he cannot articulate the exact item that is lost but that sense returns when greeted and treated as a local rather than as a stranger. Today's typical tourist with their credit cards, cash, and points may not feel truly lost; nevertheless, to one extent or another there exists a disorientation. This is addressed indirectly in *Devarim* (22:1): "לא תראה את שור אחיך או את שיו נדחים והתעלמת מהם השב תשיבם לאחיך—If you see your brother's ox or sheep going astray, you must not ignore them. You must return them to your brother." The Torah then expands to other lost items as well (ibid., 22:3): "וכן תעשה לחמרו וכן תעשה לשמלתו וכן תעשה לכל אבדת אחיך אשר תאבד ממנו ומצאתה לא תוכל להתעלם—You must do the same to a donkey, an article of clothing, or anything else that your brother loses. You found it; you must not ignore it." The *Ohr HaChaim HaKadosh* teaches that the ox of your brother refers to people, who are compared to animals but are nonetheless holy. We must return them to their brother, meaning to their homes, we must make them feel comfortable so that they can serve Hashem properly. This verse speaks to the righteous Jews who are commanded not to turn away from those who were pushed aside, but rather return and bring that sense of security and warmth of home back to them. There are many aspects to this:

- The saintly Chafetz Chaim, Rav Yisrael Meir Kagan, in his *sefer Chomas Hadas* writes that if the Torah went out of its way to show the value of returning a lost animal, which is of monetary value, how much more so the need to show mercy upon every Jewish soul who has "strayed" from the path of the Torah.

- Rav Yosef Yoizel Horowitz, the Alter of Novardok, writes in his *sefer Madreigas Ha'adam* that the lost objects of your brother include the loss of his body to health issues, both physical and emotional.

- Rabbeinu Bachya teaches us that when the Torah says, "Do the same for your brother's donkey," which is a nonkosher animal, it continues by emphasizing that we must return a lost garment—which is not even a living creature. The Torah concludes that this applies to all lost items of your brother. Not only is it speaking of returning physical objects, but also to doing anything to help a fellow Jew in need. It may be to remove any potential damage or to move your brother away from anything dangerous, including making him feel at ease and at home. This is all categorized under the mitzvah of *"V'ahavta l'rei'acha kamocha*—Love your neighbor as yourself."

I am now in the midst of experiencing a major, difficult decision in my life. It is not a mid-life crisis but rather a decision regarding my personality make-up. Throughout my life I have consistently resisted change. When I find something I like, and I understand that it works well for me, I basically stay with it. I tend to keep the same brand, color, and style with no need to even consider any other options. Whether it is suits, shoes, or even my daily routine, I prefer to stick to that which I am used to—until now. For years I have been "married" to a Blackberry phone that unfortunately broke before its time. I waited patiently for the newest Blackberry device (temporarily filling in with a cheaper, inferior replacement phone) only to find out that the new version might not meet my needs. And now, after many years, I need to choose between two other options—both new—causing me to dread having to face this choice of a new option. I need to overcome my ultra-conservative ways and actually make an effort to face making a change. This, for me, is drastic.

The cliché, "The apple doesn't fall far from the tree," appears throughout life's experiences. The mannerisms of the apple, the child, do not fall far from those of the tree—the parent. Obviously, every child is the product of two parents, so from which "tree"—the mother or the father—does the apple fall? I started to think about my own children, considering from which tree they "fell" off: mine or my wife's? The jury is still out. Some have fallen off the tree and others are still ripening. Nevertheless, the shaping of the size, taste, texture, and fabric of who they are can be seen in all of them and...in both of us.

Putting aside how our children look, be it the boys looking like each other or the girls not, there is something that distinguishes them as well: their personalities. Although people most often refer to type A personalities, there are actually four types of personalities: A, B, C, and D.

- Type A personalities are competitive, high achievers, and have a strong sense of time urgency.
- Type B personalities are the opposite of type A. They are relaxed, laid-back, and not easily stressed. While type B can be achievers too, they tend not to be as competitive as Type As. Type B personalities can delay work, completing it at the last possible moment. Some of them can turn into procrastinators, a tendency that type A's avoid like the plague.
- Type C personalities love details and can spend a lot of time trying to find out how things work, making them very suitable for technical jobs. Type Cs are not assertive at all and they suppress their own preferences even if this makes them uncomfortable or inconvenienced.
- As for the type D…well…the "D" stands for distressed. Type D's have a negative outlook toward life. They are pessimistic. A small event that is not even noticed by a type B can ruin a type D's day.

The classification of personality types into the four major categories A, B, C, and D is quite accurate in most cases. However, there are a few points that must be taken into consideration about any theory regarding personality type. The human personality is simply too complex to be described in terms of just one theory:

- You might find that you have type D personality traits but still find that you have some personality traits from another type such as type C.
- There are multiple personality traits that are not covered at all by a single theory. This is why one-personality-type-theory-fits-all is certainly insufficient to help you understand yourself very well.

By looking at my children's personality categories, I can detect if they are genetically predisposed to either myself or my wife. I am not going to reveal my children's personalities, but each does reflect back to one of their parents.

Differing personalities add much to life on many levels. The different personalities of children in a family give character and texture to the family. The diversity within families and the ability of family members to coexist despite their different personalities (starting with parents and continuing with the children) is the beauty of every family. If the individual family is the microcosm, the macro is the Jewish People who also should exist as one large family. The state of coexistence has eluded the Jewish People for centuries and is the impediment to the ultimate redemption.

The Torah states in *Shemos* (35:1): "ויקהל משה את כל עדת בני ישראל ויאמר אלהם אלה הדברים אשר צוה ה' לעשת אתם—Moshe assembled the entire community of Israel and said to them, 'These are the words that God has commanded for you to do.'" *Rashi* informs us that the day of gathering was the day following Yom Kippur when Moshe came down from Har Sinai the second time around.

Rabbi Shlomo Lunschitz, in his commentary *Kli Yakar*, explains why Moshe specifically gathered the Jewish People immediately after Yom Kippur. Earlier (*Shemos* 18:13), the Torah describes Moshe, who sat judging cases of dispute the day after Yom Kippur. The *Kli Yakar* explains the need to adjudicate cases among the Jews so that monies that would be donated to the building of the *Mishkan* would come from funds that clearly belonged to them and had not reached their pockets in an illegal way. The building of the *Mishkan*, God's abode in this world, needed to be built upon complete honesty, totally devoid of animosity between the parties regarding to whom the money really belonged. Therefore, prior to the campaign to raise money for the *Mishkan*, Moshe settled all monetary disputes among the B'nei Yisrael. The *Mishkan* was a symbolic place for all Jews to be together, to openly come together for a common cause.

Due to the need to assure communal wholeness, Moshe Rabbeinu needed to capitalize, bringing all the Jewish People together at a time when they were a wholesome group, and there was never a more appropriate time than immediately after Yom Kippur. Yom Kippur is the day on which we need to forgive each other before approaching Hashem to forgive us, and we were therefore naturally on the best of terms with our fellow Jews.

Historically speaking, the Jewish People are most vulnerable when split, and invincible when unified. Repeatedly throughout our history, we were attacked when we were "spread out" and far apart from our fellow Jews. The story of Purim is no exception. To the contrary, it was Esther and Mordechai who rallied the Jewish People to come together with an *achdus* and brotherly love just as it was the day after Yom Kippur when Moshe descended from receiving the second *luchos*. More than ever we all need to look at the different "Jewish personalities" and come together despite our differences, conscientiously making every effort to connect and become that one large family of Klal Yisrael. Let us all fulfill the commitment of *"kiyemu v'kiblu"*—to accept and fulfill that which we did previously in the time of Moshe. Let us all work to join together as one to become the greatest people and the shining-star family among the family of nations of the world. Amen!

San Diego is a destination city for business and pleasure throughout the year. This is not only true for the general population, but for Jews alike. Although we have Jewish tourists all year long, there are a few specific times when there is a greater influx of observant Jews.

Jews of all religious stripes come to visit San Diego throughout the year, and I want to address the attitudes expressed by Jews from the entire spectrum, particularly from the *chareidi* or right-wing camp. As a disclaimer, I—Heaven forbid—am not being critical of any of our visitors from any area, I am just bringing out an observation. Here is a sampling of some of the questions that I receive on a regular basis:

- After providing the time for *Shacharis*, the questioning visitors will typically ask, "What time is the latest minyan?"
- When it comes to locating those handy places to eat outside of our homes, our visitors will ask, "Where is the pizza shop?" "The dairy restaurant?" "How about the meat restaurant?"
- And, here's the real topper: "Which gas station sells cholent on Thursday nights?"
- When it comes to education they ask, "Are there schools and yeshivos here?" "Is there a *kollel* in San Diego"?
- The most general question is, "What do people do here?" (Translation: "like, for Jewish fun?")

After I inform them in the negative on most of their initial questions, there is typically a follow-up that applies to all the inquiries, mainly, "How do you survive here?!"

There is another group of older tourists who have been to other vacation destinations and are not as sheltered as the group I previously described. They are not taken aback by a small amount of "Jewish materialism" such as kosher eateries, bakeries, and such. What really amazes them is that people actually succeed in living here and raising observant families. This second group knows that there are Jews who reside outside of the large, concentrated cities where most Jews seem to live. Nevertheless, they are still surprised to see religious, genuinely observant Jews living here in San Diego! Personally, I don't know why they think this way, but they do. They also ask questions similar to those asked by the first group, only they do not respond in disbelief, but with genuine surprise.

The short answer to these questioning and frequently flabbergasted tourists is that in small communities like San Diego, we not only survive, but we also thrive! It is true, we may not have many places to go out to eat or have round-the-clock minyanim with cholent available 24/7. But those amenities are not what make a Jewish community. We are a close group of Jews who come together from different places. In a larger city, there would be a natural tendency for a group to break away when they attain a critical mass. Like a large family, the children tend to branch out, exploring different areas of interest. In a smaller community, we learn to treat each other as brothers and sisters despite differences in personal areas of expertise. Everyone teaches and speaks about tolerance, but there are those who not only preach but do. Everyone is welcomed warmly when they enter our homes. It is the challenges that make us bond together, strengthening each other spiritually; we depend upon each other as fellow Jews and children of Hashem.

This is exactly what Hashem requests from us, as the Torah states in *Devarim* (14:1): "בנים אתם לה׳ אלקיכם לא תתגדדו ולא תשימו קרחה בין עיניכם למת —You are children of God your Lord. Do not cut or mutilate yourselves and do not make a bald patch in the middle of your head as a sign of mourning." The simple understanding of "*lo tisgodedu*—do not cut yourself" clearly refers to the prohibition of excess mourning and acting as the non-Jews do when addressing death and mourning. Practically and metaphorically speaking in today's times, it is the idea of *not* making yourselves into groups that are different from each other. A practical example of an easy cause for separation is when the members of one minyan hold by different practices. For example, they may end up having separate minyanim for those who wear tefillin on Chol Hamoed versus those who do not. The spiritual challenge is maintaining a community with different *hashkafos* or philosophical outlooks on Judaism and focusing on different aspects of Jewish life. This is the true beauty of a smaller Jewish community, which, perhaps because of its size, can demonstrate a unique example of how the Jewish People are intended to be. The opposite of "not making groups" is respecting people who are different and keeping them together.

The midrash on the words "Do not band together" (*Yalkut Shimoni, Re'eh* 891) teaches us that when we *do not* stand apart from each other, the first part of the verse, "We are children to Hashem," comes to light. The comparison comes from Korach. The midrash states that we should not group ourselves together and end up arguing and separating from each other. Such a rift will create a plague among us, in the same way Korach separated himself from the rest of the Jewish People. He created a cut between himself and Moshe. The irony of the midrash using the word "*korcha*—making a bald spot," is that it shares the root letters of the name Korach! Rabbi Shimon Bar Yochai takes these words to a higher level by looking at the next *pasuk.* Here Hashem calls us "*banim*—children." To Hashem, His *banim* are incredibly endearing. Immediately following this line, once we have reached this level, we are now referred to as an "*am kadosh*—a holy people." Once we have earned the relationship of being Hashem's child, we then become holy, concluding with the declaration, "*U'vecha bachar Hashem*—And Hashem has chosen you from all the nations on the face of the earth."

The route for the Jewish People to acquire the title of "chosen nation" can only come when we live respectfully together, side by side, despite all our differences. In other words, we strive to become "chosen" by working together to accept each other for who we are. This does not mean everyone must agree with everyone else; we must respect and honor our differences, focusing on building a Torah-observant community. This is our core belief.

Every Saturday night following the conclusion of Shabbos, we call out "*Ah gut voch*" or "*Shavua tov*," meaning, "Have a good week." Sometimes, a person senses a certain omen indicating whether the week will be good or bad, with the tone set by how the week began. We should all keep in mind that the words we utter can be very powerful—whether for good or for bad. It is important, therefore, to remember that wishing someone "a good week" really means something.

Rabbis, in general, have varying relationships with their congregants, often depending on whether the congregant chooses to share personal and confidential information. Some rabbis have close contact with some of their constituents and are more directly involved in their daily lives, thereby knowing more of the challenges the family faces. When that is the case, the rabbi checks in on the individual or family to see how things are going, by giving encouragement, advice, and even a *berachah*.

One Saturday night, I wished someone a *shavua tov* and a *mazeldike voch*. As we have grown closer over the years, this individual confided to me some major things going on in his life that may seriously affect him, his family, our community, and ultimately, Klal Yisrael. That coming week would possibly signal the arrival of the big challenge. As I wished him the magical words, I squeezed his hand with more intensity and greater *kavanah* than the usual, casual blessing. I paused and thought about the words I was wishing him and then looked him in the eye and reviewed the intent of what had just transpired. Hopefully, my typical after-Shabbos greeting, along with those of everyone else who wished him the same greeting will be fulfilled.

This is the way we should begin our week following the power and influence of Shabbos.

It was over twenty-five years ago that I, then a young rabbi, was officially installed as the new rabbi of the congregation, the oldest Orthodox synagogue in San Diego. Rabbi Berel Wein, along with local city dignitaries attended the beautiful affair. Things that endure over time inevitably go through many changes, and this axiom applies particularly to people. Over the years, not only is there turnover within communities, the demographics and group dynamics change as well. The continuity of a shul and its congregation is dependent upon new members joining, especially young families, thereby keeping the cycle of life going. As simple as it may sound, effectively balancing the seasoned members and the new members, the young and the old, and of course, the different levels of observance, involves many trying situations.

Before arriving, I was warned of the different groups that existed within the shul, particularly the tension that existed between the older, more established, long-standing members, and the newer young families. The feelings were so strong that when my wife and I were invited to spend a Shabbos with the congregation to get to know people, lead the services, speak, and have my wife give a ladies' class, we were also expected to attend two *melaveh malkahs*: one for the "older" members and one for the "younger" member families. After being offered the position and accepting it, one of the first things on my agenda was to rid the shul of this separation. The Torah warns and commands us with a mitzvah of *"Lo tisgodedu*—Do not make separate groups"; figure out a way to be together.

The portion of the week of the installation dinner was *Parashas Bo*, and my speech addressed this issue. Following the eighth plague, Pharaoh's officials said to him, "How long will this man [Moshe] continue to be a menace to us?" Moshe and Aharon were brought back to Pharaoh, who said to Moshe: "Go serve God your Lord." Additionally, Pharaoh inquired, "But, exactly who will be going?" To which Moshe replied with the powerful words (*Shemos* 10:9): "בנערינו ובזקנינו נלך בבנינו ובבנותינו בצאננו ובבקרנו נלך כי חג ה׳ לנו—Young and old alike will go. We will go with our sons and our daughters, with our sheep and our cattle. It is a festival to God for all of us."

There is much to understand in this verse:

- The *Kesav Sofer* explains that the reason Moshe began with the young before the old was because Egypt was considerably more dangerous for youth, more so than for the elderly. Children are very impressionable, and the youth were susceptible to the influence of Egyptian idolatry. The older generation, who remembered the *Shevatim*, were stronger in their Judaism, and therefore less threatened.

- The Ponovezher Rav, Rabbi Yosef Kahaneman, explains that the usage of "young and old" was because an individual is an orphan when he does not have parents, but a nation is orphaned when there are no children.

- Rabbi Yitzchak of Volozhin explains the verse to mean that "it will be a *chag* [i.e., a holiday] for us when we depart from you [Pharaoh] and go to our own land."

- The *Netziv* explains the holiday aspect as follows: It is impossible to celebrate a festival and be happy without sons and daughters, and we need the sheep and cattle for the holiday's sacrifices and offerings. We need our children and animals to celebrate properly. What kind of joy would we have if our children remained in Mitzrayim? It states later in the Torah: "*V'samachta b'chagecha atah u'vincha u'vitecha* — You will rejoice in your festivals, you, your sons and your daughters" (*Devarim* 12:12).

- The Gemara in *Shabbos* (119b) recalls the words of the Sages: "Yerushalayim was destroyed only because the people diverted the schoolchildren living in Yerushalayim from their Torah studies." Rabbi Yehudah Rosanes, in his *sefer Parashas Derachim*, explains that it was in the merit of the children's learning that the Shechinah settled on the Jewish People. As long as the Shechinah rests upon the Jews, no nation is able to rule over us. This was what worried Pharaoh: if the children would go to learn, he would lose control over the Jewish People. On the other side of the spectrum is the older generation. Without the elders, who would there be to teach the children and to be role models for them? Without the older generation, how would the young connect to our *mesorah*? Therefore, it was just as critical to include the older generation.

We sometimes feel more comfortable with those who are like us—the same age and the same socioeconomic background. That is understandable. But a community requires *everyone*.

Every year our shul puts out a beautiful calendar for all members and other interested people. The calendar contains the basics of any standard calendar: the year, months, and days of the week. Alongside the secular dates, our calendar also includes the Hebrew calendar. Included with the two synthesized dates—secular and Hebrew—are the candle-lighting times for the start of each Shabbos and Yom Tov, the davening times, and additional Jewish holidays, as well as secular "holidays." One of the major events of the year for our congregation is the annual spring picnic: everyone who attends has a terrific time. There are wonderful grilled hamburgers and hot dogs, socializing, ball playing, hill climbing, and just lots of fun. There is no davening or learning, yet everyone gets credit for coming to shul!

At the last picnic, we all joked, making facetious cracks about how people enjoy the social side of getting together more than the religious things we do in shul, particularly on Shabbos. As I thought about this a little more seriously, I realized how important it is to enjoy each other's company in a neutral environment outside of the shul. Shul is not the place to socialize, play ball, bring pets, and simply schmooze and socialize together. It takes good, smart people to recognize that certain activities are appropriate in shul while other activities are not. Focusing on the physical and social events outside of shul while keeping the appropriate holiness inside shul is the way to create a close, cohesive, and growing cross-generational community.

The Jewish Community Center (JCC) gathers on a Sunday and other weekdays to work on our physical life, but the *beis ha'k'nesses* is the spiritual JCC. One of the most important lessons a person needs to attain in life is knowing when and where it is appropriate to do things.

The shul's role is for *ruchniyus* (spirituality), while the JCC and other shul outings may be for *gashmiyus* (physicality). The distinction and importance of this segregation is paramount to keeping the holiness of the Jewish People and calls our attention to proper behavior. It is especially important to point this detail out particularly in our day and age when there are so few boundaries left that separate the holy from the non-holy:

- It is critical to create the time and place for the activities directed to the mundane things that we enjoy and in which we should participate; with the caveat, of course, that the activities are proper and appropriate.
- Once we know that the fun and games are relegated to the picnics and such, we can, in turn, come to the realization that when we walk into shul, our primary focus and goal is to create and enhance the special relationship we have with God.

With this recognition we will be able to experience the promise that all of the *batei k'nessios* and *batei midrashos* in which the congregants acted properly will be relocated to Eretz Yisrael, where we will experience the rebuilding of the Third Beis Hamikdash in *Yerushalayim ir ha'kodesh*!

I received an early birthday present from my first cousin who is only four months my junior. When I turned fifty, he saw fit to send me an anti-shock cane that has a flashlight and compass on the handle. He insisted on sending this and included it with a note stating that I am in a *much* higher age decade than he is, at least until October when he will join the same ranks.

As mentioned in *Pirkei Avos* (5:25), fifty is significant; it is the jubilee year and is also the age for giving counsel or advice. It is important not to forget that there is also a different kind of milestone: as we churn out the years: we also should be appreciative of greater responsibility.

As children grow up, parents grow older. Newlyweds turn into young couples who then have children, becoming young families. Eventually, parents of young families enter their thirties, and then forties, with teenagers now running the household. The turning point of forty to fifty is the mega change to becoming middle-aged. As the young group morph into the middle-aged group, the empty nesters reach the age of retirement. The newly retired, in their late sixties, are suddenly facing their mid-seventies, and those "young" retirees are now almost in their eighties. Eighty-year-olds are quickly entering their nineties, and all of us look around and wonder where the years have gone.

When a community loses members, especially active members, there is shock and disbelief. There are certain people who are the bread and butter, the fabric of the minyan, and it is the minyan, of course, which provides the core purpose and role of a shul. We know the custom is for a mourner to stay home during the week of shivah and avoid being part of society, which is why a minyan gathers in the mourner's home, allowing the mourner to say Kaddish. Many small communities do not have the resources and manpower to maintain multiple services daily, especially when a minyan is required for a shivah house. No one can have a complaint about this situation, but on the other hand, frustration grows when there *are* enough people around to make multiple minyanim but people either show up late or do not show up at all! It is difficult to comprehend what many are thinking. Do they expect to have services provided for them yet are unwilling to help others? It is irrelevant whether a person knows the individual who needs a minyan. If someone needs help to celebrate an occasion or to make a minyan, community members should avail themselves, regardless of their relationship to the person in need.

In *Vayikra* (26:42), the Torah states: "וזכרתי את בריתי יעקוב ואף את בריתי יצחק ואף את בריתי אברהם אזכר והארץ אזכר—I will remember My covenant with Yaakov and also My covenant with Yitzchak, and also My covenant with Avraham will I remember, and I will remember the Land." *Rashi* and other commentators ask why the Patriarchs were listed in reverse order? This happens to be the only place in *Tanach* that the order in which the names of the Avos are written is not chronological! *Rashi* quotes *Toras Kohanim* (8:6) and explains: "As if to say, Yaakov, the youngest of the Avos, is sufficient for this; that the Jews should be redeemed through his merit. And if he is not worthy, see now that

Yitzchak is with him. And if he is not worthy, see now that Avraham is with him, for he is worthy."

Rabbi Yaakov Lurenbaum, in his *sefer Nachalas Yaakov*, questions *Rashi*'s comment by stating: "Wasn't Yaakov Avinu the choicest among the forefathers"? How can *Rashi* begin with an assumption that Yaakov Avinu was not worthy on his own merits to help take Klal Yisrael and lead them out of the exile?

Rabbi Lurenbaum explains that the intention of *Rashi* is based upon a different *Rashi* in *Shemos* (33:13). There, *Rashi* explains the mentioning of the forefathers as follows:

- If the Jewish People are liable for the punishment of death by burning, we have already been absolved because Avraham was thrown into a furnace—for us.
- If the Jewish People, are accountable and deserve to die by beheading, Yitzchak Avinu already offered that by stretching out his neck during *Akeidas Yitzchak*.
- If the Jewish People are subject to *galus*, Yaakov Avinu has already paid the price for his children since he was exiled and paid in full for the future.

In our verse in *Vayikra*, the Torah begins with the least severe punishment, exile, then beheading, and finally the worst type of death—burning. Therefore, it is understandable to say that if this punishment of exile by Yaakov—the lightest punishment—does not work, we move up to the member of the Avos who is associated with the next level of punishment.

Thus it follows that when *Rashi* uses the words "not worthy" it does not imply that Yaakov was not worthy; it is referring to the level of punishment endured by the Avos that will merit us to enjoy redemption. If we are not worthy to merit redemption with the lightest punishment, which Yaakov endured, then we will call upon the merit that Yitzchak endured. And, if necessary, we will summon the merit of Avraham, who was thrown into the furnace.

We, as a group and as individuals, must see to it that we are worthy of helping the Jewish People. It is our investment of time, money, and effort that makes a meaningful difference. It is not only for the community at large, but for each one of us to make a great impression on our own families. The best *chinuch* (education) to teach our family, our children, our friends, and all members of our community is to set the example of taking the next step. Each one of the Avos stood for the Jewish People; each of them was ready to take the next step of responsibility when it came to communal affairs. They did not sit back and rely on the previous generation's dedication and work. They not only stepped up to the plate, but they started swinging and hitting as well.

A Jew must realize his or her responsibility to step up and swing. The benefit to you, your family, your shul, and your community is at stake. Every one of us is essential, and together we must meet our responsibilities as members of our community, which, in turn, impacts us all.

Chapter II

CHINUCH
Seeing What We Don't See

ONE of my mottos regarding educating and raising children is "school is for information; home is where they learn." The average Jewish family spends hundreds of thousands of dollars on Jewish education—the information which, in turn, feeds applied learning. Those dollars are invested in our children's future, and, surely no less than any other investment, active involvement is required. It is imperative that our children's needs and progress be checked and nurtured to yield the best results. Jewish schools are crucial.

The home, however, is the epicenter for our children to learn how to conduct themselves and to develop a depth of understanding of the values that their parents hold dear. Home is where the information our children receive in school or yeshiva is truly "learned." A good chef uses prime ingredients, treating each item with great care in order to create a masterful meal. Our children receive information (ingredients) from school and bring them home to "digest." The home is the crucial environment for creating the best possible level of applying those pieces of information, nurturing a matrix that synthesizes the ingredients for a life of clarity of values, proper conduct, and respect.

For a master chef, proper cooking utensils, precise temperatures, and timing are essential details. The learning acquired at home has many components that, in a profound way, relate to the production of food by the master chef. The home is not limited to parents. It includes siblings, nutrition, safety, security, and so forth. Everything contributes to the end result!

In a sense, money spent on tuition is the cheapest part of educating our children. It is easier to write a check than to guide, nurture, and ultimately help our children truly learn through synthesizing the information they receive at school. It is the real learning that takes place in the home that is so challenging and, in many cases, ignored or overlooked.

As parents, we have an obligation to nurture the information that our children receive. We must also incorporate discipline techniques that serve to benefit our child's chances of succeeding in life. Reprimanding and guiding are essential for instilling the desired behavior. However, we must evaluate our own strategies to ensure that we are not just reacting. We should be putting careful thought into averting situations that can cause damage to the physical, spiritual, or emotional makeup of the child.

A parent is one who will sacrifice from the moment the child is conceived until their child reaches independence. As parents, we need to understand that we must sacrifice, not only for our children's physical well-being, but also for their spiritual well-being. When a child asks for something spiritual (within reason) that may cost time, money or effort, the parent must figure out a way to nourish and nurture that request. If we desire our children to grow up with sincere religious and observant commitment, then we need to display our commitment to that very goal, even when it may be inconvenient. If a child wants to grow more connected to Judaism, we should do whatever it takes.

Imagine a scenario in which a child is striving to always daven with a minyan. As an extreme example, consider the child who arrives home from Israel in the late evening. After a long and grueling day, he wants to catch the last minyan. Surely there are kids at that point who would be happy to go straight back home and daven privately without a minyan. Indeed, many parents at 9:30 p.m. would rather drive straight home than straight to shul! The parent in question now has the perfect opportunity to show and encourage the right thing to do. Not only does he not complain, he is overjoyed by the commitment and dedication of his son.

We must do whatever it takes, within the limits of possibility, to ensure that the child receives the religious training, learning, and positive experience despite the hardship that may fall upon the parent. These are the attributes we parents need to inculcate within our persona, openly expressing the desire to our children that we will do anything spiritually and religiously for them.

This has been the case for parents and children throughout history. We sometimes find tragedy when proper supervision is not provided, especially when it comes to adult children. We find this in the incident of the death of Aharon's two sons Nadav and Avihu. In *Vayikra* (10:1), the Torah states: "ויקחו בני אהרן נדב ואביהוא איש מחתתו ויתנו בהן אש וישימו עליה קטרת ויקריבו לפני ה' אש זרה אשר לא צוה אתם"—Aharon's sons Nadav and Avihu each took fire pans and placed fire and then incense on them. They offered it before God, but it was unauthorized fire, which God had not instructed them to offer."

Nadav and Avihu "gave their all" for this mitzvah. In truth, a Jew must do and perform every mitzvah by giving of himself to such an extent that his soul is spent—to the degree that he is listless and completely out of energy after doing a mitzvah. Yet, if that were the case, would it not be nearly impossible to do another mitzvah after expending all one's energy on just one command? Rav Pinchas Yustman explains that because each mitzvah is commanded by Hashem, it's performance arouses a person and gives him renewed strength and vigor, helping him look forward to doing the next one. He quotes the words, "*V'chai bahem*—And you shall live by them," which Chazal understand to mean, "not to die from them." Even if we "kill" ourselves over a mitzvah, the very act of doing the mitzvah with all our being allows us to become stronger and do more mitzvos.

Nadav and Avihu did the service in the *Mishkan* with the highest regard and with an incredible measure of *mesirus nefesh* (self-sacrifice). They gave it their all. However, their lofty endeavors of self-sacrifice resulted in their deaths. Why? Why did this act not elicit the renewed energy that a mitzvah always yields?

A mitzvah literally means something we were commanded to do. In this case there was no command; Nadav and Avihu did it on their own. This is noted by the special cantillation mark *mercha kefulah*, a double *mercha* on the word "*lo*" meaning they were *not* commanded. As great as they were, Nadav and Avihu acted on their own, without direction from Hashem. Their father Aharon knew that they were great and righteous men and could therefore not fathom them doing something wrong.

Parents need to guide their children to do mitzvos when we are commanded to, and to not do them when we are not commanded to. It's not about us, and it's not for us to determine if or when. According to the time that Hashem requires us to fulfill His mitzvah, we do it. We need to be all-encouraging, to consistently nurture the desire of our children to fulfill their *avodas Hashem*. This, in turn, will give them the strength, courage and attitude to want to do more.

One of Rabbi Wein's classic statements regarding raising children is "God punishes children by making them parents." My Rosh Yeshiva has keen insight into relationships—family, business, and, in particular, child-rearing. His consistent focus has always been to create a "mensch," who would by definition be a *ben Torah*; yet, it didn't used to be that you had to be a *ben Torah* to be a mensch. Rabbi Wein has witnessed two, sometimes three, generations of father-to-son child-rearing. He would note the varying patterns of behavior between the parents and children when they were young, often sharing significant similarities when they grew older.

We all, at least one time in our childhood, have made the cavalier statement, "When I have kids, I will never do that!" Or, "I will never do to my kids what my parents did to me." Of course not! But, lo and behold, just one generation later, those children-turned-parents find themselves doing exactly as their parents did.

One of my own children once remarked, "Did I act like so-and-so when I was their age?" Indeed they did! When a child acts out in a certain way, the parents tend to treat their children the way they were treated when they were that age. There is also the added dimension that parents make certain decisions based upon information only they understand. The children may know what is happening but do not really understand why. Children cannot fathom that they do not have the right to know why their parents treat one child differently from their siblings. It is important that parents explain to their children that they do not need to know every reason for a parent's responses to specific behaviors. There is no entitlement for a child (of a certain age, of course) to know everything. The child's questions of "why, why, why?" may be answered with "because, because, because."

Nevertheless, a good parent will add a statement such as, "One day you will understand," or "Right now you may not understand but one day you will." This is a legitimate response to an inquisitive child. With time and patience, the cycle of children becoming parents and raising them as they were raised is then remembered. As the old saying goes, "What goes around, comes around." This works and applies for both good or poor parenting.

Chazal say that the recipient of a miracle does not recognize the miracle as it unfolds. There is no question that the amazing, wondrous miracles that are witnessed and seen by all, such as the splitting of the sea, is known by all. Chazal are referring to the hidden miracles that are not noticed and appreciated as miracles until much later.

For example:

- There was no reason to surmise that the killing of Vashti by King Achashveirosh was the preparation for all that would follow.

- Three years later, Esther was selected to be the next queen and was taken to the king's palace. No one had a clue as to what was unfolding.
- A while later, a plot of two of the king's chamberlains to assassinate Achashveirosh was discovered by Mordechai, and told to Esther in the name of Mordechai. These apparently random occurrences did not initially seem significant.
- Haman was elevated to become the second-highest official in the country. Who would have thought a Jew-hater's rise to power would end well?

The *Chasam Sofer* remarks that only at the end, after the major miracle witnessed by all, did everyone understand that the killing of Vashti was "like" a *k'rias Yam Suf*. This is because the recipient of the miracles does not have the angle in their vision to see and appreciate the miracle of the One who performs it. This concept is echoed in the words of David HaMelech in *Tehillim* (136:4): "לעשה נפלאות גדולות לבדו כי לעולם חסדו—He who does great wonders, *alone*, for His kindliness endures forever." Only Hashem Himself, who performs all miracles, knows no man can grasp the miracles as they occur.

Nevertheless, it is a mitzvah and incumbent upon every man to discern all the good Hashem has done for him from beginning to end. Everyone should recognize and perceive how the events in his or her life were a perfectly sewn tapestry, taking care to tell it over to their family. Describing and telling over the miracles of one's life to their children and grandchildren is a crucial component of education. The lesson to be learned by the child and grandchild is that they, too, should see and recognize the independent events as having a purpose and pattern that Hashem has performed for them.

The *Chasam Sofer* writes that there is a hint of this when the Torah describes Moshe meeting God on Har Sinai. The verse states "*V'ra'isa es achorai u'fanai lo yei'ra'u*—And you shall see Me from behind, but My face will not be seen" (*Shemos* 33:23). When something occurs in the world and people are perplexed, they ask: "Why did God do this?" Only after some time are they able to see and understand, retroactively, that all these seemingly small, insignificant events were a preparation for Hashem to arrange a desirable outcome.

A person who reviews the events and recognizes the master plan of Hashem strengthens his *emunah* in Hashem and receives great reward. How much more so the person who reacted with *emunah* as the questionable events were taking place. A person receives the greatest reward for having *emunah* by the mere fact that he can identify a seemingly negative or benign occurrence and interpret it as the hand of the Almighty. A child does not have the intellectual capacity to fully appreciate a parent's decision involving the child's life. But we as adults should have the intellectual ability, unlike children, who lack this awareness, to realize the limits of our intellect, and that Hashem (like parents to children) has infinite wisdom that we cannot grasp. Therefore, even without having the answers or knowing the big picture, we should recognize that Hashem, our Father in Heaven, has set up these events to contribute to the greatest miracle: the redemption of the Jewish People.

This is the lesson we need to repeat to ourselves—and to our children.

I studied just shy of two years in Israel post–high school. I attended an American yeshiva for boys who had not seized the opportunity to learn Torah in high school and had unfortunately never been introduced to learning in a non-threatening, no-pressure atmosphere. The climate in the *beis midrash* was adjusted to each student's needs, and there was an appropriate *rebbi* and method of teaching for everyone. The yeshiva was located on top of a mountain while the community was down below, a good five-to-ten-minute walk depending upon which direction you were coming from. In addition to the incredibly dedicated *rebbeim* and staff, the yeshiva took advantage of having an English-speaking *kollel* in the community. Two nights a week, some of these otherwise-insulated *kollel* men came to learn with the raucous, uncouth post–American high school students. There was a clear generational and societal gap between the black-hatted, white-shirted *kollel* guys and the ripped-T-shirt-and-jeans boys.

I had the merit to learn with a young man who was the most respected in all of Telz-Stone. My *chavrusa* from the *kollel* was a man named Alter Yachnes, who taught the youngest class in the cheder. His job was to introduce the children to *aleph-beis*, eventually teaching them how to read. Although an extremely humble man, when Reb Alter Yachnes walked into a room full of adults, everyone stood up to honor him.

The profound respect accorded to him was on par with the heads of the yeshiva and rabbi of the town. Why? Because he taught the fundamentals to the next generation. He used his expertise and talent in a successful manner. The children privileged to learn from him were given the building blocks to become great Torah scholars. There are two great lessons to be learned from this:

- In *chinuch*, the respect bestowed on a person often arises not from his position but rather from his efforts and success in making others into strong and committed Torah Jews.
- The foundation of a building is the most critical contribution to that structure. It is only with a strong, solid foundation that the building will survive any turmoil or trauma. Similarly, the roots of a person take hold from the beginning; the best teachers give each student the tools to succeed. When we use the expression "the ABC's of life," these are not limited to reading and writing—but also to life's experiences.

Whether we are discussing raising a child from birth, or nurturing an adult who is finding his or her way back to Judaism and religion, the foundation is critical. This rule applies tenfold when introducing a potential convert who is trying to become Jewish with the laying of the new Torah foundation on top of a preexisting belief. A *ger tzedek* (convert) needs instruction to replace the old foundation when starting anew with a Torah foundation, to take extreme care that it be laid carefully and correctly. The first person to lay such a foundation, creating the beginning of all Judaism, was Avraham Avinu.

Hashem famously instructed Avraham to take his entire household and travel to Eretz Canaan. In *Bereishis* (12:5), the Torah states: "ויקח אברם את שרי אשתו ואת לוט בן אחיו ואת כל רכושם אשר רכשו ואת הנפש אשר עשו

בחרן ויצאו ללכת ארצה כנען ויבאו ארצה כנען—Avram took his wife Sarai, his nephew Lot, and all their belongings, as well as the people they had gathered, and they left, heading toward Canaan." The words "*asher asu b'Charan*," literally, "the souls that they had made in Charan," can be interpreted to mean the servants they had acquired. According to *Rashi*, this refers to the people that they had converted to God's cause. Sarai had taught the women (converting them) while Avram taught the men (converting them), bringing them to believe in monotheism.

Rabbi Chanoch from Alexander, the Alexander Rebbe, asks: "What happened to all those who converted? We do not hear from them; we do not hear anything about them. Where did they disappear to?" He explains that after Avraham died, they did not seek to learn from Yitzchak because they did not properly look up to him; they did not consider Yitzchak as important and noteworthy to follow as they did Avraham. These people—whom Avraham and Sarah converted to monotheism—were, upon Avraham's death, devoid of a *rebbi* and *manhig*, a teacher and a leader. They had no future, no continuation. There was nothing to keep pulling them along because the spring—the source of their growth—was gone. Once their source of direction and inspiration dried up and their teacher and leader was no longer present, the people who had been nurtured by Avraham Avinu and Sarah Imeinu reverted to their old ways.

Every person, in order to continue to grow and to maintain his knowledge and belief, needs to seek out ways to fill any void that arises once the current source of learning Torah and mitzvos is gone. If it is not filled appropriately, the old lifestyle will call once again, making it easy to return to the previous way of living. Experience has shown that no major effort is required to return to the ways one had previously been accustomed to living.

Eventually, the leader of a generation passes on. Someone eventually comes to replace him. People should be careful not to say that the *Gadol*, the leader, of this generation is not as great as the one who came before him. A person must look at the current leading rabbi as the *tzaddik* of *this* generation, as it says, "*Yiftach b'doro, k'Shmuel b'doro*." The leadership of each generation reflects the people of that specific generation. When someone leaves a yeshiva, seminary, or a community, it is imperative to follow through with a new rabbi or mentor in their new location. Even the best foundations need reinforcement from time to time; we cannot remain solid upon our original teachings alone. We learn in *Pirkei Avos*, "*Asei lecha rav*." Make sure you have a rabbi to whom you can ask questions and from whom you can receive clarity and guidance.

In terms of parenting, in particular, we all need advice and direction from time to time. Foundations are crucial but need to be followed up. Let's not get lost like the students of Avraham. All of us need to cling to the next person who fills that role, continuously solidifying and building ever more deeply upon the foundations laid by our original rabbis and teachers.

When I grew up, school always started immediately after Labor Day. Maybe this "traditional" start date for the new school year is a northeastern practice, because in the south, schools typically open a few weeks earlier. There is an air of excitement connected with this time. Teachers are busy setting up their classrooms with new materials, students are excited about purchasing all their new school supplies, and parents are ecstatic that the summer is over, signaling that their kids will soon be out of the house (and hair) for a major part of the day.

Nevertheless, with all the preparations, we tend to lose focus on the primary purpose of school. With all the excitement about buying supplies or purchasing new school uniforms, we tend to forget that the most important aspect of going to school is to learn!

For many schools, one basic method is used to teach. Thus, large groups of students are exposed to similar teaching techniques for everyone. This method of teaching is the antithesis of Shlomo HaMelech's words: "*Chanoch la'naar al pi darko*," that we should "educate every child according to his way"—*his* way and not necessarily the way that works for everyone else. This is surely a very challenging objective considering the curricula of our current school systems, but it should not thwart a concerted effort to try to teach each child according to his or her ability and learning style.

The overall education system, inclusive of Jewish education, has made great strides in providing a learning forum for students who have unique learning challenges or special needs. As important as it is to address these specific needs, labeling children as such tends to detract from the overall message that each student has a unique learning style, especially the emergent learners in the primary grades.

In truth, *every* child's education needs to be special in the sense that education for each child is catered specifically to nurture their success. Every single student is entitled to "special education," and individualization of teaching and learning is exactly what Shlomo HaMelech was referring to when he stated that every child needs to be educated "according to his ways," applying whatever special way is necessary to reach that youngster.

Labeling something or someone in the world is often necessary, but it should never come with negative drawbacks. One must be very careful not to define a student with very general language because such description often will identify students incorrectly. Such is the case with using the term "special education." The Lubavitcher Rebbe is quoted as saying that he did not use the Hebrew word *beit cholim*, a "home for the sick" for a hospital. Rather, he would emphasize the positive, referring to a hospital as a *beit refuah*, a "house of healing." We all need "special education," and the flip side is that educators need to know how to teach specifically and appropriately to each student.

Unfortunately, it does not take much to create a child who feels like a failure. Children are fragile; they can be broken at the very outset. They can turn to negative behavior in order to receive positive reinforcement or approval from their peers through mischief. A child who has been labeled a failure by his or her teacher will very likely seek approval for inappropriate actions and behaviors. Children vie for attention from their parents and peers and will do almost anything to achieve it.

Judaism is a beautiful religion and the Torah is what makes it so beautiful. Everyone starts off being part of the "inside"—part of the larger group. It is only after something happens that either forces the child—or the masses—to rebel and become part of something else in order to gain acceptance. This is a result of not being taught according to their own, unique way. It is often the lack of special education from teachers, parents, and others that could have influenced and nurtured the child according to his or her special needs. This is a huge responsibility, but knowing the upside of such quality education, we must all embrace it with the greatest of sensitivities and the utmost time and devotion necessary for the future success of our nation.

With technology improving and medicine advancing, health care for all generations, including the very young and the aging, positively increases as well. Over the past fifty years, average life expectancy has increased globally by almost twenty years, from 46.5 years in 1950–1955, to 65.2 years in 2002. In the United States, life expectancy at birth increased by almost nine years between 1960 and 2011. To see three-generation families today is somewhat common, and we are now witnessing more and more four-generation families! Historically, this is a great blessing.

Of course, there are a host of challenges that must be faced regarding attending to the needs of aging parents. We feel guilty because we cannot help enough, and this feeling arises primarily because we do not have the time, resources, or physical capacity to do the job. At the same time that we are struggling to allocate adequate time for raising our children while dealing with the burden of society's challenges, we are also bombarded with the responsibility (and privilege!) of taking care of our parents. This trial is common to many people in the Jewish and non-Jewish world.

There is another significant, uniquely Jewish crisis that looms for the "sandwich generation" and has existed only within the last generation or two. I am referring to the Baal Teshuvah movement. Newly observant Jews face a challenge with their nonobservant and sometimes non-Jewish parents, while at the same time raising their own children who often surpass their knowledge of Judaism. Thus, on one side there are the parents who are bereft of Jewish knowledge and practice, while on the other side are their children who are receiving a stronger and more intense Jewish education. Certainly these parents (in the case of the *baalei teshuvah*) are thrilled that their children come home from day school and yeshiva knowing so much Torah and being able to learn above and beyond their own levels. Nevertheless, these parents need to find the right balance vital for effective parenting while still maintaining a proper perspective regarding their new lifestyle. This perplexing conundrum can lead parents to question their new lifestyle. How do we address the need to appropriately continue to educate both sides of the family's generations—the ones who preceded them and the ones who follow?

Here is a recommended suggestion, which is not intended as a perfect solution. At the end of *Shemos*, we learn about the *Mishkan* and all it contained. The *Mishkan* is the house where Hashem's presence resides in this world. But it also stands as a model for every Jewish home as well. The Jewish home is the place to raise our children, educate them, and create harmony within all generations of a family.

The Torah states in *Shemos* (27:20): "ואתה תצוה את בני ישראל ויקחו אליך שמן זית זך כתית למאור להעלת נר תמיד—You [Moshe] must command the Israelites to bring you clear, illuminating oil, made from hand-crushed olives, to keep the lamp constantly burning." *Rashi* explains the word "crushed" to mean that the olives were crushed in a mortar; they were not ground with a millstone. This was done to ensure that there would not be any remaining sediment. Only after obtaining the first drop would he put the olives into a mill and grind them. The second drop of oil would be unfit for the candlestick, but would be fit for the meal offerings, as it says, "Beaten for the light," but it is not essential that it be beaten for meal offerings. Rav Alexander Levinson explains that the difference between the oil used for candles and the oil used for the offerings mirrors the difference between two approaches to serving Hashem:

- Some serve God because they are commanded to do so. This person is like a servant who follows the command of his master without knowing why, without understanding the purpose for doing the mitzvah.
- Others serve Hashem with the alacrity of a deer, yearning to oblige. In the sense of the deer, a person serves Hashem through an inner desire to get close to Him. The innermost voice tells him to do the mitzvah.

Both methods of serving God are observed, and both methods are necessary.

- Taking an olive and crushing it to take the oil for lighting the menorah was strictly a commandment. The command represents the first drop of oil to ooze out from the crushing process. This resulted from the obligation of the mitzvah itself.
- The second drop of oil for the *Minchah* offering was not from the crushing. The *korban Minchah* was brought to show gratitude and give thanks for all the goodness Hashem bestows upon us. This sacrifice and offering came from within our essence, from a deep desire to get close to and cling to God. As it states in the beginning of *Vayikra*, it was the *nefesh* of the person that offered it, referring to the emotional side rather than the physical. The word *nefesh* is only mentioned by the *korban Minchah*.

Each person serves Hashem within his or her own capacity, some needing a direct command, others willing to do it on their own. A similar distinction is sometimes suggested between the *baalei mussar* and the Chassidim:

- *Baalei mussar* follow the halachah precisely and meticulously, with emphasis on the commandment aspect.
- Chassidim, on the other hand, represent the inner joy in performing the commandments as a mechanism to come close to Hashem.

Of course, the above is a simplification; in essence, these two paths or philosophies need to be implemented in *every* single Jew, at times emphasizing one, and at times the other.

Regarding the different generations, we need to assign different methods to each group:

- When *baalei teshuvah* deal with their nonobservant relatives, Torah must be taught through *tzivui*, meaning "command," i.e., "This is what we do and this is how we do it." We educate them to the basic tenets and rules of the Torah.
- When it comes to the educated children of *baalei teshuvah*, the parents need to display an inner spiritual desire to get ever

closer to Hashem. Parents from all backgrounds need to teach by example and display the fire that burns within them to get close to Hashem. The ritualistic component is of course essential, but educating our children must come from within and from the sincere desire—not just the obligation—to do the mitzvos.

Our hope and prayer is to educate from both sides and bring the family together, showing and displaying a love of Torah and fulfilling the mitzvos because we are commanded to do so and because we want to do so.

There are many different pleasures each of us look forward to throughout our lives. Pleasure is a broad class of mental state that humans and animals experience as positive, enjoyable, and worth seeking. These include more specific mental states such as happiness, entertainment, enjoyment, ecstasy, and euphoria. The early psychological concept of pleasure, referred to as the "pleasure principle," describes it as a positive-feedback mechanism that motivates every living creature to recreate particular experiences they have found pleasurable in the future—and to avoid situations that have caused pain in the past.

The experience of pleasure is subjective, and different individuals will experience different kinds and quantities of pleasure in the same situation. Many pleasurable experiences are associated with satisfying basic biological drives, such as eating and drinking. The appreciation of cultural artifacts and activities such as art, music, dancing, and literature is often pleasurable.

There are also situations in which the pleasurable experience is physical but causes an internal sensation. Any professional gets satisfaction when his or her experience and skill set is used. I have experienced joy and a sense of fulfillment from those things that typically give pleasure to rabbis and teachers. A rabbi is a teacher, and a teacher enjoys teaching. When someone asks me a question, I immediately have a good feeling in the sense that the person wants to learn, and I have the opportunity to help them, teach them, and nurture growth.

Last week I had an incredible experience that gave me an enormous amount of pleasure. I received a phone call from two young siblings, about eight and five years old, who said that they had a question for the Rabbi! I was ecstatic as I carefully listened to their question about a young fruit tree, asking me when they could derive benefit from the tree by eating its fruit. I decided to show them how important it is for children to ask questions and not feel intimidated by the idea of "asking the Rabbi." By the way, there are other children who come over with their parents to ask a question on Shabbos. In this case, I went over to the children's house and looked at the fruit tree and discussed the relevant laws associated with fruit trees. I get such *nachas* when children ask questions and when parents arrange to have their questions asked and taken seriously. This is a level of *chinuch* that can only be learned at home. The rabbi of a community is a resource for everyone and is happy when his expertise is sought.

A *ben Torah* and all who truly value the Torah continuously search for growth. Every Jew must live with a Torah *hashkafah*, a perspective or outlook that centers around the growth of Torah and mitzvos for themselves and their family. There are several indicators that contribute and make up a good Torah *hashkafah*. The case of children asking questions is one of those gauges. Someone who does not ask is not in growth mode. That person is instead using up their original resources, which will eventually dry up. The message of Torah *chinuch* cannot be stated more clearly than what Chazal say about *chinuch* at the very outset of *Sefer Vayikra* (6:2): "צו את אהרן ואת בניו לאמר זאת תורת העלה....—Relate the following instructions to Aharon and his descendants: This is the law of the burnt elevation offering..." *Midrash Rabbah* (end of 7:3) teaches why there is a tradition for children to begin learning Chumash from *Vayikra* and not from *Bereishis*. Rav Assi asks: Why do young school children begin to learn *Toras Kohanim*, the book of *Vayikra*, and not *Bereishis*. "It is because young children are *tahor*—pure and innocent; let it be the pure and wholesome ones who come to learn about *taharah* [i.e., cleanliness and purity]."

However, in *Vayikra* (1:1), the Torah states: "ויקרא אל משה—And [Hashem] called Moshe." *Midrash Eichah Rabbah* (1:33) states that there is a *mesorah* that the *aleph* of the word *Vayikra* is small. Rabbi Yehudah said: "Come and see how dear the *tinokos shel beis rabban*—the young school children—are to Hashem." God exiled the great Sanhedrin, but the Shechinah, God's presence, did not go into exile with them. God exiled the *mishmaros*, the watch groups, but the Shechinah did not go into exile with them. But when the schoolchildren were forced into exile, the Shechinah went into exile along with them. We gather from the midrash that the essence of Hashem's presence was primarily there because of the young children learning Torah. In the merit that their mouths were full of Torah and empty of nonsense, there was no sin, hence Hashem's presence was glad to be with them even if that meant leaving Eretz Yisrael. This resulted in the Jewish People benefiting from the children's learning; it kept the Shechinah close to the entire Jewish People in the *galus*.

Rabbi Yosef Zundel of Salant, in his *sefer Be'er Yosef*, connects this to the *Aron* in *Shemos* (25:22). "I will commune with you [i.e., meet with you at set times] there, speaking to you from above the ark cover, from between the two cherubs that are on the Ark of Testimony. In this manner I will give instructions to the Israelites." The Gemara in *Sukkah* 5b asks: "What is a *keruv* (cherub)?" Rabbi Avahu says: *Ke'ravia*—It is like a baby, for that is how a baby was called in Babylon. This hints to the fact that it was in the merit of the young children that Hashem placed His Shechinah in between the cherubs. This was done to teach Torah and mitzvos to the nation of Israel.

Adults and parents need to recognize that it takes Torah learning—*especially* for our young children—to have the Shechinah live in our midst. Now, more than ever before, we who are living in the *galus* of the *galus* need to see the primary importance of Torah learning at all levels. We need to reassess our *hashkafah*, the outlook, we have on the primacy of Torah in our schools, shuls, and communities. Communities grow by bringing in more Torah personalities and families who have a proper Torah *hashkafah* to help influence the proper path we need to be on.

Our shuls and communities should continue to grow in Torah and *yiras Shamayim*. We need to listen to the call of Moshe to raise the bar of Torah in our midst and be a shining light so that we, too, can listen to the sweet words of Torah emanating from the cherubs running all around us.

A few weeks ago, I was learning with one of my *chavrusas*, Lionel Kahn, who is actually my longest-standing *chavrusa*. We have been learning together for more than twenty years now. Our weekly learning is exactly that: *learning*. We have very few interruptions or sidetrack discussions. Any outside discussion is directly related to the subject matter at hand. Without going into the details of the Torah-related matter we were discussing, Lionel made the following statement, which I felt contained a lot of wisdom: "An old person looks back at the past while a young person looks toward the future." As the old saying goes, "Age is only a number," and in this sense it is absolutely true:

- I have been with chronologically young people who are constantly talking about the past, which indicates being old.
- I have been with chronologically elderly people who are still looking toward the future, and they are really young!

Looking back, recalling with nostalgia the days of old, shows a person is living in the past with little hope of the future. On the other hand, someone who looks toward the future remains young. Just as a person in his youth looks to accomplish, grow, and experience new things, they too still look to accomplish and grow.

Moshe Rabbeinu was considered forever young despite his age of one hundred and twenty. Moshe, until the very last day of his life, hoped to enter Eretz Yisrael. He did not recount his days from his youth in Egypt nor did he dwell on the trek of the last forty years in the desert.

Throughout life we look forward to what the future will bring while at the same time we look back at what happened in our lives. One important reason to look back on life is to make sure we do not repeat past errors and to learn from our mistakes. In the Torah we read about the past and the future, but sometimes looking at the past gets us into trouble.

In *Bamidbar* (11:5), the Torah states: "זכרנו את הדגה אשר נאכל במצרים חנם את הקשאים ואת האבטחים ואת החציר ואת הבצלים ואת השומים—We fondly remember the fish that we could eat in Egypt at no cost, along with the cucumbers, melons, leeks, onions, and garlic." The Jews complained, remembering that they had such good food in Egypt, that now their spirits are dried up with nothing but *mann* to eat, which would fall before them day after day. Despite the fact that the *mann* from heaven could taste like anything they desired, they still complained. On top of the complaints came a questionable claim of having had such delicious fruits and vegetables and fish in Egypt! Did B'nei Yisrael lie straight out or was this perhaps the *eirev rav* speaking? How could B'nei Yisrael, who had been slaves in Egypt, possibly claim they had eaten such delicacies in Egypt? The commentaries give an answer for each food type they claimed to eat and explain why this statement was not a lie. Rabbeinu Bachya points out that the word used for fish is not *dag*, but rather *dagah*, with a *hei* at the end. *Dagah* refers to fish that is already four or five days old since it was caught; it had already dried up. The fresh fish that was caught daily was not on the Jew's menu—only the Egyptians ate the better-tasting fresh fish. In at least two other places in *Tanach* we find this same word *dagah*, and in both instances it refers to older dried-out fish:

- In *Shemos* 7:18, after the first plague of *Dam* turned the Nile into a river of blood and caused all the fish to die, the river became putrid and repulsive. Who would even want to eat fish that died in a river of blood?
- In *Yonah* (the haftarah on Yom Kippur afternoon), after God summoned a large fish to swallow Yonah, the verse states (2:2): "ויתפלל יונה אל ה' אלוקיו ממעי הדגה"—Yonah davened to Hashem from the belly of the *dagah*." These depths of the stomach of the fish were like death.

In truth, the Jews did have fish, fruits, and vegetables in Egypt, but they were not really edible. Yet the main point is not whether they had these foods. It was rather the lack of foresight with regard to looking ahead at the beauty of Eretz Yisrael. By looking back, they were acting old, ready to give up and die rather than look forward to life and living on. Psychologically, it may be tiring to look forward when you are older; it may seem easier to live in the past rather than make a new future. But success lies in the young or the young-at-heart who want to look to build and accomplish more and not rely on past successes. In every aspect of life, we should not dwell on the past. We should always look forward to the potential of the future.

It is hope and the anticipation of the future—the times of Mashiach—that has made the Jewish People an ageless and vibrant nation. It is with this sense of hope and optimism that we need to raise our children—and ourselves!

As a pulpit Rabbi, I am interested and intrigued when I visit other shuls. I enjoy witnessing some of the identical scenarios I encounter at my shul. I typically read the bulletin, the weekly announcements and any other signs around the shul that give a genuine flavor of the fabric and dynamics of that particular shul. Commonly, every professional or laborer scrutinizes others who hold jobs or positions similar to his. Recently, I saw a beautiful sign in a shul which reverberated within me. In fact, I am sure other rabbis would also react in a similar fashion. Visiting a different shul one day, I noticed a sign at the entrance of the sanctuary stating: "We ask our members to please remember that there are no reserved seats in our shul. If you should find someone in your usual seat, please do not ask that person to move. It is far more important to welcome newcomers to our shul with a smile than to sit in your *makom kavua*." I cringe in my seat when I witness that exact scene unfolding in front of me, watching a disgruntled member of the shul kicking a guest out of his or her seat, doing the exact opposite of what the abovementioned sign suggests!

Historically, our rabbis typically encouraged a person to have a *makom kavua*, a permanent seat in their place of learning and davening. This helps a person focus and not be distracted by their surroundings, which might otherwise be unfamiliar if he or she always sits in a different location. A *makom kavua* is important, but not at the expense of embarrassing or insulting someone. I was thinking about *makom kavua* from a halachic viewpoint: Is it a permanent place, determined by where the table or chair is, or is it the actual place in the room where the person is situated? For example, if I sit on the left side of a certain table and that table and chair get moved to the other side of the room, should I move with the furniture or not? Does the *kedushah* (sanctity) that a person brings with his learning or davening move with the individual or does it stay in the same place?

The answer can be related to the only place in the world where there was an original *kedushah*, holiness, which maintains its sanctity no matter what. That place is the Beis Hamikdash. Other structures, regardless of their age, lose their sanctity. I believe the *makom kavua* is special due to the presence of the individual and is only special if that particular person is there. Once the person leaves, it is no longer special as a *makom kavua*. Furthermore, is there a statute of limitations for how long a person can retain the rights to his *makom kavua* once he has left that shul or *beis midrash*? Following my understanding, once a person moves on to another place, the original *makom kavua* is no longer unique or specific to that individual.

I am convinced that this theory is supported in the Torah. In *Devarim* (11:19), the Torah states "ולמדתם אתם את בניכם לדבר בם בשבתך בביתך ובלכתך בדרך ובשכבך ובקומך—You shall teach them to your children to discuss them, while you sit in your home, while you walk on the way, when you retire and when you arise." Rav Moshe Schreiber, better known as the *Chasam Sofer*, explains that Hashem is placing an obligation upon fathers to teach their sons and educate them in Torah. Not only to teach them while they are sitting in their home, but on the road as well. The obligation is to teach them in the identical manner on the road as in the home, and that children should behave on the road just as they would behave at home. Rav Shmuel Binyamin, better known as the *Kesav Sofer*, the son of the *Chasam Sofer*, explains that the Land of Israel is our home—we have established it for ourselves from our fathers. This differs from the exile, in which we are strangers in a foreign land—one day we are here, the next day we are out. This is supported by the verse: "*Va'yis'halchu mi'goy el goy*—And we have gone from one nation to another" (*Tehillim* 105:13, *Divrei Hayamim I* 16:20). The *Kesav Sofer* explains "*b'shivtecha b'veisecha*—when we are sitting in our homes" to mean when we are dwelling in tranquility in Eretz Yisrael, and "*u'v'lechtecha va'derech*—walking on the road" to mean when we are in *galus*. No matter what, where, or when, we need to take with us the teachings from the home and always have them close at hand.

The great teaching of Shlomo HaMelech—"*Chanoch la'naar al pi darko*"—adjures us to educate every child according to *his* way; meaning, "*u'v'lechtecha va'derech*," teach them for those times when they will be on their way.

Many girls and boys who learned for many years in yeshivos and great learning institutions eventually foray into the exile known as the world. The formative years of study in the yeshiva are similar to the home in which we are taught. Eventually, we leave the comfort of that environment and need to adjust in *galus*, whether in college or in the workplace. It is imperative to not only immerse ourselves in the teachings we receive during our years of school, but more so, to pack them up with us for the journey of life. There are many men and women who learned a lot in yeshiva—but unfortunately left it all behind.

The significance of Shlomo HaMelech's genius of educating each person according to his way, must include teaching every person how to transfer his learning to the outside world, to educate him regarding how to maintain his learning and religious observance in the *galus* of the outside world and not only in the confines of the *beis midrash* or the halls of the Bais Yaakovs. The single most important lesson we must transmit to the next generation is the ability to maintain the best of both worlds by continuing to live and breathe a religious learning and growing lifestyle even outside of the study halls and into the workplace. Remember to take your *makom kavua* with you wherever you go!

Everything in life has its pros and cons. With the invention of modern innovations and conveniences, our personal lives seem to become more comfortable, easier, and, in the case of child-rearing, safer. But the progress of modern technology brings with it some non-monetary costs. One of our most widely used technological conveniences is the smartphone, a device that has made life so much easier on many levels. And yet we are becoming increasingly concerned with the negative impact this amazing device is having on our society. There are myriad examples of inventions that improved our lives on some level, yet also came at some cost, creating a negative effect in tandem with its positive contribution. Despite this, I am not suggesting we remove them from our world. Rather, what we all need to do is develop strategies to more effectively curb the damaging effects of these advances upon society.

I have witnessed the introduction of many useful inventions, gadgets, and *tchotchkes* throughout my life. I cannot recall exactly when specific great innovations hit the market, but I can definitely remember the excitement of seeing new gadgets appear during my teen years that had not existed previously. For example, childproof devices such as outlet plugs, preventing children from sticking things into outlets, thereby protecting them from electric shocks. Cabinet locks were designed to keep children out of cabinets, such as those containing poisonous chemicals.

There is no question that these simple devices have saved thousands of injuries and deaths to toddlers and unsuspecting children. What I am about to say should *not* be misinterpreted as implying that we should get rid of these protective devices. What I am saying is that having these locks and barriers can also contribute to inhibiting a child's curiosity. While the locks and gates are intended to avert or prevent harm, they can also be used to block and even inhibit a child's natural quest for exploration.

I once heard an educator speaking about the difference between today's young children and similarly aged children from previous generations. Today's young child, according to this educator, and also supported by emerging research, tends to be less inquisitive and overly accustomed to being told "no" than children of previous generations. Observing parents disciplining their children, one frequently hears, "No! Don't do that" or "Don't touch that" (not in regard to hot or dangerous objects), and so forth. These words are verbal inhibitors that can negatively affect the child's natural desire to seek out and to explore. Safety devices, created to protect children, should not be used to stymie a child's curiosity. Parents, when putting safety latches on cabinet doors, need to be aware of the importance of allowing cabinets containing sources of "safe wonder" such as linens, pots and pans, lids, plastic goods, and so forth, to remain open. The mess created is a source of great learning and creative play for the child. While we should embrace products designed to protect our curious toddlers and young children, we need to also allow our children the ability to explore various places in the home, keeping at least some doors unlocked, so a toddler's curiosity can still be sparked and nurtured. There is something wonderful about watching a child pull out pots and pans, allowing him the opportunity to play with them—always, of course, under parental supervision. Handling objects, exploring their feel, taste, and even their sounds all contribute mightily to a child's growing understanding of the world he lives in—and the excitement that children should naturally have.

Perhaps the main ingredient lacking in today's Jewish world is excitement and enthusiasm when it comes to performing mitzvos, learning Torah, and in observing Shabbos and Yom Tov. One time last year, I was so glad to hear one of the children reacting to one of our superb children's programs called *Mishmar*. This incredible program runs on alternate weeks for boys and girls. I was surprised and happy to hear one of the children say, "We only have *Mishmar* every other week? Why?" I could detect this child's strong desire for more Judaism in his life. This is the critical guidance we need to give teachers and educators to create more significant Jewish education.

The Golden Calf was undoubtedly the greatest national sin done collectively by the Jewish People. On its own, it was horrible, disgusting, and repulsive—yet, it did contain an element from which we can learn, namely, the incredible hype and enthusiasm the Jews had for this event. The negative fallout of the worshipping of the Golden Calf is obvious, but the positive spin should not be overlooked so that we may learn from that experience. The people wanted to engage and to be part of a spiritual experience. They were excited and forthcoming in participation, undeterred by the expense of donating their gold. Where do we find the key in keeping our children engaged and excited about life, and especially about Judaism?

Hashem appoints Betzalel to be the architect of the *Mishkan*. The *Mishkan* was built as a *kapparah* (atonement) for the sin of the Golden Calf. In *Shemos* (31:2), the Torah states: "ראה קראתי בשם בצלאל בן אורי בן חור למטה יהודה—See, I have called by name Betzalel son of Uri, son of Chur, of the tribe of Yehudah." The Sages (*Sanhedrin* 69b) reveal to us that Betzalel was only thirteen years old at the time God commanded Moshe that Betzalel was to work on the *Mishkan*!

Finding the appropriate person to construct the *Mishkan* with all its intricacies was no simple task. Actually, it was impossible to find someone who had such ability and expertise, someone well-rounded in all areas of construction and design. This was because the Jews had been enslaved in Egypt, forced to do back-breaking work, making and carrying huge amounts of bricks and mortar. They did not have the skills necessary to design or construct the fine details of the *Mishkan*. There was no one who was skilled and trained to work with fine metals such as gold, silver, copper, and precious gems. The people had never seen them in Egypt; they were slaves. It would be a great wonder to find someone capable of such highly skilled work among the Jewish People. In fact, after Moshe heard the list of items needed to be built, sewn, and crafted for the *Mishkan*, he asked out loud, "Who is able to build and create all of this?" He asked, "Who will be chosen and who could come close to performing all the necessary tasks?"

Immediately, Hashem said to Moshe, "See this great, talented man whom I 'called' from the earlier generations before the Jews went to Egypt." Furthermore, God said, "During the time of the Six Days of Creation it came to mind that this generation, and in this year, the *Mishkan* would be built. Therefore, I am preparing now the child who will be born and will be that builder and architect of the *Mishkan*."

During the Six Days of Creation, Betzalel's soul was with God, hence the name Betzalel, which means "in the shade of God." During the days of creation, Hashem prepared the *neshamah* of Betzalel, giving him the creative force and all the necessary tools for building the *Mishkan*. The midrash says that Hashem "showed" Moshe the book that was given to Adam HaRishon (the first man), which contained the names of all the generational leaders. Betzalel's name was written there, as the one who was to build the *Mishkan*.

We derive from the midrash that Hashem had prepared Betzalel long ago for this day. Hashem nurtured Betzalel, encouraged him, and gave him the opportunity to explore and to grow, to polish his talent.

The point for us is that we cannot stunt a child's learning and curiosity. To the contrary, it is our responsibility, our privilege as parents and teachers to fuel each child's natural quest to discover and to learn, allowing curiosity to be sparked to flourish. From the very earliest stages of development we must encourage our children to be curious and to seek out adventure, albeit with parental supervision—monitoring, but not inhibiting. Hopefully, if we instill these qualities of seeking out and exploring, we will be paving pathways for our children to grow and thrive as confident, inquisitive, creative individuals.

Warning: The idea I am about to share applies to everyone—observant and nonobservant alike. Please read these words with care. You might find the following words offensive, destructive, unpleasant, and even aggressive. This was written with the knowledge that you are mature, intellectually honest, and ready to be open-minded and accepting.

Parents and donors spend thousands of dollars on Jewish education to raise our children...for what? I vividly remember a fifth-grade girl in the Binghamton day school, who was taught by my wife, asking the following question: "We just learned about the observance of Shabbos in the Ten Commandments, so why don't we observe Shabbos at home?"

What kind of message are we giving our children when we tell them to learn about something, but we don't follow through by practicing what they learn? Would we want to have our children taught that we are not allowed to steal and then take them on a family shoplifting spree?

Parents, teachers, principals, rabbis, youth leaders, and all others who have the precious responsibility of teaching our children need to shoulder the burden of not only teaching Torah and mitzvos, but of observing them as well. Please explain the difference to me. If an educator teaches that fighting is unacceptable in the schoolyard, would you expect to find two teachers fighting in the schoolyard? Why is it, then, that if we are charged with the responsibility of teaching our children the Jewish way of life, we violate it? If we represent ourselves as Torah-observant Jews, then we must *behave* as Torah-observant Jews. We cannot just pay lip service to the youth; we must carry what we teach into our own personal lives.

Of course, we need to incorporate the words of Shlomo HaMelech, who wrote: "There is no righteous man in this world who does not sin." Everybody slips once in a while, but it cannot be a constant way of life for a role model. We should all know by now that if the words of Torah and learning are not backed up by observance, then the words of Torah become meaningless and will fall away. Think about it: all that time, money, and effort—all a waste. To achieve fulfillment in life is to practice that which we learn and to incorporate what we learn into our daily lives.

This lesson is readily found in the Torah itself. In *Bereishis* (24:67), the Torah states: "ויבאה יצחק האהלה שרה אמו ויקח את רבקה ותהי לו לאשה—And Yitzchak brought her into the tent of Sarah his mother, and he took Rivkah and she was a wife to him." The *Targum Onkelos* on this *pasuk* says, "Yitzchak brought Rivkah into the tent and witnessed that her actions were the same as his mother's [Sarah] and then went ahead and married Rivkah." *Rashi* quotes the famous *Midrash Rabbah* (60:16) denoting the different elements and miracles of Sarah's tent. There were four constant open miracles which took place in and around Sarah's tent:

- The Cloud of Glory hovered above.
- The doors of her tent miraculously widened, allowing anyone to enter.
- Blessings were sent into her dough.
- A lamp would remain lit continuously from Friday night to the following Friday night.

When Sarah died, these four miracles ceased but returned when Rivkah took up residency in Sarah's tent. The *Targum*, however, states that Yitzchak took her as a wife only after he saw Rivkah doing the things his mother Sarah had done., It was not enough that the four miracles returned once Rivkah occupied Sarah's tent; Rivkah had to actually do—to observe and practice—the same things Sarah had done in order for Yitzchak to marry her.

Specifically, Rivkah separated challah under conditions of purity; she even separated her unconsecrated dough under conditions of purity. The fifth item mentioned in the midrash differs from the first four, as the four are miracle-related while the fifth was something Rivkah naturally aspired to do, and it happened to be the same thing Sarah did.

Rivkah, like Sarah before her, performed the mitzvos naturally. She did not need to rely on miracles. It was this strength of character that led Yitzchak to recognize her greatness, and take her as his wife. The question is, why did Yitzchak need this proof—particularly as the previous *pasuk* explains how the servant Eliezer informed Yitzchak of all the *chessed* Rivkah had done for him. Why did he need more assurance than that? Rabbi Yitzchak Zev Soloveitchik, the Brisker Rav, explains that the secret of how Yitzchak determined whether Rivkah was a suitable mate was not dependent upon miracles being performed *for* her, it was whether she herself *did* mitzvos above and beyond the ordinary requirement. It was not about what others said; it was about what she did.

There are no guarantees in life regarding how our children or students will turn out. Nevertheless, we must stack the odds in our favor to bring about the most desired results. We have already witnessed three to four generations after the Holocaust. By and large, those Jews who chose to live and lead an observant lifestyle saw their children and their children's children follow suit. Unfortunately, those individuals who only spoke in terms of identifying as Jews, but did not invest in practicing our rituals and laws, lost their children to everything except their identity of being Jewish. And some have tragically lost their children to the point of not identifying at all with Judaism.

No one ever said that following the rules of the Torah is easy. Everything worthwhile and precious requires continuous commitment and, when required, even pain and sacrifice. The golden rule in life is that when you work hard for something—when you sacrifice for it—you will retain it and you will be rewarded with long-lasting results. Without commitment and hard work, your efforts will fade away. My responsibility to do that which I tell others to do is constant, and the message I give must be consistent. If I am teaching or asking others to teach Torah to my children and to my students, I have a responsibility to be an example to them. I must reflect the very conduct I desire in others.

The previous discussion focused on the requirement to observe Torah as a prerequisite to teaching Torah. In a similar vein, with a subtle difference, our next insight delves into the requirement for our behavior to be consistent with our Torah values in order to pass on our traditions.

I believe the primary method for staying on track spiritually and physically is through the study of Torah. The structure of the Torah and following its course shapes each of us, guiding us to develop into healthy human beings. There is a concept of being a *"menuval b'reshus haTorah,"* a person who behaves in a manner which is marginally within the guidelines and permission of the Torah, while not behaving within the spirit of the law. Perhaps this individual did not have the opportunity to receive a proper education, but it is also likely that his innate nature caused him to look for ways to stretch the letter of the law, without restraint regarding the spirit of the law.

In the *Shema*, it says (*Devarim* 6:6–7): "והיו הדברים האלה אשר אנכי מצוך היום על לבבך ושננתם לבניך ודברת בם בשבתך בביתך ובלכתך בדרך ובשכבך ובקומך—And these words that I command you today shall be upon your heart. You shall teach them to your sons and you shall speak of them while you sit in your home and while you walk on the way, when you lie down and when you rise." This is a very comprehensive commandment of thinking and learning Torah *all* the time. Even more important than learning is teaching and carrying on the message to our children and to future generations.

A very sad but poignant story is told about the *Chiddushei HaRim*, the Gerrer Rebbe. The *Chiddushei HaRim* had thirteen children. All of them died in his lifetime. Through each of the tragedies he stood strong and firm and did not shed even one tear. He would comfort himself by saying the words of Shlomo HaMelech: *"Hashem nasan va'Hashem lakach*—God gave and God took back" (*Iyov* 1:21).

That all changed when his last child died. He was no longer able to control himself and broke down, crying bitterly and uncontrollably. One of his relatives asked him why he was crying only at the time of the last child's death and not when the other twelve died. He replied that he was not crying because of his child's passing—that he accepted as a decree from Heaven. He cried because he could no longer fulfill the mitzvah of teaching Torah to his children.

Many people are blessed with children and have the opportunity to learn and transmit the very same Torah, mitzvos, and way of life to their children and yet fritter the opportunity away. The irony, of course, is that in today's day and age, we have many tools at our disposal to learn for ourselves and to teach our children. It's not the way it was fifty or sixty years ago in America, when learning and teaching was not the norm. Somehow, despite the opportunities, the situation for the bulk of the Jewish People does not look as we would have hoped. Where have we gone wrong?

First, one must acknowledge that it is incumbent upon each of us to educate the next generation. There is a double language in the words, "You shall teach them to your children and speak to them these words." Rabbi Pinchas Shlomo Pollak, in his *sefer Minchas Marcheshes*, explains that the word *"v'dibarta"* comes from the word "to act." A person must live and act in the same way that he teaches his children to act. The old adage of "Do as I say, not as I do" is the antithesis of Torah ideals. *Rashi* explains the word *"v'shinantam"* as meaning, "to sharpen," like a *shein* (tooth) is sharp. The process of teaching children must be sharp, clear, and inspiring in order for them to gravitate toward the learning and to accept the teaching. Taking this reasoning to a deeper level, the word "sharpen" in Hebrew is *chidud*, which has the same root in Aramaic as the number one. The teaching of the Torah to children and the actions of the parents must be *one and the same* so that the message can take hold. Our actions must be the same whether we are at home, at the store, or away on vacation. The Torah must be taken with us from the moment we get up in the morning until we go to sleep at night. Each of us must be consistent in our observance and fulfillment of the Torah at work, at home, or at play. If we do not behave properly, consistently applying Torah principles in this manner, then we will not be able to teach our children anything.

It baffles my mind that so many people are willing to spend thousands of dollars on tuition for their children's Jewish education and yet fail to support that investment with meaningful, sincere support, learning, and practice. Furthermore, the cost of Jewish education is a bargain if we complement it and back it up with our own learning and growth. But it is throwing away good money if we don't. I am completely bewildered when I see parents behaving in ways that are contrary to the very education and teaching they are offering their children. Is there any doubt that a child who receives mixed messages from their parents will be confused? That confusion will only last a short time because as soon as the child reaches the age of making their own decisions, they will likely follow the weak decisions of his parents.

Hashem, as our Father, is very consistent with His teaching and actions, so that His children may learn properly. Hashem's messages are clear and consistent regarding the way a parent should raise a child. We are obligated to understand those teachings and to fulfill them ourselves, so that we may give them over to our children. Before we stretch the limits of the law, or worse, violate the law, as parents, we should consider whether we fear that our children's behavior will be a product of our behavior.

Some parents think that the mitzvah of teaching our children is over at a certain point. The mitzvah of teaching our children is incumbent upon every parent until his very last breath. Indeed, the mitzvah of teaching and guiding children knows no limits. Being a parent is ongoing as long as there is a child. It is an honor and a privilege to learn Torah and to fulfill the mitzvos. It is also an honor and mitzvah to teach those valuable lessons and way of life to our children as the Torah is timeless, continuing forever from generation to generation.

Historically speaking, most movements have been started in order to right a perceived wrong.

A benign example is the creation of sugar substitutes. Saccharin, one of the earliest sugar substitutes, was created to curb weight gain or to serve as a substitute for sugar.

While sometimes necessary in the short term, in the bigger picture, this approach misses the real underlying issue. The Band-Aid approach is not a true solution to the problem it purports to solve. In our example, instead of creating the substitute, man should learn to compensate by eating foods without adding sugar, or by exercising more, or by eating less.

In terms of Jewish outreach, the task of reaching out to mankind became necessary as a result of the failure of man to do the right thing in the first place. Once mankind strayed off the righteous path, a new concept labeled "outreach" was born to correct that which was lacking.

If we were to ask, "Who was the first person ever hired to do outreach, and face all the hurdles it entails?" the answer would clearly be Noach. Noach was declared a *tzaddik* by the greatest source: the Torah. *Rashi* comments that some understand this declaration to mean that Noach was a *tzaddik* in *his* generation, although not compared to Avraham's generation, but nonetheless, he was still the *tzaddik* of his time. He was effectively hired by God to give *mussar* and rebuke to the people of the world and enjoin them to follow the commandments of the time. He faced a colossal task because his generation was sufficiently evil before Hashem as to warrant complete eradication. Noach approached his task in a seemingly detached manner. He did manage to pique many people's curiosity regarding why he was building a mammoth structure. He had 120 years to go out and attempt to prevail over the wickedness of the generation and teach them to correct their ways. However, Noach chose to pursue an unpretentious course, focusing on building his *teivah* (ark). He thought his single-minded and determined effort to build this *teivah* in preparation for the massive flood would surely penetrate the hearts and minds of his generation.

Yet Noach's unassertive tactic seemed not to work; it influenced no one but his own children. What was Noach hoping would transpire as a result of his conduct?

Perhaps we can suggest that while Noach's effort to try and save the world was noble, it didn't work. It wasn't that Noach failed; it was that the people of the world failed to absorb his teachings. Noach did not necessarily do outreach by tapping people on the shoulder or cold-calling to invite them for services. Rather, Noach's forte was somewhat unique and perhaps lacking in our day and age. In my humble opinion, the method Noach used was the process of gradual or subconscious assimilation of ideas: knowledge defined as "osmosis." There are many things a person knows not through overt teachings or aggressive stimulation, but rather through the process of osmosis.

A key factor influencing the return of nonobservant Jews to Torah-true Judasim is whether their experience with and perception of observant Jews involves *chillul Hashem* or *kiddush Hashem*. Why would a nonobservant Jew want to become religious if they witness observant Jews desecrating God's name? (I am not referring here to sins that fall within the normal category of "For there is no man so wholly righteous on earth that he always does good and never sins" [*Koheles* 7:20].)

There are plenty of unassuming, quiet Jews who go about their business and are known to be honest, who only have a good word to say about others, who treat others with respect regardless of whether they know them or not. The power of *kiruv* (outreach) can be accomplished through the process of osmosis. If a Jew acts like a Jew is supposed to act, quietly demonstrating *middos* and honesty, he is essentially emanating an effective method of bringing others close to home.

Midrash Rabbah (Bereishis 26:2) quotes from *Tehillim* (92:14): "שתולים בבית ה' בחצרות אלקינו יפריחו—Planted in the House of Hashem, in the courtyards of our God they will blossom," and (ibid., v. 15): "עוד ינובון בשיבה דשנים ורעננים יהיו—They will be fruitful in old age; they will be full of sap and freshness." The midrash explains that the one who was "planted in the House of God" is referring to Noach, whom God planted in the *teivah*. "In the courtyards of our God they will blossom," refers to Noach having children named Shem, Cham, and Yafes. "They will be fruitful," refers to Noach, while, "they will be full of sap and freshness," refers to Noach bearing his three children. The analogy of Noach being "planted" is because plants and flowers are looked at and inhaled by those in their surroundings.

Hashem held back the birth of Noach's children until he was five hundred years of age, while all the other men in his time had children in the age range of one hundred to two hundred years. Normally, people have more energy and strength to raise children when they are younger. Hashem made this point to show Noach's greatness—that his children survived the flood despite having been raised by an old father. They saw and experienced the sincerity of their father, and even though he was older, they absorbed his parenting and teaching through osmosis.

The midrash is commenting on *Tehillim* 92, which is the *shir shel yom* (psalm of the day), for Shabbos. By experiencing and observing a perfect day of Shabbos, we plant ourselves in the House of Hashem and will ultimately blossom. The blossoming process is that which surrounds all of us; whether our own children or those around us in the courtyard of life. The responsibility of observant Jews is to become better, more dedicated Jews. By raising the level of existing religious observance and attitude, we will, in turn, raise the consciousness, dedication, and observance of nonreligious Jews around us. In today's day and age, the best kind of Jewish outreach—and inreach—is just being a good all-around Jew and letting people see. Jews who are suspicious of religious Jews are keen enough to discern between lip service and sincere service to Hashem. Noach lived a righteous life and survived while the men of his generation did not pick up his uniqueness in serving Hashem. To the contrary, they poked fun at him, and despised and ridiculed him. We know what happened to that generation, and we saw how Noach was able to rebuild a new world. We, too, should stand up to the ridicule and pressure by just acting in a manner that creates a *kiddush Hashem*, taking notice of how many people start coming closer to Hashem. One does not necessarily need to go to them; they will seek out the truth and come to you.

Chapter III

TORAH

The Blueprint
or the Architecture?

DO you ever pick up your cell phone and feel that it's very hot and the battery is drained?

Do your eyes and forehead ever hurt when you're trying to read?

When fasting, do you ever feel uncomfortable, listless, and hear your stomach rumbling or feel your muscles straining?

All these examples—cell phones heating up, eyes hurting, stomach muscles straining—share something in common.

Cell phones search for a signal from their carrier, and the search continues trying to connect until it finally links up to a strong connection. During this search, the battery continues to work, burning itself out trying to make the connection. Once the link-up occurs, it cools down.

As I approached middle age, my nearsightedness became an issue. Without the appropriate corrective lenses, my eyes strained to see properly. Our eyes make ever-increasing effort to focus so that the more we try, the greater the strain is on the eyes. I've noticed that as soon as I put on my new reading glasses, everything comes into focus and the strain is immediately relieved.

On a fast day, we feel increasing pangs of hunger. As our stomachs empty and don't refill, our bodies search for nutrition from all sources, pulling from the area where food is normally stored. Our stomachs' constant search for food causes strain and discomfort. As soon as we eat, the muscles searching for nutrition start relaxing.

The fascinating common denominator is feelings of strain and uncertainty when dealing with a lack of needed energy or correction. Quite often, while enduring such a difficulty, we are troubled and cannot accept the fact that once the situation is resolved everything will again be calm. We cannot grasp that once the battery cools down, the vision clears up; with glasses, the headaches will go away; and with food, the hunger pangs will subside. Often, we only recognize why we went through something after the cure is revealed. We begin to appreciate why things are unclear only after the issue is resolved. As they say in the vernacular, "Hindsight is twenty-twenty."

We, in this world, can only discern the present situation. We train our minds to believe that this is only a part of a bigger picture. Even though things in life may appear bleak and dark now, we believe it is for a reason. We struggle to deduce how the difficulties are necessary for the future. This concept straddles both worlds, from bad eyesight enabling us to recognize the benefit of good glasses and the beauty of vision, to recognizing that difficulties in the present can lead to something good in the future.

Often in life, we can't understand why certain events take place. Some of us merit to live long enough to see how later events bring clarity to events that transpired earlier in life.

During the last century, Jews have lived and experienced this phenomenon. Chazal teach us that we do not have clear vision and understanding of why and what happens in this world. Whether the issues are about each one of us personally, our families living in Eretz Yisrael, the Jewish People at large, or the entire world, it is only at the time of Mashiach that we will be able to truly see the entire picture and understand why certain things had to happen. In the time of Mashiach, the world we live in today will become clear not only to the Jews, but to all the other nations as well. With clarity and certainty, the nations of the world and the Jewish People will see everything.

At the conclusion of every service, we stand to say *Aleinu*. The final lines of *Aleinu* proclaim: "Through the Sovereignty of the Almighty…all humanity will call upon Your Name, to turn toward You all the wicked of the earth…They will offer and accept the yoke of Your Kingship that You may reign over them. Then will Hashem be King over all the world. On that day shall Hashem be One and His Name One."

In other words, the only true clarity will be in the future. What about now? How do we gain a little more clarity about life? We keep our Torah and mitzvos and we await the future Redemption, and that provides us with some measure of clarity.

Every morning I try to be as cheerful as possible, saying good morning to people with a smile. Recently, I encountered one of my regular congregants and said the usual good morning, but I did not have that pearly white smile on my face. Surprisingly, the person said to me, "No smile today?" To which I quickly replied, "The smile is there; it is just covered by my mouth and lips."

There was a famous line by Alan Alda, an actor who portrayed an emergency Mobile Army hospital surgeon during the Korean War. When necessary, the surgeons would work around the clock, sometimes for thirty-six hours straight, as the flow of wounded soldiers seemed to never cease. Sometimes there was a lull in the fighting, giving ample time to rest, but once again, after a long shift, they would be inundated with more casualties. One time, completely exhausted, he lay down to catch some sleep—only to be awakened by the corporal, who questioned him, "Why are you sleeping?" He replied, "I am not sleeping, I am just checking the inside of my eyelids." In other words, our eyes are always open, but the lids cover them up!

There is a prayer we recite once a month call *Birkas Ha'chodesh*, the blessing of the incoming new month. However, the very same term,

Birkas Ha'chodesh, is used in the Talmud to designate a very different ritual—a blessing praising God for the new moon, recited outdoors while glancing at the waxing moon at the beginning of the month. This ritual, which some Jews are unfamiliar with, is known as *Kiddush Levanah*, loosely translated as "sanctification of the moon." The source of *Kiddush Levanah* is in the Gemara, *Sanhedrin* 42a. It is not one of the 613 mitzvos; it is a Rabbinical mitzvah that was instituted to help us realize the greatness of Hashem through His wondrous creation. Men are required to recite *Kiddush Levanah*, but because this is a time-bound commandment, women are exempt.

To recite the blessing, one must see the moon at night for at least a moment. In certain locations, weather poses a great challenge to fulfilling this mitzvah. In the first half of the month, after the evening prayer, there is at least one person in any given shul throughout the world who goes outside to see if the moon is visible. Invariably, they come back inside and either report seeing a beautiful moon, or if it is cloudy and covered over, no moon at all.

Now if they report that there is no moon, what do they really intend to say—that the moon disappeared? We all know that just because we cannot see the moon doesn't mean it is not there! To the contrary, even though we cannot see the moon, we still know it is there; it's just covered up by clouds.

Clouds were an integral part of the Jewish camp when they traveled through the desert. Clouds come in all different shapes and sizes and their function or purpose varies according to the need or situation. A cloud typically obscures something, creates a blur, creates a sense of vagueness, making things unclear. So what exactly was the purpose of the cloud that covered Har Sinai during the world's greatest moment of clarity?

The Torah describes the giving of the Torah in great detail. However, not only do we read about the actual commandments that were received, but also the incredibly wondrous and exciting manner in which they were received, yielding a lasting impression of awe.

The aftermath was just as critical as the events leading up to the giving of the Ten Commandments. The Torah states in *Shemos* (20:18):

"ויעמד העם מרחק ומשה נגש אל הערפל אשר שם האלקים"—The people kept their distance while Moshe entered the *arafel* where the Divine was revealed." What was the *arafel*?

- Rashi describes the *arafel* as a mist.
- Rabbi Hirsch, based upon the *Radak*, explains the *arafel* as a heavy cloud.
- According to other opinions, namely Rabbeinu Bachya and *Me'am Lo'ez*, it was a "glowing light."
- *HaKesav V'HaKabbalah* calls it a "blinding light."

On this verse, the *Mechilta* says that Moshe went through three partitions to stand before God. The three partitions were darkness, a cloud, and the *arafel*:

- The outer layer was darkness.
- Inside the layer of darkness was the cloud.
- Within the cloud was the *arafel*.

The verse says that Moshe approached the *arafel*, an image paralleling the Kohen Gadol entering the Holy of Holies on Yom Kippur. As Moshe entered and went in deeper, he got closer to Hashem, and a greater light was revealed into the *arafel* on top of Har Sinai.

The *Malbim* explains that darkness can completely shut out any light, preventing it from shining at all. In the cloud there was a degree of light, but the cloud created a separation between Moshe and the great light. The cloud gathers all the light and holds it together, preventing access to this light. The *arafel* is in an area that spreads the light that is being held back. As Moshe infiltrated the series of partitions, he was able to get closer to Hashem, reaching a greater level of understanding of God than any other man. With this understanding we see why the verse concludes with the words, "where the Divine was revealed." Moshe reached a level of understanding of Hashem's presence and place in the world because Hashem's presence fills the world.

We live in a world of darkness because we are not able to access the light. Moshe worked on himself to reach a level where he could gain access to the light and see clearly God's presence in the world. We must realize that there is light that provides clarity and reality to the world.

The trouble is that due to the physical components of the world, darkness blocks out the light. If we could get beyond the physical, we too would also enjoy the brightness and truth of the world as Moshe did. We strive on a daily basis to get a glimpse past the cloud that obscures the light in order to see and feel the Shechinah. Even if we are unable to reach the level of Moshe, Hashem will nevertheless one day remove the cloud that covers the light.

We should all be blessed with the strength of removing the darkness and displaying the light through a good eye, a big smile, and seeing through the clouds!

The practice of spying or using spies, is typically conducted

by government agencies employed to gather intelligence on domestic activities, as well as on friendly and unfriendly governments. People should keep in mind that the spy business is usually a two-way street. Just as one individual is attempting to gather information on someone else, that individual may be also gathering information on the first individual simultaneously. If you are old enough to remember the original television show (or the reruns) called *Get Smart*, you may recall the names of the two spy organizations: "Control" and "Chaos." These two organizations were constantly spying on each other. This holds true in the real world as well. There are currently seventeen intelligence agencies in the US, all of which fall under the umbrella of the Department of Defense.

Whenever I go out into the world, whether it is to go shopping, ballplaying in public, a sporting event, or some type of recreational activity, I always bring my "spy glasses" with me. Call me neurotic or paranoid, but whenever I enter a restaurant, or any unfamiliar room, I always sit facing the entrance because I hate having my back to the door. In a sense, I spy out those who enter, simultaneously surveying my surroundings, helping me to feel safe in the new, unknown environment. Whether this is truly effective or not, I hope never to find out. Realistically, I am not only looking at everyone else, but I am aware that everyone else is also looking at me—most probably all for the same reasons. Putting aside the strange room and seating scenario, I am constantly being eyed by people who question whether I am Jewish and whether I am also a rabbi.

When out and about, I generally try avoiding the questioning eye about religion. Typically, people try to lure me into conversation by speaking in a bland, nonthreatening tone. Once engaged—either because I have a few extra minutes on hand, feel up for a good fight, or am simply caught off guard—I get peppered with questions about Judaism. Most often, I am asked the obvious questions about my yarmulke and tzitzis. These questioners even openly wonder if I always wear a suit and tie! Some cashiers will ask if a special holiday is coming up, looking at the quantity and assortment of typical Jewish foods. The range of questions knows no bounds, covering topics dealing with Israel, Zionism, the Talmud, Jewish law, and even the location of the synagogue. The worst is when a questioner innocently begins speaking of Judaism and then turns the question into a nasty diatribe ridiculing Judaism and Jews, finally espousing his religion upon me. Recently, I was stopped and asked the usual question, "Are you a rabbi?" I quickly ran through a mental analysis of my time, patience, and desire regarding whether to answer in the affirmative or not. The instant evaluation led me to say, "Yes, I am a rabbi." I then took a deep breath waiting for the next question or statement to roll out about me and my religion. I was pleasantly surprised to receive a confrontation I'd never had before. Hearing that I was a rabbi, this individual calmly asked me, "Rabbi, please teach me something."

I was completely caught off guard but regained my composure and calmly quoted the famous verse from *Vayikra* regarding loving your neighbor as yourself. When a spy is caught by another spy, he must always be prepared in advance with answers he intends to divulge to the other side.

It was such a refreshing response from anyone, let alone a non-Jew. For the record, most of the interactions I encounter regarding the topic of learning with Jews is typically, "Why do we need to do this or that and why can't we do this or that?" Rare is the time someone approaches me with a request of "Rabbi, please teach me something." This was a refreshing perspective on how people react differently in different situations. I felt this person's sincerity and desire to learn. This, Heaven forbid, does not mean to discount the many Jews who ask me questions of "why" and "what," because, most often, they are coming from a good place. When the gentleman asked me the question, I started to think of another angle as to why his question was different. The answer is connected to the names of the spy agencies of *Get Smart*, mentioned above. The good spies were called "Control," while the bad spies were called "Chaos." These names represent the core principle of Judaism: the Torah was given to us to control our lives while the *yetzer hara* was created to challenge the Torah and create chaos.

It is interesting to note that both types are referred to as "spies."

We tend to sympathize with the first, conventionally noble group and may even want to join their lines. Moshe himself sent out twelve "equal spies," yet after the fact, most commentaries view them as ten bad spies and two good spies. Most *mefarshim* give a bad rap to the ten spies, but there are some who find merit in their words and actions. One such commentary is the *Tzvi Yisrael*, commenting on the opening verse in the *parashah*. In *Bamidbar* (13:2), Moshe sends out one spy per tribe, describing the worthiness of each man. The purpose and benefit of sending spies was to create the impression that it would be a challenge to conquer the land, and that only due to God would we capture it. If spies were *not* sent, the concern was that future generations might say, "The inhabitants of Canaan were weak and the Jews—our ancestors—conquered the land through natural means." Perhaps, therefore, Hashem would have acquiesced to B'nei Yisrael's request to send spies, thereby alleviating this concern. The spies would come back, and we would have on record that the inhabitants were giants and very strong, but despite all that, we were able to conquer the land because of Hashem. The hint to this lies in the words in the *pasuk*: "אשר אני נותן לבני ישראל—That which I [Hashem] gave to the Children of Israel."

The attitude is what makes the whole difference:

- The good spies look out for ways to protect the Torah and its ability to control our *yetzer hara* and push our *yetzer hatov*, encouraging a life of achievement and joy.

- The evil spies, who create chaos, look for ways to disrupt the design of the Torah, its mitzvos, and the ways to adhere to it.

We are all spies and messengers. For the most part, Orthodox Judaism works for the spy agency known as "Control," although sometimes we forget and become spies for "Chaos" in our *hashkafah*, our philosophical outlook in life. It is so easy to create chaos and it is always difficult to control, but that is our challenge in life. *Hatzlachah* to all those who ask questions!

One never knows how near or far our teachings may reach. A few weeks ago, I received a phone call early Sunday morning from a *rav* in Baltimore whose sister had passed away here in San Diego. I did not know this rabbi and I had never met his sister, so I asked how he got to me. The rabbi's niece, the daughter of the *nifteres* (deceased), explained to me that her mother had told her that if her brother (the rabbi in Baltimore) could not come to officiate at her funeral she wanted me to perform the *levayah* service. Somehow, the daughter received my weekly message, printed it out every Friday and shared and read it with her mother every Shabbos. I had never met anyone in this family beforehand, and I was touched beyond belief.

One of the challenges for someone working in the spiritual field requires patience in order to see the fruits of their labor. In much of life, we must accept the fact that we may never see results or growth from our efforts. We can only try to sow the seeds and hope that people will be nurtured and eventually produce the fruits that we planted. Unfortunately, there is never a guarantee that a person (whether a child, student, or friend) will develop the seeds planted within them. However, even if those seeds do not take root for many years, they may eventually blossom even if we never know about it.

For most educators, we often do not see the fruits of our labor because we are busy with direct, one-on-one impact on each student, yet eventually, it may be a student's child or grandchild who reaps the benefit of the learning.

We are all taught and trained from the time of our youth that the reward for mitzvos and good deeds are reserved for the World to Come. It is with deep faith that we continue to persevere and fulfill the Torah with the conviction that we do not want the reward in this world and would rather wait to receive it in the next world.

The words of Torah leave an everlasting impact on everyone who learns it and shares in its beauty.

A few weeks ago, out of the blue, as I was walking, I caught my-self favoring one foot over the other. I found it difficult to put pressure on my left foot, especially when walking barefoot. For some reason it felt better and less acute when wearing socks and even more so wearing shoes. After I gave up on my usual stubbornness and natural tendency toward martyrdom, I decided to actually look and see why my foot hurt. Lo and behold, I had a nasty callus that had just appeared out of nowhere. A similar condition comes from a cousin of the callus known as the corn. From where do calluses and corns come?

Calluses and corns are thick, hardened layers of skin that develop when the skin tries to protect itself against friction and pressure. They most often develop on feet and toes or hands and fingers. Corns and calluses can be unsightly. If you are healthy, you need treatment for corns and calluses only if they cause discomfort. For most people, simply eliminating the source of friction or pressure makes corns and calluses disappear. Callous comes from the Latin root *callum,* meaning "hard skin." Walking barefoot excessively can cause feet to become calloused. I needed an over-the-counter treatment, which, within a few weeks, killed the dead skin around the callus and eventually peeled away, leaving new fresh skin underneath.

I began to wonder why I had this callus and what I did wrong to deserve the discomfort it brought me. I thought about the concept of *middah k'neged middah,* "measure for measure," and tried to calculate which mitzvah I had perhaps neglected. Of the 613 mitzvos, most are performed by the hands, mouth, or by just being in attendance, while very few are accomplished through use of one's feet. Although some of the *baalei mussar* emphasize that it is our feet that bring us to the places where we fulfill mitzvos or commit *aveiros*, it is not the feet themselves that actually commit the sin. Or is it?

We usually use the word "callous" in the metaphorical sense, referring to the emotionally hardened. If someone is unmoved by other people's problems, one might say he shows a callous indifference toward human suffering; his feelings and emotions are deadened. Generally, this definition is associated with relationships between man and his fellow. Perhaps it is appropriate to suggest that callousness includes man's relationship with God.

In *Parashas Emor*, we read about the festival cycle beginning with Pesach and ending with Shemini Atzeres. Although the commandment to "go up" to Yerushalayim is found later in the Torah and limited to Pesach, Shavuos, and Sukkos, we nevertheless understand that the concept is implied here in *Emor* as well. In *Vayikra* (23:4), the Torah states: "אלה מועדי ה׳ מקראי קדש אשר תקראו אתם במועדם"—These are God's festivals that you must celebrate as sacred holidays at their appropriate times." The Gerrer Rebbe, Rabbi Yitzchak Meir Alter, explains that these appointed, appropriate times are called "sacred" times—they draw the person to holiness. Therefore, only three verses later does the Torah state: "ביום הראשון מקרא קדש יהיה לכם"—The first day shall be a sacred holiday for you," i.e., that you will be called and drawn to holiness.

We may ask, "Who exactly is being drawn to holiness and given an opportunity to become holy—the Torah scholars or the average Jew?" Rabbi Avraham Lichtenstein, in his *sefer Kanfei Nesharim*, writes that it is speaking to the general population—the average Jew—who is not involved in Torah study all the time. Often, laypeople are busy with work, business, and other activities. This limits their time and involvement in pursuing Torah study, which are the very tools necessary to reach ever greater spiritual heights. These appointed times are designed for the average *balebos*; to use Shabbos and Yom Tov to study more Torah and be drawn more deeply into holy pursuits. The Torah is a book of life from which we learn and absorb a deeper understanding of the mitzvos. Shabbos and Yom Tov are imbued with holiness, and they are times that allow us to draw into ourselves a special *ruach ha'kodesh*—a certain

Divine, spirited inspiration to receive and understand more of the Torah. Similarly, the concept of having a *neshamah yeseirah*, an extra soul on Shabbos and Yom Tov, a means by which we receive physical nourishment and we also draw spiritual and intellectual nourishment from that same extra *neshamah*. Shabbos and Yom Tov are a call to become spiritually replenished. These holy days are imbued with the charging device and the time to do so.

One of the distinctions between Yom Tov and Shabbos is the fact that we, not Hashem, determine when Yom Tov will fall out based upon the sanctification of the moon. The mitzvah of *Kiddush Ha'chodesh* was the first mitzvah given to Klal Yisrael as a nation. Apparently, up until that point, the decision to calculate the holidays was still in God's court, not the earthly court. This is supported by *Shemos Rabbah* (15:2), which states: "HaKadosh Baruch Hu said before the Torah was given that the *mo'adim* [i.e., festivals or appointed times] belonged to Me. From now on, they belong to you." The midrash says that the festivals were originally "*mo'adei Hashem*," but they were given to Klal Yisrael, who determine when the new month begins: "*Asher tikre'u osam*—that which is now determined by them."

The mitzvah of going up to Yerushalayim on the festivals encourages us to take the right steps in order to grow closer to Hashem. *We* establish when these holidays will occur, placing the initiative directly upon us. Nowadays, while we cannot formally fulfill this mitzvah in the absence of the Beis Hamikdash, we can take Yom Tov seriously, seeing it as a time to get closer to Hashem. Perhaps I did not use my time during Yom Tov carefully enough to strive to be *oleh regel*—to use my feet correctly to "go up." I therefore needed to be reminded of my "callousness" toward Hashem by developing a callus on the part of the body that, metaphorically, did not take me where I was supposed to go.

Preventive medicine is always better than deferred maintenance, but nevertheless, some people feel that since they are healthy, why bother going for regular check-ups? Others are afraid to go to the doctor for fear that they may find out that something is wrong. *Baruch*

Hashem, I feel healthy and therefore have no problem going to the doctor at least twice a year. In preparation for my physical examination, I have blood drawn to give the physician some internal information prior to the exam date. For the best and most accurate results, blood should be drawn while fasting, except for drinking water. I choose to have the blood test taken as early as possible, but as a result I must skip my morning cup of coffee—the "fix" that gets me going for the day. Upon my return from the doctor's office, I make a beeline for the coffee machine and enjoy that cup with an overwhelming sense of satisfaction usually accompanied by an "ahhhh"—an expression of relief and pure delight.

There are a few natural, guttural responses to sensory and emotional experiences:

- When I take a sip of my first cup of coffee in the morning, I let out a sigh of "ahhhh."
- A hot cup of tea that follows a heavy dinner is "uhhhh."
- At the shul *kiddush* I hear reactions of "ooooh" when someone drinks a new scotch or bourbon they have never tasted before.
- If someone eats something delicious, the typical reaction is "mmmm."
- Even the different sizes of the blue prize boxes at parent-child learning programs receive different level of "ooohs" and "ahhhs."
- When we worry about something, it's either an "*oy vey*" or "*ai yai yai*."

There are also a few facial expressions that soundlessly communicate very clear emotions. This kind of expression is magnified in our times due to the emojis and emoticons people use while messaging and writing communications via their computers and handheld devices. Sound or facial expressions are often made at the beginning of something such as the start or at the end of a message. Every individual decides where and when to use an expression, and the question is, where is its use most effective?

On a more serious note, which is greater—starting or finishing something? As we proceed through life, we begin many things, but we do not necessarily complete them all. And everyone knows that if you never begin, you will never have the wherewithal to finish. I believe both starting and finishing are equally important; both provide a sense of accomplishment. Ultimately, when a person finishes a cycle of something or begins something completely new, the end or the beginning should motivate a person to strive for greater heights.

I have noticed that as human beings, we all have different reactions, some physical and some emotional. In addition, we each react differently at the start or end of an event. The taste and impact a "sweet" has on a person's stomach will vary based upon whether it is eaten at the beginning of a meal, on an empty stomach, or at the end of the meal for dessert, on a full stomach. The reaction and response toward a situation will vary according to when it occurs. This idea is found in the amazing description of the giving of the Torah.

The Torah states in *Shemos* (20:15): "וכל העם ראים את הקולת ואת הלפידם ואת קול השפר ואת ההר עשן וירא העם וינעו ויעמדו מרחק—All the people saw the sounds, the flames, the blast of the ram's horn, and the mountain smoking. The people trembled when they saw it, keeping their distance." The *Ibn Ezra* explains that when it says they "saw the sounds," it is referring to hearing. In a similar vein, in *Bereishis* (42:1), the Torah writes that Yaakov saw that there was food in Mitzrayim. Obviously, Yaakov did not actually "see" that there was food down in Egypt—rather, *Rashi* says he "heard." The sense of sight would typically refer to vision, to mentally processing what the eyes "see," just as the sense of hearing refers to mentally processing the sounds that the ear is "hearing." However, the five senses—seeing, hearing, tasting, touching, and smelling—all have more than one meaning. The *Rambam*, in *Moreh Nevuchim*, writes that the definition of "seeing" means feeling and reaching an understanding. Another example of this is in *Bereishis* (27:27): "ויגש וישק לו וירח את ריח בגדיו ויברכהו, ויאמר ראה ריח בני כריח שדה אשר ברכו ה'—And he [Yitzchak] said, 'See the fragrance of my son...'" Yitzchak did not literally "see" the fragrance of his son, but he *understood* the fragrance. Whenever the verse mentions the concept of seeing, it implies a level of understanding, of inner perception.

The *Rosh*, Rabbeinu Asher, writes that "seeing the voices and sounds at Har Sinai" actually means one benefited from the sounds. There are other references in the Torah that infer that the term "saw" is defined as receiving some type of benefit from what was seen. Rabbeinu Bachya explains the verse in *Tehillim* (29:7): "קול ה' חצב להבות אש"—The voice of Hashem hews out flames of fire." They would *see* the fire at the giving of the Torah and then, as it says, they *saw* the voices and the sounds.

There are many ways to communicate information, news, and feelings that we want to share with one another. We must be careful of the little gestures we make, both consciously and subconsciously, because subliminal messages can be very powerful. We need to realize that it takes no more than a little sigh to let everyone around us know how we're feeling. People will "see" you through "hearing" some of the things that just come out, intentionally or not. Let the noise and the sounds people hear be those of satisfaction and appreciation for all that we experience. In order to really allow Torah to become part of us, let it enter all our senses!

There is nothing in life that does not require *siyata d'Shmaya*, Heavenly assistance. Every waking minute, from the time we open our eyes in the morning until we rest our heads on our pillows at night, God helps us with everything. But as the old saying goes, "God helps those who help themselves." In both my personal and professional life, I try to manage things on my own with direct assistance from the One above. Nevertheless, there are emergency situations that none of us can manage alone, and these require the assistance of others. One such emergency is when the local *eiruv* goes down at a point in the week, past the ordinary time that would enable us to fix it. Due to the late hour, our *eiruv* maintenance company cannot schedule the job to fix it in time for Shabbos. Help! I need *siyata d'Shmaya*, and I need it through the help of others. *Baruch Hashem*, I have some great people around to help, think, and brainstorm for a solution. Particularly during times of heavy storms, I've had to rack my brains to keep the *eiruv* as operational as possible in time for Shabbos.

What is the definition and history behind the word "brainstorming"? Alex Faickney Osborn (1888–1966) was an advertising executive and the author of the creativity technique named "brainstorming." Osborn began developing methods for creative problem-solving in 1939. He was frustrated by his employees' inability to develop creative ideas for ad campaigns. In response, he began hosting group-thinking sessions and discovered a significant improvement in the quality and quantity of ideas produced by employees. Osborn outlined his method in the 1948 book, *Your Creative Power*.

Osborn claimed that two principles contribute to "ideative efficacy": deferring judgment and reaching for quantity. Following these two principles, his general rules of brainstorming were established with intention to

- reduce social inhibitions among group members,
- stimulate idea generation,
- increase overall creativity of the group.

Here were his rules:

1. **Go for quantity**: This rule is a means of enhancing divergent production, aiming to facilitate problem-solving through the maxim "quantity breeds quality." The assumption is that the greater the number of ideas generated, the bigger the chance of producing a radical and effective solution.

2. **Withhold criticism**: In brainstorming, criticism of ideas generated should be put "on hold." Instead, participants should focus on extending or adding to ideas, reserving criticism for a later "critical stage" of the process. By suspending judgment, participants will feel free to generate unusual ideas.

3. **Welcome wild ideas**. To get a good, long list of suggestions, wild ideas are encouraged. They can be generated by looking from new perspectives and suspending assumptions. These new ways of thinking might give you better solutions.

4. **Combine and improve ideas**: As suggested by the slogan "1+1=3," this is believed to stimulate the building of ideas by a process of association.

Osborn notes that brainstorming should address a specific question, and he held that sessions addressing multiple questions were inefficient. Osborn envisioned groups of around twelve participants, including both experts and novices. Participants would be encouraged to provide wild and unexpected answers. Ideas receive no criticism or discussion. The group simply provides ideas that might lead to a solution and applies no analytical judgment as to the feasibility. The judgments are reserved for a later date. Ultimately, working together makes people learn, grow, and offer solutions to challenging situations they would unlikely be able to resolve on their own.

So now, back to our very stormy weather and the *eiruv* situation. After much brainstorming with some of the best and brightest minds of our generation, we were on our way. It took a good number of hours during the week to come up with a plan of action that, while far from perfect, would hopefully be a stopgap measure to temporarily keep the *eiruv* up in that section. I'm not sure I alone could have resolved the issue; this was a collective effort that met success.

As there is nothing new under the sun, where in the Torah do we find the strategy of brainstorming?

I will take literary license to point out a very subtle scene that is over-looked by most of the commentaries regarding Moshe brainstorming the plan to take the Jews out of Egypt. The Torah states in *Shemos* (4:28–29): "ויגד משה לאהרן את כל דברי ה' אשר שלחו ואת כל האתת אשר צוהו: וילך משה ואהרן ויאספו את כל זקני בני ישראל—And Moshe described to Aharon everything that God had told him about his mission. And Moshe and Aharon went to Egypt, and they gathered all the elders of Israel." At first Moshe tells Aharon, his brother, all that Hashem had told him. Then both Moshe and Aharon gathered the elders of the Jewish People.

Why was all this necessary? The *Ramban* is one of the few commentaries to shed some light on this situation. The *Ramban* explains which words Moshe told over to Aharon, which in turn were told to the elders. Moshe told Aharon all the words that were spoken between Him and God and all about how he had resisted the mission. Moreover, he, Moshe, had been sent against his will. This is the meaning of the word *kol*, "all." Moshe told Aharon not only what he had been instructed to do and say in Egypt, but all the words—even those surrounding Hashem's choice of him (Moshe) to be His emissary. Perhaps Moshe was still eliciting feedback on his ability to lead the Jews out of Mitzrayim. Perhaps he wanted to discuss the situation with his older brother and with the elders, whom he greatly respected. Presumably, Moshe went to inform and discuss the plan of Hashem; that he was the man tapped for this job. He was seeking out responses to his concerns. This signals Moshe's humility, and he would continue in this fashion throughout his life.

The strategy called "brainstorming" is a tool that can not only be used in business, but as an incredible instrument for family building, classroom and student unity, and overall team development. Once again, we witness Moshe Rabbeinu teaching Am Yisrael through example; modeling the idea of brainstorming with others rather than relying solely on himself. This is a sign of *anavah*, humility, of which we can all learn to take a dose occasionally.

Stadiums, arenas, and theaters share some common areas and design. Among the items they all have in common are seating, lighting, restrooms, and, of course, the staging area and/or playing field, in other words, where the action takes place. Many shuls today share all the necessary components to qualify for this list.

Most of today's shuls function both for davening and learning. For the most part, the areas designated for anything related to *tefillah* are fixed. On the other hand, when it comes to Torah, learning can take place anywhere. It is extremely important to daven in shul with a minyan, but learning and teaching of Torah has no "restriction"; it can be basically anywhere, anyplace, any time. The main sanctuary of Beth Jacob uses three different platforms for delivering a class or a *derashah*: the pulpit or main podium, the *bimah*, or a *shtender* immediately in front of the pews, which I refer to as field level.

Since the beginning of time, communication has been central to the existence of man. In today's world we have technology that allows us to communicate from the farthest distances with speed and clarity. Whether by email, text, Twitter, or phone, its reach is far in both physical distance and the number of people connected at one time. Nevertheless, the most effective means of communication is face-to-face. I speak differently to people in person than through electronic communication, and I express my thoughts in a different manner to different people; one message is not for all. Furthermore, speaking from a distance is not as intimate as speaking in close proximity, and the message is typically more generic.

A speaker has a unique perspective when giving a talk. A speaker feels "safe" when speaking from a distance, either physically or electronically. As the distance lessens, anxiety tends to increase. Nevertheless, the closer people are when presenting ideas and concepts, the greater the form of communication. Therefore, when speaking at "field level," a person will communicate more effectively than from the pulpit itself.

When the Torah was given at Har Sinai, it was the communiqué of the relationship between God and the Jews. The *midbar*, desert, was the place of this communication and this was specifically because of the effectiveness this venue offered. There are many different channels that Hashem could have used, but ultimately Hashem felt that this was the best place to teach and give the Torah.

The midrash explains that the *midbar* was chosen as the place the Torah would be given because it is truly no-man's-land. The desert is *hefker*, owned by no one. It is open and devoid of distraction, unlike the city or the confines of our homes where we are drawn to a myriad of distractions. The desert is a place to think, to process, to concentrate, making it ideal for Torah learning:

- *Midrash Rabbah* teaches that whoever does not make themselves *hefker* (ownerless) like a desert is not able to acquire wisdom and the Torah.
- The Gemara (*Nedarim* 55a) states: If a person makes himself like a desert, in an ownerless state, then the Torah will be given to him as a gift.
- The midrash states that the Torah was given with fire (*Shemos* 19:18), water (*Shoftim* 5:4), and earth (i.e., the desert, as in *Bamidbar* 1:1). Just as these elements are free in the world and

no one owns them, so too, the Torah is ownerless and whoever wants to take it can do so.

Thus, we see that Torah can be absorbed in many circumstances. It can be picked up from far away on your computer or phone, it can be taught and learned in the *beis midrash* or shul, and—most in line with the original acquisition of Torah—it can be deliberated over in the *midbar* or the equivalent thereof. Finding that time of tranquility, with no interruptions and minimal distractions, when you can think clearly with optimal focus, can bring untold benefit from your pursuit of learning. Even five minutes of quiet can yield much gain in learning, as you emulate the original and ideal acquisition of Torah.

Last Shabbos, as the *aron kodesh* opened, a feeling of sadness fell upon me. The *aron* in our shul normally houses three *Sifrei Torah,* but to my dismay, only two out of those three were present. At first glance I was shocked, and then alarm and panic gripped hold of me. Immediately, I thought it might have been borrowed without permission. Then...emerged the dreaded thought, *Was it stolen?* As my mind raced during those few seconds while singing the words of *"Va'yehi bin-so'a ha'Aron,"* I began to focus, remembering what had happened only a few weeks prior. Here is a description of what led to my apprehension.

Throughout life, many people, in their respective professions, learn and prepare for unique situations, possible emergencies that they hope will never materialize or come to fruition. It is almost like buying insurance: we need it and must have it but hope never to use it.

This applies even more so in the Rabbinate. Many laws and halachos are learned and studied, mostly for the theoretical possibility—as remote as that may be—to know what and how to proceed in a situation when a split-second decision is needed. Sure, there are times when a question arises and there is ample time to go back and review the law, but often one needs to act immediately, relying on memory, expertise, and a lot of *siyata d'Shmaya.*

During our *semichah* training many years ago, Rabbi Wein reviewed many scenarios, including this most recent one. It was an ordinary

Shabbos morning, and we were rolling along, zipping through Torah reading. During the sixth *aliyah*, my eyes were trying to focus in on a word, working to decipher the letters. The word was distorted. As I peered in closely, my heart sank, realizing that the ink had begun to fade on some of the letters. One letter, a *yud*, had almost completely disintegrated. Emotionally, or perhaps psychologically, I was trying to figure out how this Torah was still kosher according to the most lenient opinion. My mind worked quickly, drawing upon all I had learned over the years regarding such a scenario, but I was left with no alternative: the *Sefer Torah* was *pasul* (invalid), and therefore not kosher for use. At that point, as I hovered over the Torah, other men on the *bimah* started to peer over, searching for the error. After I declared it *pasul* and motioned to the *gabbai* to bring another *Sefer Torah* out, a group of men moved into action, helping to take care of the invalid Torah. It reminded me, and others, how if God forbid, a human being needs medical attention, a crowd will quickly gather around to help. A few of the guys helped dress the *pasul* Torah while others quickly brought out another Torah to continue the *leining*. During this commotion, I and all those around me felt a keen sense of connection to this now-*pasul* Torah, as though it was a living human being.

The Torah, which is the *eitz chaim*, the "tree of life," was now injured, perhaps critically. It needed to be carried away while all of us hoped for the best. There was a sudden strong feeling of loss that gripped everyone who had witnessed the Torah "going down"—a sense of defeat and despair permeated through the shul. The good news is that a *Sefer Torah* can always be repaired. Unlike tefillin or a mezuzah, which, when a letter is cracked or missing, will often be declared permanently invalid, a Torah can always be repaired and brought back to life.

It is interesting to note that the word *meis*, "dead," is used to describe something that is permanent and final. When the Torah records the death of the great leaders, the word "dead" is not used. Instead the phrase "he was gathered" or "departed" is used, signifying that dying is not the end; the body has died, but not the soul.

When telling the story of the Egyptians drowning in the Yam Suf, the Torah is reluctant to state that all the Egyptians "died." Instead, in

Shemos (14:28), the Torah states: "וישבו המים ויכסו את הרכב ואת הפרשים לכל חיל פרעה הבאים אחריהם בים לא נשאר בהם עד אחד—And the waters returned and covered the chariots, and the horsemen, even all the host of Pharaoh that went in after them into the sea; there remained not so much as one of them."

The language, "that there remained not so much as one of them," is also used when describing the end of the fifth plague in *Shemos* (9:6): "ויעש ה׳ את הדבר הזה ממחרת וימת כל מקנה מצרים וממקנה בני ישראל לא מת אחד—And Hashem did that thing on the morrow, and all the cattle of Egypt died; but of the cattle of the Children of Israel died not one." David HaMelech, in *Tehillim* (106:11), uses the same expression, "אחד מהם לא נותר—that not one of them remained." We recite this in the paragraph leading up to the morning *Amidah*. One of the *Baalei HaTosafos* writes: "*Lo nishar bahen ad echad*," explaining *ad* to mean that one did remain. He uses the rule of "up until, but not including" the last part of a statement (e.g., I am told to answer math problems 1–10, so I do "up until, but not including," i.e., only problems 1–9). Who was the one person that survived the drowning from the Red Sea? It is explained that Pharaoh survived and that "not one of them" refers to his people, who did not survive. The midrash explains that the *malach* Gavriel came and submerged Pharaoh in the water for fifty days as a direct punishment for having exclaimed, "Who is God?" The word *mi* in Hebrew also spells out the word "water," which has the numerical value of fifty.

The *Mechilta* records a dispute as to what happened to Pharaoh:

- Rabbi Yehudah says even Pharaoh drowned.
- Rabbi Nechemia says everyone died except for Pharaoh.
- A third opinion is that Pharaoh went in last and drowned.
- The *Midrash Seichel Tov* tells us that Pharaoh did go down into the water and Hashem turned him on his face and the water covered him, but his soul did not leave him. At that point, an angel of Hashem plucked Pharaoh out of the water and brought him to the city of Nineveh. Hashem spared Pharaoh so that he could relate the amazing feats that the God of the Jews performed for them against him. Hashem wanted Pharaoh to reveal His name

throughout the land of Nineveh and throughout the world. The Rabbis say he ruled over Nineveh for five hundred years and brought them back to repent. How awesome it was for the man who denied and rebelled against Hashem to promote and bring greatness to His name, whereby Pharaoh himself declared, "Who is as great as the God of the Jews!"

For this reason, Hashem saved him so he could be the messenger to bring about a revolution of *teshuvah* among the non-Jews of the world. Therefore, the verses do not use the word "dead" as if there were none who returned. To the contrary, when there is a little bit of life left, it has the capability to accomplish many things.

Although our *Sefer Torah* "looked dead," it was not! It was temporarily out of commission. If we do not attend to its aging, it might eventually deteriorate beyond repair. When I see the empty space in the *aron*, I remind myself that this Torah is being taken care of. It is being repaired and will be brought back to life. Not only will it be brought back to life for its own sake, but it is being brought back to life to be the Living Torah, whose purpose is to spread the word of Hashem to us and all of humanity!

The Torah gives life—for it is alive!

The Jewish calendar contains the High Holidays, the minor festivals, and the three pilgrimages known as the *Shalosh Regalim*. Two out of the three—Pesach and Sukkos—are longer holidays with multiple commandments, preparations, and a set of intermediate days that break up the first and second half of the Yom Tov. The third holiday, Shavuos, is not accompanied by any one specific mitzvah, and being only one day (two days outside of Israel), there is no Chol Hamoed. Pesach and Sukkos can be stressful, expensive, and a lot of hard work, while Shavuos is relatively inexpensive and not too difficult. Perhaps the reason we have a Chol Hamoed is to unwind and stretch out a bit from the Yom Tov experience, and therefore Shavuos does not require one.

Many families go on Chol Hamoed trips, and our family is no different. This year, like most years for our family, we ended up doing some type of bike riding. By pure chance, my son and I shared a surrey bicycle with two steering wheels and two sets of pedals. Peddling incorporated the efforts of each rider, with either rider on his own or both riders together affecting the bike's movement. Steering, on the other hand, was a bit different; despite having two steering wheels, only the driver's side controlled the direction. The second steering wheel (that's the one I got) was a "dummy wheel." It did absolutely nothing, no matter how many directions I turned it. The irony, though, was that as we were riding, my instincts as the guy in control of the wheel kicked in. Whenever I felt we veered too far to the right, I turned the wheel to the left, and as I felt we were veering off to the left, I quickly turned my wheel and steered to the right! Even though I consciously knew that my steering wheel was doing absolutely nothing, I still acted upon the situation, thinking I was in control.

We go through life thinking that we are in control of our lives. There is no question that our actions can influence certain outcomes, but ultimately, we are being carried by Hashem. We try to steer the wheel in a certain direction even though we are literally just spinning the wheel. It is true that "בדרך שאדם רוצה לילך בה, מוליכין אותו—In the manner or road a person wants to travel, he will be led on that path" (*Makkos* 10b, *Bamidbar Rabbah* 20:11). That path can be for the good or the bad.

The Torah was carried in the *Aron* throughout the period that the Jews traveled in the desert on their way to Eretz Canaan.

The tribe of Levi—Gershon, Kehas, and Merari—were responsible for carrying the disassembled parts of the *Mishkan* in the desert. However, Chazal teach us that the *Aron* "carried itself" because it contained the two sets of *Luchos* and the original *Sefer Torah* that Moshe wrote. This, in turn, teaches us that we do not carry the Torah, the Torah carries us:

- In *Shemos* (25:15) the *pasuk* states: "בטבעת הארן יהיו הבדים לא יסרו ממנו—In the rings of the Aron the poles shall be, they shall not be moved." Chazal comment that anyone who removes them at any time receives *malkos*, "lashes."
- Both in connection with the *Mizbei'ach Ha'olah* and the *Shulchan*, the Torah confines the poles remaining in place to when the

vessels are being transported. It is only the *Aron* whose poles must remain in place permanently.

- The *Meshech Chochmah* ascribes this to the midrash that states that the *Aron* represents the Crown of Torah, available to whoever wishes to wear it.
- The *talmid chacham*, he explains, requires constant support, as Chazal say in *Pirkei Avos*: "If there is no flour, there is no Torah."
- That is why the Gemara (*Pesachim* 53b) praises those who help *talmidei chachamim* by means of lending them money with which to do business.
- The *pasuk* (*Shemos* 25:15) supports the *Yerushalmi's* praise (*Sotah* 7:4) of a person who, while he is unable to learn, teach, or to observe mitzvos, regardless of his financial situation, still supports those who do learn Torah.

All of this is hinted through the poles, which permanently support the *Aron*. The poles represent all the supporters of Torah, whose physical, emotional, and philosophical assistance is constantly required.

The *Meshech Chochmah* also discusses another explanation, which he bases on the *Rambam*. This affirms that the Kohanim must kindle the *Menorah* in the *Beis Hamikdash* not only at night, but also by day, as part of the *hatavas ha'neiros*, preparing the lights. The *Meshech Chochmah* explains that since Chazal have pointed out that God, in whose House the *Menorah* is lit, does not require physical lights by which to see, the mitzvah of *hadlakas neiros* in the day emphasizes that God commanded the kindling at a time when lamps are unnecessary. By the same token, once Chazal have taught us that the *Aron* carried itself and did not need the *b'nei Kehas* to carry it, the Torah commanded that the poles should not be removed. This serves as an ongoing reminder that just as the poles are not required when the *Aron* is lying in its place in the *Kodesh Hakodashim*, so too, they were not required when Klal Yisrael was traveling in the desert, since the *Aron* was perfectly capable of carrying itself.

Perhaps we can take the message from the *Meshech Chochmah's* second explanation and adapt it to elaborate on the first one. If the *Aron* was able to lift the Kohanim, who were seemingly carrying it, and fly them over the Yarden River in the time of Yehoshua, then it was certainly able to carry itself. And so too with Torah. The Torah is sufficiently capable of looking after itself and providing the *talmidei chachamim*, who study it diligently, with all their needs. Then why does the Torah expect the wealthy to support them? The truth is that it is not they who support the Torah, but the Torah which supports them! And the prohibition of removing the poles from the *Aron* is not to teach us that the *talmidei chachamim* need the benefactors constantly, but rather that the benefactors constantly need the Torah learning of *the talmidei chachamim*, not only for the spiritual inspiration and guidance that it affords them, but also for their continued success in their financial endeavors. For who knows whether their material blessing is not conditional on their sharing it with *talmidei chachamim*, and that the moment they withdraw their support that blessing will come to an end?

Chapter IV

MITZVOS
The Materials

WE often reckon the passage of time by generations, but just how long is a generation? As a matter of common knowledge, we know that a generation averages about twenty-five years—from the birth of a parent to the birth of a child—although this obviously varies in individual cases. We also generally accept that the length of a generation was closer to twenty years in earlier times when people married younger and life expectancies were shorter.

I have been in San Diego long enough to see the transition from one generation to the next. This community, just like all other communities, witnesses people and families come and go. Some move to other cities or other countries, while others move up to a different world. In any case, there are many interesting people and characters who make up the flavor and personality of the community. Some people are quiet, reserved, and keep to themselves, while others are boisterous, overt in their opinions and feelings, and always visible.

One such colorful man who lived in the Beth Jacob apartments for many years was Mr. Solowitz, z"l. For those who knew him, there is no need to describe him. This is not the place to elucidate his uniqueness and special qualities for those who did not know him. Nevertheless, there is one detail that I will share—one thing that he and I had in common—the New York Yankees baseball team.

Mr. Solowitz had a very sharp and insightful mind. The Yankees had won the World Series four out of the last five years at the end of the century and then went cold. He shared a great insight with me as to why the Yankees team at that time would not win again. He said the players had lost their hunger, their drive, their enthusiasm, and even their adrenaline to win again. There was very little left for such a dominant team to prove their prowess any longer, and without the inner motivation to do so they could not win. Other teams who had the drive and need to prove their prowess and had young players who were hungry for recognition and success would assume the top and win a World Series.

The lesson of being "hungry" for something—whether in sports, education, or relationships—is the key to success and winning. Momentum is a critical part of continued growth, and once that begins to slow down, it is only a matter of time before we start to lose, giving back some of that which we gained. This principle can certainly apply to our ambitions in Torah.

One of the keys to success in life in general—and religion in particular—is the ability to continue and maintain momentum, to create a snowball effect to build on past successes. In my career I have seen the continued upward growth of individuals and families in spirituality and overall service of Hashem. Unfortunately, I have also witnessed the unraveling of hard work and self-sacrifice of other individuals and families. The reason for growth—or negative decline—is determined by how determined each person is to maintain that desire and hunger for more, as opposed to giving in to a feeling of complacency encompassed by the inner gnawing of the refrain, "Come on. How much more do you want me to do? What do you want from me?" People are tired and just want to get a break and take it easy. Many of the good, religious habits they once prided themselves on become just memories. The mitzvos, learning, davening, *chessed*, etc., that were part and parcel of their identity begin to gather dust and cobwebs. Religious observance could almost be viewed as a passing fad that came and is now gone—a "been there done that" phenomenon. This notion is counter to the philosophy of the Torah where we actively apply the rule "there's no rest for the weary." The Torah famously teaches this in *Bereishis* (37:1): "וישב יעקב בארץ מגורי אביו בארץ כנען—And Yaakov settled in the area [Chevron] where his father had lived in the land of Canaan."

The most common traditional interpretation of "*Vayeishev Yaakov*" is the opinion of *Rashi*. Yaakov wanted to dwell in peace, but then the troubles of Yosef sprang upon him. Hashem said, "Is it not sufficient for the righteous that which is prepared for them in the World to Come, but they seek to dwell in peace in this world also?"

On the surface, it appears as though Yaakov had lost his drive, his sense of wanting more. Yaakov does indeed want to dwell in peace, but not the peace we described earlier—of wanting to have it easier and take a break from Torah and mitzvos. To the contrary, Yaakov saw the opportunity to sit and learn in the *beis midrash* all day and not have to go to work!

The *pasuk* comes to teach us that when Yaakov was in *chutz la'aretz*, outside of Israel, he was focused on fulfilling his obligations to work. His diligence to perform his work successfully was second to none as he completed his responsibilities to Lavan. This is supported by the statement in *Bereishis* (31:40): "By day I was consumed by the scorching heat, and at night by the frost." But upon entering the land of Canaan, Yaakov immediately declared a religious asylum. He no longer felt it appropriate for him to continue to work. When he came to his father's house in Eretz Canaan he was ready to serve Hashem from two dimensions:

- From the place where his father Yitzchak and grandfather Avraham had lived.
- From the greatness of the land itself—our holy land, the sanctified land that God chose for him and his descendants.

Yaakov no longer saw it as a time to amass physical wealth and items of this world. Rather, he felt the only reason he had worked so hard when he was outside of Israel was so that he could retire from the physical and focus solely on the spiritual, just as his predecessors Avraham and Yitzchak had done. He no longer wanted to go out to shepherd his flock as he had done before. Avraham and Yitzchak, in their old age, separated from money and acquisitions in order to devote themselves completely to Hashem and prepare to receive prophesy, living fully under the influence of God. Yaakov wanted to do the same thing as Avraham and Yitzchak: to sit in peace and tranquility, to learn Torah, and do as his fathers had done.

Yaakov wanted to dwell in peace and tranquility, separate from the life of *gashmiyus*, physicality, and put his efforts into *ruchniyus*, spirituality. The hunger and drive were just revving up again in pursuit of loftiness.

Today, we may be witnessing a regression. Perhaps, as life grows less demanding, we take our Yiddishkeit for granted, which may lead to this deterioration. Or perhaps even the opposite may be true: as we grow older, we face more stresses—more pressures either from within our families or from without, and from our personal disappointments. Regardless of the causes for this potential deepening malaise, everyone reading this needs to think back to a time when they were doing more, when they were actively and enthusiastically growing spiritually. This is not the time to only focus on *olam hazeh*, forgetting or neglecting all the Torah and mitzvos we fought and struggled for.

There is room for both. Make some time to get back to the greater heights of our past and bring them back into the present.

The most dominant technological device to emerge and steadily improve in sophistication, ease of use, and coverage over the last ten years is the cell phone. On average, people tend to upgrade or purchase a totally new cell phone every two years. Clever marketing plans presented by cell phone companies constantly present supposedly bigger and better deals to their customers. Cell phone manufacturers perpetually tweak their products, working to eliminate the glitches or hiccups in their products. One such issue that is slowly but finally being phased out is the voice command feature, a wonderful tool when you cannot actually push the buttons. Unfortunately, one of the side effects of this feature is that it sometimes activates without the user intending it to do so. As Murphy's law dictates, this feature activates at the most inappropriate times, typically causing the cell phone possessor to hear, "Please say a command." After a while we grow frustrated with this unintended occurrence and yell back, "Be quiet!" or "Leave me alone!" or something worse.

There are times in life when we hear "commands" from people of authority. Whether from parents, teachers, or law enforcement, there is a level of obligation requiring us to take heed. When I was in yeshiva in Israel, one of the *rebbeim*, Rabbi Price, was nicknamed "the sheriff." A few times a day—before davening *Shacharis*, a few rounds during the late morning, and even in the early afternoon—he would walk through the dormitory banging on the doors trying to wake up the guys. His famous line after pounding on the door was, "Open up in the name of the law!" causing us to endow him with his nickname. Over time, Rabbi Price was able to round up more and more students to come learn and daven due to his extraordinary efforts. It was especially difficult to ignore Rabbi Price, who schlepped himself to wake us up; he himself lived with a debilitating muscle disease, making it difficult for him to walk.

At times, we find ourselves "having to do something" that centers around religion. Once again, a parent, teacher, or authority figure tells us to do something and we ask, "But why?" The most common answer we receive is, "Because the Torah says so!" This is the automatic and ultimate response when the authority has no answer other than God commands it and therefore we must do it.

I would like to suggest that the types of commands described above can be viewed through the purview of the Torah. The Torah teaches about the mitzvah of the *parah adumah*, the red heifer. Many of the commentaries explain that this mitzvah is a *chok*, a law that we do not understand and therefore cannot explain the reasoning behind it. A quick synopsis of the mitzvah is to take a completely red heifer, slaughter it, burn it, and mix the ashes with water, making a compound that will be sprinkled on the third and seventh day upon a person who came in contact with a corpse. Odd as it may seem, the person doing the sprinkling requires a purifying process after purifying the impure person. The one who did the act of sprinkling becomes impure (albeit not the same degree or kind of impurity).

The general understanding of mitzvos places them in two categories: *mishpatim* and *chukim*—laws and statutes. These categories speak to the understanding and reasons behind the mitzvos:

- *Mishpatim* are mitzvos we understand, that we as human beings would have come up with ourselves if we needed to create a legal system. For example, not to kill, not to steal, and so forth.
- *Chukim* are mitzvos we do not understand. These are mitzvos we would not likely come up with on our own as we are not able to grasp the reason behind or benefit of these mitzvos. For example, forbidden mixtures such as *shaatnez*, and meat and milk; throwing the he-goat off the cliff during the Yom Kippur service; and the *parah adumah*.

Rabbeinu Bachya lists two sets of categories that each contain three categories, and these two lists make up the two parts of a *chok*. The three categories of *chukim* he lists are:

- *Mitzvos muskalos*—intellectual mitzvos
- *Mitzvos mekubalos*—accepted mitzvos
- *Mitzvos she'ein taaman nigleh*—mitzvos that do not seem to have any rhyme or reason.

He explains that there are three categories of mitzvos in general: *chukim*, *eidos*, and *mishpatim*. *Mishpatim* are the mitzvos mentioned earlier, such as not to kill or steal. *Eidos*, meaning "testimonies," are a kind of *chok*, and are represented by mitzvos such as tefillin, tzitzis, bris milah, sukkah, shofar, lulav, etc. While we cannot fully understand or appreciate the significance of these commandments, we know that they are nevertheless a testimonial about God and His maintenance of creation.

I think the cell phone is an example of the *mishpatim*. Just say a command that is easily understood. The voice command feature is intellectually useful. In the second example above, the sheriff represents the *eidus*, testimony: we know we have to get up to daven, because to do so connects each of us to our history and heritage as Jews. Learning and davening are the key reminders of who we are as individuals and as a people in the history of the world—past, present, and future. The third example of "Just do it because I said so!" is the *chok*—the mitzvah without further explanation or even the need to understand. Shlomo HaMelech says in *Mishlei* that even he did not understand the mitzvah of the red heifer. This means that even the wisest of all men performed a mitzvah that he could not understand.

I often hear protests from people who challenge strictly following the Torah's observance today. They argue that some of the mitzvos no longer apply to us today. They fool themselves into thinking that science, medicine, and technology have shown things contrary to some of the practices mentioned in both the Written and Oral Law of the Torah. Hashem reserved one mitzvah, the *parah adumah*, as the quintessential *chok*, which is inexplicable to everyone, anywhere in the world. This sends a message that just as this mitzvah is not understood and one may try to give reasons why it should or should not be followed or practiced, we still fulfill it without question. So too, with the *mishpatim* and *eidos* categories of mitzvos. We must comply to the letter of the law and not come up with our own reasons of why we should or should not do something today.

We do not know *all* the reasons behind *any* of the mitzvos and therefore must follow the Torah, regardless of what society comes up with—for or against. Let us figure out ways to fulfill the mitzvos and observe the laws of the Torah with faith and commitment to Hashem and His laws instead of trying to argue why we should not have to follow certain mitzvos. At the end of the day, the mitzvos are Divine and we mortal humans are not able to comprehend their purpose or meaning.

In August 2013, *Time* magazine published an article about how singing can affect changes in the brain. When we sing, musical vibrations cause the alteration of our physical and emotional landscape.

Group singing, for those who have done it, is the most exhilarating and transformative of all. It takes something incredibly intimate—a sound that begins inside the singer—which then merges and shares that sound with a roomful of people. The musical vibrations pouring out in harmony make that combined melody even more thrilling. It is not surprising, therefore, that group singing is on the rise. According to Chorus America, 32.5 million adults sing in choirs, up by almost 10 million over the past six years!

Music and song are very powerful tools that profoundly influence both our bodies and our souls. Jewish music is commonly played at many of our *simchos*, whether bar or bat mitzvas or weddings. However, while the lyrics are all in Hebrew, the tempo and intent often feels as though we are trying to imitate a different culture and world; although at least it is Jewish music. Unfortunately, I heard that the music accompanying graduations of some of our local Jewish schools play non-Jewish music. How is it that a Jewish school promotes the negative influence of non-Jewish music? We cannot control what type of music people listen to in their homes, during exercising, walking, and driving in their cars, but we can direct teachers not to play non-Jewish pop or rock music in the classroom. We could put our foot down and make a policy that only Jewish music should be played in our schools. I even found myself guilty of holding a movie night for kids, but from now on that is not a necessary activity for the shul to offer to educate our children. Most children today get enough television, movie, or video time every day; they do not need to come to shul for more.

Music of all kinds has the potential to profoundly influence us. The words and especially the style of a good bit of English non-Jewish music today influence and even extol many forbidden things. We live in a world that seems to have lost its moral compass and value system. Pop singers, especially those who have reached rock star status, become idolized by our youth. The influence of their music and on-stage performances has the power to destroy basic decency and the moral fiber of their fans. Jewish music with Hebrew lyrics, on the other hand, brings holiness and spirituality to those who listen to and absorb the words and meanings of the holy songs. Like so many things in life, a person needs to develop an appreciation for this.

Unfortunately, in the davening in many shuls and yeshivas, singing is looked down upon as perhaps being too "modern." Do people only sing in nonreligious environments? Are people simply concerned that davening will take too long and become too dragged out? I am not sure what will happen during the time of the Third Beis Hamikdash, when the Leviim sing. What will people say then? Or maybe this attitude is simply due to a lack of understanding and appreciation of how singing and the use of beautiful melodies can inspire our *tefillos*. This, of course, applies to singing the words instituted by the Men of the Great Assembly who organized the *tefillos* for us.

The Torah (*Bamidbar* 4:47) states: "מבן שלשים שנה ומעלה ועד בן חמשים שנה כל הבא לעבד עבדת עבדה ועבדת משא באהל מועד—From thirty years old and upward and unto fifty years old, everyone who entered in to do the work of the service, and the work of bearing burdens in the tent of meeting." Rabbeinu Bachya points out the extra words of *"la'avod avodas avodah—*to do the work of the service." He explains that the components of the *avodah* are the physical service, the *shir* (singing), and the *simchah*. He stresses the point that the *simchah* is required in order to fulfill mitzvos.

Shlomo HaMelech explains that having *simchah* at the time of performing a mitzvah is a mitzvah itself. In the same way that we perform mitzvos for Hashem, so, too, the joy over doing the mitzvah is known as a mitzvah itself. Singing with the mouth alongside an instrument brings the *nefesh*, soul, of a person to a level of *simchah*. It was with this intention that the Leviim performed the service in the *Beis Hamikdash*.

Chazal explain that the *avodah* is the song sung by the Leviim. The Leviim were commanded to sing and bring elation for the mitzvah of the bringing of a sacrifice. This was done so that the mitzvah of the offering itself would be performed with *simchah* and this was accomplished expressly through their singing. In other words, the very act of this mitzvah, and every mitzvah for that matter, must be done with joy. The single most effective way to raise a person to the level of *simchah* necessary was through song. David HaMelech (*Tehillim* 100) states:

"עבדו את ה' בשמחה—Serve Hashem with joy." That service is our performance and fulfillment of mitzvos. One of the reasons that the Leviim
only "worked" until the age of fifty was because a person's voice starts
to weaken at that age.

We are fortunate that in today's day and age Jewish music is more
readily available than it has ever been. There are many more Jewish
movies and videos for children that were not available a generation
ago. Years ago, there was no choice of the kind of movie or song to be
used (besides the fact that the non-Jewish songs were somewhat more
kosher—maybe not *glatt*—but a little less *treif* than now). But today
there is no excuse not to use the Jewish content and good music and
song for our children and families.

The battle to maintain our religious levels is ever challenging in today's society. We consistently need to redirect our resources to pump
positive music and singing into the souls of our youth and adults. There
is a lot of good material to enhance our Yiddishkeit and not destroy
it. Non-Jewish pop and rock music is a silent but deadly killer of our
neshamos. Why bring this upon ourselves? The *shir shel yom*, "song of
the day," is not only the preparation; it is the mitzvah of the day. This
is but one of the small things that has the potential to either promote
great influence or, on the other hand, damage, to one's spiritual state
of mind and being.

When the opportunity to connect to music comes along, we must
first determine if it is going to be beneficial or harmful to our souls and
only then decide to listen (or sing)—or not. Let us sing songs the way
the Leviim sang their songs—as an expression of *avodas Hashem*, the
ultimate service to God.

One of the scariest and most dangerous things I do as
I get older is look in the mirror. Looking in the mirror is sometimes a
shocking but awakening experience. A few years back I had a completely
black beard—not a hint of gray—until that dreaded morning when my
beard received a visiting white hair. Although the black hairs thought
the white hair was funny-looking and different, they put up with it,

thinking it was only there temporarily. Before they knew it, more white hairs had moved into the area and were not only visiting, they were here to stay. Nevertheless, in the beginning the white hairs were completely outnumbered by their black counterparts. Before long, I noticed that my beard was black with some white patches. Now my beard has become mostly white with a few black patches.

The only benefit I would grant to having white hair is that some measure of wisdom comes along with it. As I have grown older, the wisdom I have gained is the growing reality that I cannot convince or effect a change in someone in an area of Torah and or *hashkafah* if they do not want to hear the other side. Some people are set in their beliefs and cannot or will not be convinced otherwise.

Some people find it bothersome that some mitzvos, namely *mishpatim*, are categorized as mitzvos that make sense (i.e., if we were to come up with rules and regulations for society, these mitzvos would be among them), while the other category of mitzvos, *chukim*, are commandments that do not have any apparent logic, at least from our human perspective. There are reasons for these *chukim*, but they are above and beyond our comprehension. Chazal have tried to give reasons for these *chukim*, but I've found that when speaking with a skeptical person, this becomes no more than a source of frustration. I often try to share an explanation or reason for a *chok*, but it will usually be scoffed at and rejected out of hand.

Because of my frustration, I will not attempt to give a reason to the well-known *chok* of *shaatnez*. Rather, I will leave it up to the great Torah commentator, the *Ramban*. This mitzvah forbids certain mixtures between animals, seeds, and materials. Traditional and Kabbalistic sources explain that wearing *shaatnez*, the combination of wool and linen in a garment, is forbidden because it "stops up" the flow of certain parts of the body if worn. In *Vayikra* (19:19), the Torah states: "את חקתי תשמרו בהמתך לא תרביע כלאים שדך לא תזרע כלאים ובגד כלאים שעטנז לא יעלה עליך—You shall observe My statutes: you shall not mate your animal with another species; you shall not sow your field with mixed seed; and a garment that is a mixture of combined fibers shall not come upon you." On the words "you shall keep my statutes (*chukosai*)," the *Ramban* first gives *Rashi's* explanation that *chukim* are decrees of the King for which there is no reason given. The *Ramban* explains that Chazal say that the reasons for these commandments are hidden from us, and that the evil inclination and the idolaters raise objections against them, except in the case of the prohibition against wearing a garment made of wool and linen, but not in the case of mating animals of diverse kinds, for which there is a reason that we will explain. Clearly, the *Ramban* says, the intention of Chazal in defining statutes as the "laws of the King for which there is no reason" was not that these are decrees of the King of Kings for which there is no reason whatsoever—for every word of God is with purpose. They meant only that statutes are like the enactments a king promulgates for his kingdom, without revealing their benefits to the people, and the people, not sensing these reasons, entertain questions about them in their hearts but they accept them nonetheless out of fear of the government. Similarly, the *chukim* of Hashem are His secrets in the Torah that the people—by means of their thinking—do not grasp as they do in the case of *mishpatim*.

The reason for the prohibition of *kilayim*, mating an animal with that of another species, is because Hashem created different species in the world, both plants and moving creatures, and He gave them a power of reproduction enabling them to exist as long as Hashem desires their existence in the world. He further endowed them with a power to bring forth only their kind and that they should never be changed, as it says in *Bereishis* during creation: "*l'mineihu*—to its kind."

The *Ramban* explains that the reason for both plants and seeds not to be mixed together is that the inner essence and strengths of each plant must be distinct; no plant should receive or give nourishment to each other. Rather, each plant and seed needs to maintain its own diet and not combine it with that of another species of plant. He also quotes a *Bereishis Rabbah* (10:6), in the name of Rabbi Simon, that every plant, every seed, and even every blade of grass in this world has a counterpart, a *mazal*, in the world above us in the *rakia*, the heavens. If one mixes these species together, it can contradict and nullify the natural state of laws in heaven, creating havoc in the world beyond our scope of understanding.

The only exception regarding providing explanations for *chukim* is the wearing of *shaatnez*, the mixing of wool and linen. The actual reason for the *chukim* regarding plants and animals was to maintain the natural state in which things were created. But the mixing of wool and linen involves more than maintaining the natural way of the fabrics. The *Ramban* refers to the *Rambam* in *Moreh Nevuchim*, who explains that at the time the Torah was given, the priests of idolatry, who were masters of sorcery, had a certain garment made of *shaatnez*—a mixture of wool and linen—which they wore when performing their rites. Therefore, the Torah eradicates their idolatrous practices, commanding us to destroy their remembrance. These are some of the "explanations" to some of the *chukim* in the Torah.

Bottom line is, don't mess with God's world when He tells you not to. Unless otherwise instructed, leave it alone—and that is the meaning of the *chok*!

The book *Men Are from Mars, Women Are from Venus* states that most common relationship problems between men and women are a result of fundamental psychological differences between the genders. The author exemplifies this thesis by means of a metaphor: Men and women are from distinct planets. Each one is acclimated to his or her own planet's society and customs, but not to those of the other. One example:

- Men typically offer solutions to problems that women bring up in conversation.
- Often, women are not necessarily interested in solving those problems, but just want to talk about them.

The book asserts that men and women can be understood in terms of distinct ways they respond to stress and stressful situations. Do I need John Gray to tell me this? The answer, of course is not! If I learn, study, and follow the Torah, I will recognize and understand the different roles and missions that males and females have to complete in this world that we live in together.

Men and women are inherently different in the obvious physical ways and in the less-obvious emotional ways. One thing for sure is that men and women are different and, no matter how many scientists, psychologists, and psychiatrists chip into this discussion, none of us really know why. We can observe *what* the differences are, but *why* there are differences we simply don't know. The main reason we don't know why is because in the Torah, Hashem chose not to go out of His way to tell us. The question is…why not?

This question sheds some light on how *chukim* work. There are things in life that cannot be explained. There are mitzvos—*chukim*—that cannot be explained. But we will now see a wonderful insight into why God withholds the reasons behind certain mitzvos, and it is not what we would normally expect.

The Torah states: "רק לא ירבה לו סוסים ולא ישיב את העם מצרימה למען הרבות סוס, וה' אמר לכם לא תוסיפון לשוב בדרך הזה עוד. ולא ירבה לו נשים ולא יסור לבבו וכסף וזהב לא ירבה לו מאוד—The king however, must not accumulate many horses, so as not to bring the people back to Egypt to procure more horses…He also must not have many wives, so that they do not turn his heart astray. He shall likewise not accumulate very much silver and gold" (*Devarim* 17:17; *Rambam, Hilchos Melachim* 3:4). The Gemara (*Sanhedrin* 21b) and the *Rambam* (*Hilchos Melachim* 3:2) explain that although polygamy was permitted, and was common for kings, the Jewish king was forbidden to have more than eighteen wives.

On the *pesukim* warning a king not to have too many horses or wives, the *Yalkut Shimoni* points out why the Torah does not give reasons for why not to do things. Rabbi Yitzchak said: Why is it that God did not just tell us the reasons behind the mitzvos? He answers that there are two mitzvos where the Torah did reveal the reasons and a person actually ended up sinning:

- The Torah, as cited earlier, states that a king should not take many wives. The reason was "*Lo yasur levavo*—So his heart should not turn astray." Shlomo HaMelech said: "I will take more wives (Shlomo had seven hundred wives and three hundred concubines) but I will not turn astray" (*Melachim I* 11:4). He thought he could handle the test and marry many wives, without them influencing him. Unfortunately, even the wisest man who ever lived underestimated—on his lofty level—the danger of the lure and temptation, and it did not please God.

- The Torah warned the king not to have too many horses and gave the reason: so that the Jews should not return to Egypt. Apparently, Egypt was the center for horses, and it would lure the Jews back there, which was forbidden. Shlomo HaMelech confidently stated: "I will have many and will not succumb to go back to Egypt."

At this, Rabbi Yehoshua Ben Levi is quoted in the *Yerushalmi* (*Sanhedrin* 2:6):

> The Book of Devarim ascended and prostrated itself before the Holy One, Blessed is He, and said, "Shlomo wishes to uproot the letter yud from me. He is transgressing the prohibition of acquiring many wives and many horses." The word yarbeh, a multitude, begins with the letter yud. Hashem replied, "Shlomo and a thousand like him may come to naught, but not a letter from you [the Torah] shall come to naught."

Shemos Rabbah (6:1) says that even the *kutzo shel yud* will not be *mevutal* from the Torah. This important midrash teaches us a fundamental approach to the performance of mitzvos. Shlomo HaMelech, the wisest of all men, looked at the reason the mitzvah was given and said that it would not affect him. And yet, despite his greatness, it did.

We have heard about the challenges and the tests that accompany a person winning the lottery and receiving instant wealth. At one point, we've all said, "It's OK. Let me win the lottery and I'll handle the tests." Basically, we convince ourselves that *we* can overcome the challenge. Clearly, if even Shlomo HaMelech was unable to measure up to avoid transgressing a prohibition, how much harder would it be for us.

We do not know why the Torah and even Chazal, for that matter, instituted certain commandments and enactments. There is a danger if we think we know the reasons—and then think they will not affect us. Even worse is if we think that those reasons don't apply to us. Some things in life will remain secrets. Many situations remain unanswerable, and we are not necessarily entitled to know why such and such is taking place. Let us work on our not judging others or judging situations which people find themselves struggling with. Ultimately, we do not know the reasons behind them, and, frankly, we are probably better off not knowing what the reasons are in the first place.

The American school system has a typical nine-to-ten-month school year with a variety of evaluation periods, depending upon the district and, in the case of yeshivos and day schools, each school's custom. In addition to being a pulpit rabbi, I teach a few classes in the local high schools. I was once asked to give reports on the progress of my students. Typically, the second and fourth quarters are marked by the midterm and final grades while the first and third marking period are deemed progress reports. The wisdom behind a progress report is the opportunity given to the students (as well as the teachers and parents) to assess where they are standing and to avoid falling behind in their work. In addition, the report helps them avoid being penalized on the permanent record if they have been doing poorly.

The term "progress" is so important because it emphasizes the positive rather than the negative—even though it is typically used as a red flag for a student who is not doing well. In calculating the grade for each progress report, I listed three components: test score, class participation/behavior, and preparedness for class. As teachers, we each want to build self-confidence within the student and try to give the best grade possible. The most common measure of a student's progress and knowledge is through test scores. Sometimes, however, students do not do well on exams but are nevertheless learning and growing. Therefore, in order to measure the big picture, teachers will include behavior, class participation, and readiness to learn when calculating a grade.

The makeup of a Jew consists of many facets, without one weighing more heavily than another. Each area has a time and place for itself. From the perspective of a pulpit rabbi, I most commonly see people in the one dimension of their service to God: prayer. As we are all aware, davening is a privilege that literally shapes our lives for better or for worse. Individual evaluation of progress in davening is every congregant's responsibility. The following checklist of items mirrors a student's activity in school. Every man, woman, and child should consider these actions to determine his or her grade makeup:

- Students who often leave class early or arrive late do not grasp the material and simply will not do as well as those students who were in class, on a daily basis, from the beginning to the end. Likewise, in shul there are those who come late and/or leave early.
- In mainstream classrooms, students must sit at their place and not wander or walk around the room, which may disturb other students or disrupt their own learning. So too in shul. A person will focus more conscientiously by remaining within a certain radius of his *makom*, place.
- Being prepared for class makes learning smoother. A student must come prepared with his books, notebooks, pens, markers, pencils, etc. We need to come to shul prepared to daven. That means wearing proper attire, using the correct prayer book, and bringing anything else needed in order to pray.

How do we measure up in our first progress report in *tefillah*? It is interesting to note that the atmosphere of prayer is an extremely important component of the success of our davening. There is a source for this in *Bereishis* (25:22), where the Torah describes Rivkah's pregnancy. *Rashi* informs us that Rivkah felt turmoil in her womb, explaining that when she passed a house of idolatry, Eisav tried to emerge, and when she passed by places of Torah study, Yaakov tried to get out. My father-in-law, Reb Tzvi Rosen, pointed out an insightful comment made by Rabbi Zalman Sorotzkin in his commentary *Oznayim La'Torah*. Rabbi Sorotzkin quotes *Midrash Rabbah* (63:6) and contrasts the reactions of Rivkah to the movements of Eisav and Yaakov. The midrash states: "בשעה שהיתה עומדת על בתי כניסיות ובתי מדרשות יעקב מפרכס לצאת, ובשעה שהיתה עוברת על בתי עבודת כוכבים עשו רץ ומפרכס לצאת—At the time Rivkah **stood** at a shul or *beis midrash*, Yaakov struggled to get out. When Rivkah passed by a house of idolatry, Eisav ran and tossed about to get out."

The nuance teaches us that Rivkah, the righteous woman that she was, would never just stand in front of a place of idolatry. She would move quickly away from it. In contrast, when Rivkah came to a holy place, she would not just pass by. She would stop and take it all in. Therefore, as Rivkah passed the house of idolatry, Eisav needed to "run" back to it. The word *ratz*, "run," only appears when referring to Eisav but not when referring to Yaakov because Rivkah stood there, allowing Yaakov the desire to go out with no need to run anywhere.

We can derive from this midrash and its explanation that the world is a place of purity and holiness. If one would just stand still, he would feel the *kedushah* and soak it in with no reason to chase it. *Tumah*, impurity and sin, are negatives that we somehow create. Even after we have passed it, we need to run back to it. When it comes to learning, davening, performing acts of kindness and mitzvos, they are usually right in front of us. It is the sins and the actions we should *not* be performing that we tend to seek out and chase after. We should learn from Rivkah that when we find ourselves in a place where we do not belong, we should pass by as quickly as possible, and when we end up in a good place, we should remain there; perhaps even take a seat and make this good place more permanent.

When davening, we create a meeting between us and Hashem and maintain *kedushah* and spirituality, right there in front of us. There is no need to disrupt it by getting up and chasing some frivolous moment that breaks the connection we have with Hashem. Let us make sure, whether at home, shul, or on the road, that our davening makes the grade.

Baruch Hashem, I have a decent library with many resources from which to find inspiration. When we walk into a room full of *sefarim*, holy books, we are usually on our feet already and there is no need to "stand up" for the Torah in the room. This in contrast to when we are sitting in a shul or the *beis midrash* and the Torah scroll is moving around; then we need to rise for the honor of the Torah. Not only do we stand when the actual Torah scroll is moved but also when a Torah sage or scholar enters a room, for they are considered a walking Torah scroll.

Recently, I had the *zechus* (merit) to host a Torah giant in the Jewish world: Rabbi Nata Greenblatt. He is, *bli ayin hara*, a man in his nineties who arrived at my house at 11:30 p.m., after finishing some business that took over four hours. He lives in the southeast portion of the US, and had left his home at 6:00 a.m. to catch a flight to San Diego. After a brief bowl of cereal, I shared with him a *dvar Torah* from a new *sefer* in my possession authored by my son Dovid, *Malchus Bais Dovid on the Parashah*.

Before sharing what transpired next, it is noteworthy to mention that the scenario in my home reminded me of the Mishnah in *Pirkei Avos* (1:4), which mentions the following: "Yosi Ben Yoezer from Tzreidah and Yosi Ben Yochanan from Jerusalem received the tradition from them. Yosi Ben Yoezer from Tzreidah said, 'Let your home be a gathering place for scholars, get dusty in the dust of their feet, and drink in their words with thirst.'" Here I was, literally waiting on this great Rav and basking in his light and the breadth of his Torah. A walking *Sefer Torah* transcends age, time, and place; the words of Torah are on his fingertips and spew forth like a fountain.

I would also like to interject a piece from Rabbi Greenblatt on *Parashas Tazria* from his *sefer, K'Rei'ach Sadeh*. In *Vayikra* (14:2), the Torah states: "זאת תהיה תורת המצרע ביום טהרתו והובא אל הכהן"—This is the law concerning the leper when he is purified, and he shall be brought and placed under the jurisdiction of the priest."

Rabbi Greenblatt asks: "Once a person knows he has *tzaraas* (spiritual ailment resembling leprosy), wouldn't you think he would run to the Kohen, why does the Torah need to say, and he was 'brought' to the Kohen?" At the outset, the person sees some type of affliction or discoloration on his body. The process of purification first begins with identifying if the skin condition is in fact *tzaraas*; if it is leprosy, the Kohen will deem him a leper on the spot. If the Kohen is not sure, he will quarantine the person for a week, check again after seven days, and then repeat the process.

Rabbi Greenblatt explains the mindset of the leper. In the beginning the person does not think anything of his skin condition and does not consider the connection between his *neshamah* (soul) and his *guf* (body);

he does not think that he might have committed one of the sins that brings about leprosy. After he realizes that this skin condition perhaps is leprosy, he gets concerned and knows that only a Kohen can decide if it is or not. At that point, a person begins to think, "Maybe I did violate a mitzvah that is punishable with *tzaraas*," and they start to do *teshuvah* (repentance). Unfortunately, he starts to doubt himself. If he did something wrong, he is not sure if he is doing proper repentance as he does not know if it is *tzaraas* or not, and is afraid to even approach the Kohen. Therefore, the Torah demands that "he be brought" to the Kohen, almost against his will. This is symptomatic of a person doubting their ability to succeed; rather than try, they choose to fail. Perhaps they did do something wrong but are unsure how to go about correcting their situation. If they do not move forward and work on improving, then they risk falling further from where they began.

Back to the encounter with the Rav in my home in San Diego. I am not recording here what my son wrote, but rather sharing my awe at Rabbi Greenblatt's response. After reviewing my son's *dvar Torah* on *Tazria* for ninety seconds, Rabbi Greenblatt recalled the words of the *Rambam* as if he'd seen them yesterday. He quoted a piece that is out of character for the *Rambam*, because, while the *Mishneh Torah* deals exclusively with halachah, here the *Rambam* writes in *mussar* fashion. In *Sefer Taharah*, at the end of the laws of *Tumas Tzaraas* (16:10), the *Rambam* explores the root cause of how a person gets to the point of speaking *lashon hara*.

> *Tzaraas is the name of a condition that includes many areas that are dissimilar to one another. Tzaraas shows up in different places and on different parts of the body depending on what the sin was. All the signs and indications of tzaraas were a bewilderment and a wonder that was above nature, something inexplicable. If he remained steadfast in his wickedness, then he began to lose everything, his house would be torn down, utensils destroyed, and clothing burned. If he repented fully at any point, it would all stop; life would resume to normal. If he still did not repent, then he would continue to be separated and*

isolated from the congregation in order that he would no longer be able to speak evil against anyone.

How did this all begin? The *Rambam* continues:

Because he did not remember what happened to Miriam when we were on the way, leaving Mitzrayim. She spoke against her brother Moshe of whom she was older, and who raised him and put herself in danger to save her younger brother Moshe. Miriam did not necessarily speak badly against Moshe but rather just equated him to all the other prophets, and even though Moshe let it pass because he was the humblest of all men, she was punished! How much more so we, the average person, would be guilty speaking ill of leaders and great people. A person who scoffs and makes fun of everything will come to make fun of the leaders and even rabbis.

This type of behavior, talking badly about the leaders of the Jewish People and even our secular leaders in positions of authority, gives the speaker a thrill and attracts the attention of those around him. It is easier, in the short run, to neglect our own growth in Torah and mitzvos and throw in the towel instead, making fun of those who are trying to lift us up. One needs to "bring himself" to the Kohen or leader and try to gain from their wisdom and insight and not make fun of them and what they stand for.

This is a lesson for us all: bring the Torah into your house, open your homes to Torah sages and scholars, and bask in the delight of their Torah. Embrace who they are and what they represent, as this is the way to reverse the destruction of Jewish homes through divorce and assimilation and to build a true *bayis ne'eman b'Yisrael*.

Throughout my rabbinic career, requests for leniency in areas of halachah outnumber those inquiring when and if it is appropriate to be *machmir* (strict) in halachah. I am all in favor of using a leniency when appropriate, but we should also recognize the significance of *chumros* and the role they play in our lives. It is not right to speak disparagingly about anyone in general, and this is particularly applicable with regard to those who seek out leniencies when necessary or *chumros* when desired.

My son-in-law, who does not eat fruits or vegetables, has quite a challenge on Seder night when it comes to the mitzvah of *maror*. Since he does not eat romaine lettuce, his other option for *maror* is ground up horseradish root. For the mitzvah of *maror*, he takes three ounces of horseradish and in two or three heaping spoonfuls, he swallows the bitter herbs, sending shock waves throughout his body as he turns red. Here is a situation where most people would look for a leniency, but he says that if people are looking for *chumros* to **appear** more observant, let them start with this one. *Maror* is a Biblical mitzvah, therefore a person should be *machmir* on it!

My *rebbi*, Rabbi Wein, used to tell over a story about Rav Eizel Yitzchak Charif, a very astute and sharp Torah scholar. His sharpness could only be matched by his wife, who obviously had to be his much-needed match to keep him in line. We are all very familiar with the prohibition of *chametz* on Pesach and the severe punishment to those who violate it. A story is told of Rebbetzin Charif, the wife of Rav Eizel Yitzchak Charif, who was extremely *machmir* when it came to *chametz* on Pesach, to the degree that she would put mittens on their cat's paws after Chanukah so that the cat would not track *chametz* around the house! One year, her husband, the Rav, said to his wife that it was ridiculous to make the cat wear mittens. The *Shulchan Aruch* provides different mechanisms through which we can be *chametz*-free when Pesach arrives. The night before Pesach, on the fourteenth of Nissan, we do *bedikas chametz* and check the entire house. In addition to that, if by chance we missed some *chametz* during the search, we perform *bittul* (nullification of) *chametz* before Pesach. On top of that, if the search does not go well, and we lacked the correct intentions during nullification, we can still sell all the *chametz* to a non-Jew. At this, the wife replied to her husband, waving her hand "Ah, *feh*, you and your *Shulchan Aruch*! My father sold me to a goy years ago!"

Chumros are real and should be taken seriously.

Chazal record that during the month of Elul and the Ten Days of Repentance, a person should accept upon himself greater *chumros* in his observance. Somewhat perplexing, however, is the fact that we do not find any requirement to continue with these observances after the *Yamim Nora'im*. There is another time of year that the Jewish People collectively rise to a level of *chumros* that are not particularly observed during the year. The *Rosh* (3:2 on *Pesachim*) states: "I did not elaborate on the laws of dough stuck on utensils as the Jewish People are holy and will clean them." The *Raavan*, quoting the *Rosh* adds: "This custom of scraping down the walls and chairs has a source in the *Talmud Yerushalmi*." The *Radvaz* (1:135) states: "The Jewish People are holy as writes the *Rosh*, and as we see that they keep extra *chumros*, in contrast to other *issurim* (prohibitions)." The *Mechaber*, Rav Yosef Karo, states (*Orach Chaim* 442:6): "Those who are *machmir* have upon whom to rely." The Jewish People are holy and go above and beyond the letter of the law on Pesach.

The *Arizal* states that on Pesach one should be careful to follow all the stringencies. Thus, we find that we are stringent on Pesach to follow a lone opinion in various areas of halachah, rather than the customary leniency of the majority approach. The *Ba'er Heitev* (467:1) says: "Particularly on Pesach we follow all the *chumros*." The *Mishnas Chassidim* says (*Nissan* 3:4): "One is to be careful regarding all the stringencies of those who are strict, and this will benefit his soul throughout the year."

Nevertheless, there is a right and a wrong way to do things. When it comes to *chumros*, we accept them and perform them, but they should be done under the following conditions:

- Do not publicize your *chumros*.
- Make sure the *chumros* are based upon a legitimate source.

A person should act modestly and keep his *chumros* to himself, in his own home, without allowing others to know. When asked a *sh'eilah* (question), one should only answer according to the letter of the law and not base the answer on a *chumrah* one has personally accepted.

Ideally, according to halachah, one is not allowed to be more stringent regarding Rabbinical matters than the stringencies of the *Shulchan Aruch*; nevertheless, regarding Pesach, the Jewish People are holy and go above and beyond the letter of the law. However, this only applies if the custom has some basis or source. One is not supposed to innovate new *chumros* that have no basis in halachah.

Many *kulos* (leniencies) and *chumros* are based upon customs that families, communities, and groups of Jews adopted throughout history for many reasons. In some instances, the reasons for the custom—and hence the *chumrah*—is known while at other times, the only part of the custom that is remembered is the practice but not the reason. Just because the reason may have been forgotten does not justify the cessation of the custom. We, the Jewish People, follow the edict "*Minhag avoseinu b'yadeinu*—The custom of our fathers is [still] in our hands." We still follow customs even when the reason seems to no longer apply to these times, because there may be other reasons for these customs which were not transmitted to us. The concept of a *minhag* is likened to law. It is a very powerful statement that cannot be discarded.

A *chumrah* does not have to be viewed as a difficulty. In fact, the concept of the *chumrah* should be taken on by someone who feels the need to use this mechanism to get closer to Hashem. Taking on a *chumrah* often provides the internal feeling that one seeks to demonstrate to God that he takes the Torah seriously and wants to take on more. Whether it is a leniency or a *chumrah*, as long as we are doing both of them *l'shem Shamayim*, for Heaven's sake, we will all become closer to Hashem!

Another question that surfaces with customs is how to know if it is indeed a custom or if it is actually halachah.

Every morning at *Shacharis*, a few interesting practices can be observed, which are followed more religiously than some actual mitzvos:

- *Tzedakah* is given at a certain point in the davening.
- The universally followed practice of covering our eyes when saying "*Shema Yisrael*."
- Some people kiss their tzitzis during the *Shema*, after saying the word "*tzitzis*."

These customs and practices are mentioned by individual authorities but not universally by all authorities, which explains why some people practice them and others do not.

Being in the rabbinate, I deal with many issues and a variety of questions. Over the years, I have found that most confusion focuses on what is considered halachah, a law that must be followed, versus *minhag*, custom. Jewish thought regarding the subject of *minhag* is vast. The examples and definitions discussed are by no means an exhaustive study of the subject. It seems that part of the confusion regarding the differences between *minhag* and halachah stems from sources and references to customs sprinkled throughout Jewish law.

Maseches Sofrim (14:18) states: "Should a custom conflict with some established halachah, the custom frequently takes precedence." The *Talmud Yerushalmi* (*Pesachim* 4:3) states: "*Beis Din* (the court of law) was equally empowered to inflict the same punishment upon the transgressor of a custom as upon the transgressor of a Written Law." The *Shulchan Aruch* (*Yoreh Dei'ah* 376:4) states: "A great rule is, the customs of our fathers are Torah." The Gemara (*Bava Metzia* 86b) says that a person should not change or deviate from the customs. My *rebbi*, Rabbi Wein, said, "It was and is the customs of the Jewish People that have kept us going throughout our history. If we would have followed the letter of the law, Judaism would have been lost. The *minhagim* have saved and somehow protected us."

With all of this, the *minhagim* must be kept in perspective. When we approach the topic of *minhagim*, we must keep in mind that there are many different types of customs:

- Customs that were made as a fence to protect the observance of mitzvos
- Customs that uproot some mitzvos
- Customs that only certain segments of society observe
- Customs that apply only to men or only to women
- Customs involving different practices at home as compared to shul
- Mistaken customs with no basis, known as *"minhag ta'us"*
- Customs based upon nonsense, known as *"minhag shtus"*

There is no question that any custom that causes a disgrace to the Torah and desecrates God's name should, without question, be abolished. An example of this would be the severe joking around during the davening of Simchas Torah. Historically, there are reasons for canceling a *minhag*, such as cases when non-Jews copied our practices. Customs were even established within certain countries, cities, and societies, among Ashkenazim, Sephardim, and Chassidim. In addition, there are specific practices and customs that apply exclusively within individual families.

The strength and beauty of *minhagim* is that many of them have been with us for a long time. In certain areas of Europe, particularly in the Mediterranean regions, some *minhagim* can be traced back to Talmudic times.

We should all take a few moments to stop and think about how many customs and practices we have inherited from our immediate families and how many *minhagim* we are transmitting over to the next generation. Truly in America, there are customs and practices that have kept unaffiliated Jews somewhat connected to Judaism. Whether a jelly doughnut on Chanukah or a little child receiving a lollipop from the candy man who exists in every shul, *minhagim* hold a valuable and precious place in our daily practices.

In *Bereishis* (25:29), we find the source of a practice we continue to this very day. The Torah states, "ויזד יעקב נזיד ויבא עשו מן השדה והוא עיף —And Yaakov made pottage; and Eisav came in from the field and he was faint." Rabbeinu Bachya states that the verse should have said that Yitzchak was the one cooking the lentil soup because it was he who was mourning for his father Avraham, who had just died. However, since the halachah stipulates that a mourner is forbidden to eat of his own food for the first meal, the *seudas havraah*, after the funeral, Yaakov, Yitzchak's son, prepared it. Typically, this meal consists of cooked lentils, which is a customary food for mourners to eat. Lentils are round, without an opening of any sort, and this symbolizes the fact that life continues. Furthermore, just as the lentil has no opening or mouth, so too the mourner is forbidden to talk, and we should keep silent in the face of death and tragedy.

Yitzchak was sitting shivah because on that very day, Avraham Avinu had died. Avraham died because Hashem shortened his life by five years so as not to witness his grandson Eisav perpetrate evil in the world. It is incredible that the *minhag* of preparing food for a mourner, which dates back to the time of our forefathers, is still practiced to this day. There is one other point easily overlooked in this entire episode. Rabbi Eliyahu Kitov points out that Yaakov was helping his father through the mourning process. The midrash says that when Avraham died, Yitzchak, Rivkah, and Yaakov cried, Heaven and earth cried, along with the hundreds of people who had been healed through the merit of Avraham. All the heads of state came to grieve and mourn the loss of Avraham. Now the obvious question is asked: Where was Eisav?

Eisav, the grandson of Avraham, did not cry or even shed a tear upon his grandfather's passing. He was not heartbroken, and, to the contrary, became exceedingly haughty by stating, "If even a great man like Avraham could die, there must not be a righteous sense of judgment, there could be neither law nor judge." At that point, Eisav revoked the notion of revival of the dead and he departed to hunt. No longer having to hold himself in check or to be embarrassed because of his grandfather, Eisav went out to terrorize the world.

We behold the lofty behavior and respect Yaakov showed toward Avraham and his father Yitzchak. Compare that to the utmost disrespect Eisav had for his father and grandfather. The actions of Yaakov are still around. To this day, Jews throughout the world follow the *minhag* of bringing food to the mourner, while Eisav's actions have been completely forgotten. Let us keep the *minhagim* that we each personally and communally share, and let us transmit them as beautiful treasures of wisdom and love to the future generations. May we be remembered for the good and not for the evil.

Chapter V

MINDSET
*Consciousness and
Subconsciousness*

THE holy *mussar sefer Orchos Tzaddikim* ("Ways of the Righteous")
plows through the *middos* (character traits) of the human being. Every
middah is mirrored with another trait that is the opposite of its counterpart. For example, haughtiness is followed by humility and mercy is
followed by cruelty. This is how the *sefer* is laid out, climbing the ladder
up to the gate of "Fear of Heaven." Every individual has strengths and
weaknesses. One of our many challenges in life is to overcome these
weaknesses and use the strengths only for good. We must be careful
that the good traits are not used in a bad way; and, similarly, we should
find ways to channel the bad traits so that they are used in a good way.
Generally, anger is viewed as a negative trait, however getting angry in
order to defend God is proper and should be exercised with proper due
diligence.

Gevurah, strength, is a necessary trait that complements many other traits. The definition of a trait has many interpretations, depending upon the source and circumstances. By definition, a definition does not tell us everything about a person or event. History has told many stories about great generals who were geniuses when it came to military strategy, yet we do not know how they treated their wives, children, or members of their families. The adjective "great" is designated solely to the description of the noun but tells us little else about the person.

In *Pirkei Avos* (4:1), a famous question is asked: "*Eizehu Gibor*—Who is a mighty one?" One of the answers given is "He who has conquered his *yetzer* (commonly translated as 'desire'). A person who can overcome the inclination to do something bad is in control and considered mighty.

I would like to suggest a different type of strength that, in my humble opinion, is reserved for a truly great person. The greatness is rarely found in today's day and age, yet I have met two such couples who are true *giborim*—incredible, great people.

My definition of a great person is "someone who shows joy for another person's *simchah* even though he will never experience that joy in his life." Most of us have encountered such special people that have shown great joy for our celebrations. In this case, the names will be left out, but I do want to share the facts of the occurrences:

- A good old friend of mine (we speak a few times a year) tragically lost a child and came shortly after that to celebrate at my son's wedding. This was the time his own child should have been getting married. No one can comprehend the pain of a parent who will never experience such a *simchah* of his own and yet, with incredible strength (there is no better word to describe it), attends my son's wedding, demonstrating total joy, dancing, and showing no hint of resentment.
- A *gibor* I have known for only a few years has not yet become a parent. He and his wife have undergone many treatments and have not lost hope. God willing, they should be blessed with children. When I had a grandchild, the husband called me to wish me mazel tov. I felt from him true feelings of joy for my *simchah*,

despite the pain he must have been experiencing. But he did not let on a bit.

I would never fool myself into thinking I could do what these two individuals did. They exhibited true greatness.

Middos are not only genetic; they are learned as well. If I am not born with something, who can I learn it from? I believe the answer can be found in *Bamidbar* (13:2), where the Torah states: "שלח לך אנשים ויתרו את ארץ כנען אשר אני נתן לבני ישראל איש אחד איש אחד למטה אבתיו תשלחו כל נשיא בהם—[Hashem says to Moshe,] Send out for yourself men and they will check out the land of Canaan that I am about to give you, the Children of Israel. Send out one man for each patriarchal tribe. Each one shall be a person of high rank." Chazal comment on the word *anashim* that they were "great" men. Unfortunately, we know the history of what ensued; only two of those twelve remained great: Yehoshua bin Nun and Kalev ben Yefuneh.

The Gemara (*Pesachim* 119b and *Megillah* 14b) comments that Yehoshua did not have any sons. A few reasons are given in various sources:

- Some say Yehoshua died without children because he offered a suggestion in front of Moshe, his *rebbi*, in dealing with Eldad and Medad.
- The Gemara (*Eruvin* 63b) mentions Yehoshua dying without children because he did not return the *Aron* to its place in Gilgal on the night before the war with Gilgal, causing the people to not be permitted to engage in procreation.

It must have been very challenging for the leader of the Jewish People to interact and manage the nation while childless. Nevertheless, Yehoshua was "great" and was able to thrive as the successor to Moshe.

The Gemara (*Sotah* 35a) on the verse in *Bamidbar* (13:30): "ויהס כלב את העם אל משה, ויאמר עלה נעלה וירשנו אתה כי יכול נוכל לה—and Calev hushed the people toward Moshe and said, We shall surely ascend..." explains that Calev appeared to instigate them against Moshe. When Calev saw them silence Yehoshua, who had begun to speak, Calev said to himself, "If I try to tell them anything, they will shut me up as well." So he said to them, "Is this all that the son of Amram has done to us?" The Gemara explains that his failure to call Moshe by name was intentionally disparaging, in the hope of making the other spies think he was on their side. In fact, the *Midrash Aggadah* (*Bamidbar* 13:30) notes that while they were in the land of Israel, the spies plotted to speak evil of the land and to tell of the might of its fortifications. They took Calev into their plot, and he told them that he would speak as they did, but in his heart, he resolved to speak of the praise and goodness of the land. Thus, when he came to speak, Calev "silenced them" (i.e., the spies) by catching them completely off guard. Calev got their attention, but they were in shock at his reversal against them.

Calev's attributes are emulated by my friend and his wife who, upon losing their child, came to explain and give true meaning of their loss to others around them. People who hear about tragedy seek to comfort the mourners, yet find doing so difficult. My friends presented the complete reverse of the emotions one would assume are experienced by such a loss. They literally silenced the crowd during the funeral, shivah, and beyond having no questions about what Hashem does or plans; not only accepting it but using it as a tool to teach others.

We should learn from these great *gedolim*—giants among our midst—who rose above the natural reactions and instincts of human beings. May Hashem continue to give them strength to continue their greatness and may the rest of us who sit in awe of their greatness try to emulate them as well.

Growing up in New York city, I never developed an appreciation for agriculture. We had a small patch of grass that made up our lawn, which was maintained by Tony the Landscaper. I never really developed a "green thumb," indeed, the total extent of my interaction with trees, or anything green, was my Friday afternoon job of dusting off the leaves of the tree in the living room in honor of Shabbos!

Moving to California changed my perspective of agriculture because we had a lemon tree in the backyard. Lucky for me (not that I knew any differently), I did not have to do a thing to the tree and lo and behold, big, beautiful lemons popped off the tree for years. Until there was trouble. From December 2011 until March 2017, the state of California experienced one of the worst droughts to occur in the region on record. The period between late 2011 and 2014 was the driest in Californian history since record keeping began. A total of 102 million trees died, with 62 million dying in 2016 alone.

One day, during the summer of 2016, I stared at my lemon tree, suddenly realizing that two-thirds of the tree was dead. I was stunned. The issue of the drought had not registered with me until that very moment. Sure, my water bill had gone up and we'd stopped watering the lawn, but the fact that my lemon tree was almost dead was unbelievable. At that point, I pruned the tree, started watering it every day, and bought garden soil specifically for citrus trees. The tree took a while to recover. The front lawn, on the other hand, received a few spritzes of water a few times a week. Most of the grass turned brown, leaving patches of earth exposed. With no end in sight, I thought about ridding the lawn of natural grass and installing a water-free landscape.

The drought came to an official abrupt end and one year later, the grass slowly started to rejuvenate. I thought of asking the gardener to re-seed the entire lawn to speed up the process, but I never did. Nevertheless, the grass is slowly growing stronger, but it is not really creating new grass where it had completely dried up. That would require tilling the earth, re-seeding, and watering daily, as though there had never previously been any grass in those areas.

I marveled at the once-mighty lawn: a lawn with strong blades of grass boasting a rich deep-green color that covered the entire area like a beautiful plush carpet. The lawn was still alive, but due to the lack of water it was drained of its previous vitality, its physical life drying up before my eyes. Theoretically, this condition could be reversed by nourishing the earth with the nutrients it once had and providing daily sustenance such as water and the grooming of its physical body. I came to realize that the lawn could have a new lease of life, like *techiyas ha'meisim*, a revival of the dead!

Every Jew has challenges within their daily lives. Life is always changing and although each of us pretty much stays the same person, we do not necessarily do the same things we did in the past. By and large, everyone at one point or another has ups and downs in their religious and spiritual journeys. Many of us go through periods of drought when the demands of life cause us to lose focus on areas of our spiritual beings that require focused care, attention, and nurturing. For many of us who have experienced a flourishing in learning, davening, minyan attendance, doing *chessed*, and performing mitzvos, we can nonetheless forget to keep ourselves "watered," and fail to realize how dry and almost dead we've become. We commonly find ourselves in a drought. But we are not helpless. It takes awareness of a drought to nurse the tree back to its former state of producing the juiciest and most delicious fruit. No one should ever think it is too late; it is *never* too late to get back and revive ourselves. We are also all intimately connected to the need to be nurtured. Like a beautiful fruit tree, we need to conscientiously care for our human roots, branches, and leaves. We must never give up hope. It is never too late to put an end to our spiritual drought, as we will see in the following narrative.

The *Navi* (*Yeshayahu* 22:13) states: "And behold joy and happiness, slaying cattle and slaughtering sheep, eating meat and drinking wine; 'Let us eat and drink, for tomorrow we will die.'" *Rashi* explains that Hashem is mourning while the Jews are eating and rejoicing. Instead of worrying about their fate and fearing God's word, they mocked the prophets and rejoiced, saying, "Since we will eventually die, let us make merry and rejoice as long as we are alive in this world." B'nei Yisrael said the *nevi'im* told them in the name of Hashem that we will not have a share in the World to Come; therefore, let us enjoy ourselves during our lifetime." The Jews at the time believed in the afterlife—the World to Come—but tragically they also believed that they would not have a portion in it. Hundreds of years later, the *Rambam* penned the Thirteen Principles, including our belief, with perfect faith, that there will be a resurrection in the times of Mashiach. In Judaism, there is no denial of an afterlife, but in the context above, the Jews at the time felt they were not entitled to it.

We believe life is not only in this world but continues into the next world as pointed out in *Devarim* (4:4): "ואתם הדבקים בה׳ אלקיכם חיים כלכם

היום—Only you, the ones who remained attached to God your Lord, are all alive today." The words "alive today" connote *today*—here in this world, and *today*—in the next world. With reference to the words "are all alive today," the Gemara (*Sanhedrin* 90b) teaches us that the same way we are alive today (physically), so too, we will be alive in the next world (spiritually). From this we see a hint, which equals a proof, that *techiyas ha'meisim* is a Torah principle.

The *Midrash Rabbah* (17:6) offers a parable to help us clearly understand how we can attain life both in this world and the next. Someone on a ship is cast off into the water. The captain of the ship grabs a rope and calls out to the drowning man, "Grab onto this rope with your hand so that I can hoist you up onto the boat or pull you to dry land. Hold tight! Do not let go of the rope! If you let go of the rope, you will have no life." So too, Hashem says to B'nei Yisrael, "As long as you hold onto the mitzvos and cling to the Torah, then you will live; if not, you are choosing to forego your life in this world and the next."

How do we address the spiritual drought? By cultivating an attitude of growing and learning. All it takes is some will and desire to cut away the dead parts and add some new ideas and nourish your soul to eat, drink, and live for today—and continue to eat, drink, and live for tomorrow.

Living in a Jewish community outside the major centers brings many challenges to Jewish life. Choices available for educating one's children is an obvious example. In the social realm, there are a limited number of kosher eateries. Some people focus on complaining about what they lack, while others have a more positive attitude, expressing appreciation for what the community has to offer. In simpler terms, is the glass half full or half empty?

A wise suggestion is that the eternal pessimist should try to look for some good, and the eternal optimist should look for some bad. This way, both mindsets will appreciate what they have and remember that both perspectives have something to offer:

- To the pessimist: It cannot be that everything in life is *all* bad. There is much good that can be found and built upon.

- To the optimist: We know that Hashem is *all* good, yet He created situations that can always be elevated to a greater level. It is therefore important to acknowledge that no situation is *all* good; there is always room for growth and improvement.

This paradigm applies to many areas worthy of discussion, but I would like to focus on how it apples to the example of Jewish day school education in a small community, where there is a large diversity of families from different levels of religious observance:

- Families on the right need to appreciate the opportunity to help less-religious or even nonreligious families grow.
- The less religious families need to understand that the core purpose of the school is to nurture each person's growth in Torah and mitzvah observance.

Each side needs to develop the maturity and honesty to identify areas that need improvement and, at the same time, appreciate the good that is present. In order to succeed, a person has to take on the opposite personality: the pessimist needs to be a little optimistic and the optimist must be a little pessimistic, at least once in a while.

The difficulty a person may have with identifying with the "other side' (or "the enemy") lies within the person's own vision of himself. Sometimes we tend to see ourselves totally as one dimensional—either this way or that way, without regard to a divergent opinion. By readjusting one's thinking, every so often, in order to truly "see" the other side, the individual will become a more well-rounded and productive person. It takes time to develop and master this way of thinking. When a person is young and inexperienced, he feels more comfortable with his own natural way of thinking. But as he grows older, he hopefully develops more self-confidence and can become a little more of a risk taker, and begin to better understand the other side. I believe an example of this is found among many leaders, who, later in life expanded their way of thinking. I would like to suggest that one of the greatest prophets of the Jewish People, Yeshayahu HaNavi, exemplifies this idea.

In *Yeshayahu* (6:8) the *Navi* states: "ואשמע את קול ה' אמר את מי אשלח ומי ילך לנו ואמר הנני שלחני—And I heard the voice of the Lord, saying, 'Whom shall I send, and who will go for us?' And I said, 'Here I am; send me.'"

The *sefer Shaar Bas Rabim* explains the function of a prophet. The job of a *Navi* is twofold. First, he is the messenger from God, sent to rebuke the people due to their evil, wrong ways. The purpose is to warn the people to turn back from their evil ways and also to inform them about their potential punishments because of their sins and rebellious acts. The second component of the *Navi*'s job is to pray on behalf of his brethren, the Jewish People, and to be an advocate for them. The *Navi* should intervene and defend the Jews before God so that He will have mercy upon them and remove the sin from their record. This is what is meant by the verse when it doubles up on the language stating, "Who shall I send and who will go," informing the *Navi* of his twofold task. "Who will I send?" refers to the job of the *Navi*, describing the sins of the Jews and explaining their negligence when it comes to fulfilling the mitzvos and to bring them back to the right path. The second part: "And who will go for us?" refers to the necessity for someone to daven on behalf of the Jewish People. Yeshayahu did not consider himself worthy of the positions on both sides of the job. He did not feel worthy to be the advocate for the Jewish People, and therefore would not be able to daven for their salvation. He felt he was only fit to rebuke the people but not to pray on their behalf. Therefore, Yeshayahu answered in a curt manner, saying, "You can send me," to rebuke them but not to pray for them.

At this point in his life, Yeshayahu felt somewhat one-dimensional; he only had the ability to rebuke. We can understand that to chastise your fellow man for sins committed is a more straightforward task. But in order to daven for them, he needed to confront God, which could be scary and overwhelming. Later in life, Yeshayahu would develop the ability to fulfill both aspects of being a prophet. When he was young and inexperienced, Yeshayahu, a rookie *navi*, acted boldly by going up against Hashem and declaring in utmost confidence, "I will pray and save them."

Part of the maturing process is to develop the ability to make statements and do things that are sometimes a little out of our comfort zone. Yeshayahu went on from this opening chapter to become one of the greatest prophets the Jewish People had, eventually doing things he had not been comfortable with when he was younger.

Our defining moments are how we react to things outside of our comfort zone and how we develop the ability to see the "other sides." As a prime example, we need a healthy combination of both pessimism and optimism in order to coexist as a functioning nation.

As we travel along the road of life, we meet many different and interesting kinds of people. Some of these encounters are brief, others are long, yet it is not always the long ones that leave the greatest impression. Some of the people we come across grow to become part of our "inner world," causing us to remember them with admiration and respect. When such a person comes to mind, I tend to give pause to reflect upon the *hakaras hatov*, the recognition and thanks, I owe that individual.

We are born with many character traits that require conscientious and continuous polishing throughout our lives. One such trait is the ability to take but the reluctance to give. Over our lifetimes, we hope to experience a transition from the need to take from those who nurture us through our babyhood and early childhood, to experiencing a need to give and to share. Ultimately, we hope to appreciate the reality that all we have acquired will be given away to others at the time of death. The question is whether giving is considered a learned trait or a *middah* which is somewhat inherent, even genetically acquired, within us? I think the answer is both; we need to be taught to give and to share, but some aspects of the act of giving seem to be an inherent characteristic of our personalities.

During the time my family and I lived in Charleston, South Carolina, we became friendly with an older couple who helped us from the time we arrived until the day we left. Billy, as he was known by everyone in the community, could not do enough to help me personally and professionally. His wife, Sidney, was always involved in the shul and was always ready to help others. On reflection about this couple, the only thing they ever requested from me was someone's phone number so that they could offer assistance or inquire about their welfare. Every year, Billy chanted the haftarah of *Parashas Va'eschanan* recited on Shabbos Nachamu. I can clearly recall how Billy would say the first words of the haftarah, "*Nachamu nachamu ami*," in his distinct deep, scratchy voice combined with a heavy Southern drawl, ensuring those three famous words of Yeshayahu would never be forgotten. I only realize now, after he is gone, that he did not only chant those words; he lived them. Throughout their lifetime, both Billy and his wife brought comfort to their people, *Am Yisrael*. Nevertheless, the ultimate Comforter is Hashem, as the *Navi* describes in the haftarah.

The usage of double words throughout *Tanach* raises the question—why? In most cases, double usage represents the notion of sincerity and endearment to its subject. In this case it represents the Jewish People. The *Yalkut Shimoni* on this verse explains the double consolation as follows:

- Comfort the upper spheres and comfort the lower spheres.
- Comfort the living and comfort the dead.
- Comfort the Jewish People in this world and comfort them in the World to Come.
- Comfort the Jewish People for the exile of the Ten Tribes and comfort them for the exile of Yehudah.
- Comfort the Jewish People for the destruction of the First Beis Hamikdash and comfort them for the destruction of the Second Beis Hamikdash.

The Jewish People then went on to say to Yeshayahu: "*Rebbi*, tell us that you did not only come to comfort us for the generation that was destroyed in your day?" Yeshayahu HaNavi answered them, "I have come to bring comfort for this and all future generations."

Comforting others is so important.

When we analyze the different kinds of positive character traits, we begin to recognize their complexities. In order to extend kindness and good deeds, a person must frequently push himself to do so. Of the many mitzvos of *chessed* that exist, almost all of them require great effort, even though they may not necessarily change a situation overtly. For example, visiting the sick has many spiritual ramifications, however, it may not improve the individual's physical situation: yet *chessed* was still done. Attending a funeral is a *chessed*, a kindness to the deceased, but that cannot change or affect anything within the physical realm to that deceased individual. When it comes to the concept of *nechamah*, comforting, the very act of giving comfort is the entire mitzvah. Comforting someone can leave a long-lasting effect on the individual who experiences the care and compassion inherent in the *middah* of *nechamah*. Every time the person being comforted remembers how you extended that comfort, a small feeling of inner comfort is again returned to them. Our recognition of people who took the time and effort to express an interest in our welfare is ongoing. If the recipient feels as if they have been comforted all over again, the donor receives more reward for that mitzvah once again. This is similar to receiving dividends on an investment. The investment of extending comfort never stops. This is illustrated by the *Yalkut Shimoni*: the *chessed* lives on in many different scenarios. Being a comforter is all about giving, and zero about taking. It is a one hundred percent commitment to give and not take, even though a person may believe he is entitled to get something back.

We must strive to turn or change our actions from being takers into givers. That is the ultimate comfort a person can give and receive at the same time.

The Yiddish word "mensch," German for "human be-

ing," is loosely translated as "a person of integrity and honor." The opposite of a mensch is an "unmensch," meaning an utterly unlikeable or unfriendly person. According to Leo Rosten, Yiddish maven and author of *The Joys of Yiddish*, the colloquial term "mensch" translates to mean "someone to admire and emulate; someone of noble character." The key to being "a real mensch" requires nothing less than character, rectitude, dignity, a sense of what is right, responsibility, and decorousness (that would be politeness and refinement). The term is used as a high compliment, implying the rarity and value of that individual's qualities. But is that the true meaning or connotation of the word "mensch"?

Rabbi Wein explains a section from the morning prayers: "*L'olam yehei adam yerei Shamayim ba'galui u'ba'seser*—A person should always be God fearing in the open and behind closed doors." Rabbi Wein, in his inimitable fashion, puts a comma after the word *adam*, "*L'olam yehei adam*," so it reads as, "A person should always be a mensch!" God fearing will follow, but first and foremost, be a human being...be a mensch.

Man was created *b'tzelem Elokim*, in the image of God. From the time he was formed, the first man is called "Adam" and continues to be referred to as such until another part of the human being is created, that of his partner, Chavah. In *Bereishis* (2:22), the Torah states: "ויבן ה' אלקים את הצלע אשר לקח מן האדם לאשה ויבאה אל האדם—God built the rib that he took from the man into a woman and He brought her to him." The next *pasuk* states: "ויאמר האדם זאת הפעם עצם מעצמי ובשר מבשרי לזאת יקרא אשה כי מאיש לקחה זאת—The man said, Now, this is bone from my bones and flesh from my flesh. She shall be called Woman (*ishah*) because she was taken from Man (*ish*)." When man and woman are together, they share the extra letters of *yud* and *hei*, which represent Hashem's name. We are fused together and built around the name of God and ultimately to represent Him in this world. The challenge we face as human beings is to always ensure that we live up to that lofty status. Shlomo HaMelech states: "For there is no man so wholly righteous on earth that he [always] does good and never sins" (*Koheles* 7:20). This seems to ruin the purity of the image we are supposed to live up to. So, what do we do about becoming and maintaining the *adam* within all of us?

The Torah states in *Vayikra* (13:2): "אדם כי יהיה בעור בשרו שאת או ספחת או בהרת והיה בעור בשרו לנגע צרעת והובא אל אהרן הכהן או אל אחד מבניו הכהנים—If a person has a white blotch, discoloration, or spot on the skin of his body, and it is suspected of being a mark of the leprous curse on his skin, he shall be brought to Aharon, or to one of his descendants, who are the priests." Rav Mordechai Leiner, the Ishbitzer Rebbe, in his *sefer Mei Shiloach*, points out that there are four levels or rungs to the makeup of an individual: *adam*, *gever*, *enosh*, and *ish*.

- Paramount on the list is *adam*, as it says in *Bereishis*: "God created Adam in His image," and, "Because in the image of God was man formed." If a Jew develops some type of skin condition, he is brought to the Kohen to regain the holiness. An *adam* on such a high level cannot merely sit and remain with the impurity; he must be brought to the Kohen so that Hashem could purify him to the level he had been at the time of creation of the original Adam, Adam HaRishon.
- Sinning is the animalistic tendency that comes out when we lose sight of the holiness of man. The term *gever* symbolizes the strength of man to overcome those tendencies.
- The term *enosh* refers to humanity, and also describes us as superior to our animalistic side.
- In *Pirkei Avos*, Hillel says: "ובמקום שאין אנשים, השתדל להיות איש—In a place where there are no men, strive to be a man." Be a man, an *ish*, read: mensch, who is constantly striving in his pursuit of the *tzelem Elokim*, the image of God. Where there is a deterioration of man, by virtue of mankind sinning, we must take control and bring back the image in which we were created; we must strive to bring back the original plan of man to live forever and never die, for it is only due to our sins that life is cut short. Adam and Chavah were removed from Gan Eden because of the sin, and death was also decreed upon them. Let us "make man" and become the shining example of a *tzelem Elokim*, a true mensch in the image of God.

When we sin, we lose a part of our stature of *adam*. It is interesting to note that man was created from the ground and, according to some commentaries, a part was taken from him and then brought back to him. In today's scientific world, this is known as regeneration, whereby cells can reproduce and regenerate, sometimes creating completely new organisms. The Hebrew word to regenerate is *aruchah*, which has the same root as "length" and "long." With *tzaraas*, the area of the skin affected must be "brought" to the Kohen and examined to determine if the skin is afflicted. If it is, it is as if the skin is not there. If it is leprosy, the skin needs to regenerate itself, making itself new and wholesome again.

We need to make ourselves in the image and form in which God originally created us. When the skin does produce again, it goes through the process of *aruchah*, literally "regenerating," signifying its continuation. With a refreshed and healthy body with which the skin rejuvenated itself, there will be *aruchah*—long life will extend to a longer life.

Candy, candy, candy! Every kid's dream diet. A universal custom in almost every shul is to have at least one candy man who has a seemingly endless supply of sweets for children of all ages (typically from three until ninety-three). A second universal custom in almost every shul is the throwing of candy during an *aufruf*, the *aliyah* of a *chassan* the week before his wedding (in the Sephardic tradition, he receives his *aliyah* on the Shabbos following his wedding, the "*Shabbat Chatan*"). On a similar vein, there is also the custom to throw candy at a bar mitzvah boy. Showering the new groom or the bar mitzvah with sweets is a beautiful way to send a message of happiness and sweetness as they enter a new, major chapter in their lives. As the anticipation grows for the release of the candies, all the children position themselves to swoop in and grab as much candy as they can hold. Or chew. It is amazing how quickly the floor gets cleaned up. In fact, so quickly that I cannot help but make my usual corny remark, "We now continue with *Yekum Purkan* as the ground crew finishes another amazing clean-up."

At a recent *kiddush* in honor of the birth of a baby girl, I overheard a parent say to her four-year-old child, his pockets overflowing with candy, "I think you've had enough sugar for today." Is it any wonder why our children are so charged up? Children have enough natural energy in their bodies without needing a sugar boost to their systems. It is interesting to note how even infants enjoy something sweet. Yet, as we get older our tastes change and sometimes we even remark about an icing or cake that "it's too sweet." Ever hear a child say something is too sweet?

The human body begins its constant change from birth. From the moment a person is born until the last breath, our bodies are constantly adjusting to our new weight, height, and shifting metabolism. We do not feel the subtle change from day-to-day, but from one decade of our life to the next we experience a fluctuation in our bodies' vital signs. The effects of change in life typically do not manifest themselves immediately. The results of a good habit or a bad habit are rarely detected early. It takes years before we realize or begin to feel the effects, whether positive or negative. With regard to sugar, most children are not negatively affected by the consumption of sugar as their bodies tend to burn it off. As we age, however, our metabolism slows, requiring more exercise and less intake of sugar in order to burn off enough calories to keep us from gaining weight.

Sugar is so sweet, yet it can be deadly.

So too, in religious life and the Torah. There are certain issues, tests, and challenges that we face as a people, and we are sometimes looking for something too good to be true.

The Torah states in *Devarim* (13:2): "כי יקום בקרבך נביא או חלם חלום ונתן אליך אות או מופת—This is what you must do when a prophet or a person who has visions in a dream arises among you. He may present you [or predict] with a sign or miracle." Based on that sign or miracle he may say to you, "Let us try out a different god. Let us serve it and have a new spiritual experience." These verses are the warning against following a false prophet. Despite the possible miracle or great feat that they may do in the beginning, one must look at how it all comes out in the end. *Rashi* explains the two words "sign" and "miracle." The sign refers to a sign in the heavens; the miracle refers to something on earth. Nevertheless, despite the performance or even validation of a prediction, one shall not listen to him, i.e., the false prophet. The *Ramban* and others ask, "Why does Hashem grant the false prophet the power to show a sign?" *Rashi* concludes, "For Hashem your God uses it to test you, to turn away from the false prophet and follow Hashem." The *Rashbam* and *Ramban* explain that there are a few people who have a special gift to know the future, but a spirit of impurity influences them to prophecy. This was the power of the prophets of the non-Jews, such as the magicians and sorcerers in Pharaoh's court. The *sefer Torah U'L'Moadim* enlightens us that these are the two reasons a person could rationalize something that is the antithesis of Torah, causing him to stray from the true Torah. The two reasons a person could stray are (1) misinformation or false wisdom and knowledge, and (2) pure desire and craving.

These reasons follow the principles of "Do not follow your eyes and heart," because thoughts based upon falsehoods and desire are born out of apostasy. The eyes can see the good, but they are simultaneously able to see the bad. We need to be the *chacham* (wise person) who is able to look to the future and understand what will transpire as a result of decisions made today.

In life, things do not necessarily emerge in the end looking as good as they did at the beginning. Sugar seems to be a wonderful treat in the beginning but may cumulatively not be good for us later. A *navi sheker* leads a person down a false path, while a true *tzaddik* or *talmid chacham* has the wisdom to perceive that the end may not seem as sweet as it was at the start. There are times when difficult, unpleasant decisions need to be made in order to avoid worse outcomes later. Rabbis need to take a stand on certain issues that are viewed as being too harsh, and devoid of the sweetness we crave. This may result in the rabbi or leader becoming less popular. Nevertheless, he is trying to evade a much worse outcome later down the road.

Years ago, when I was just beginning my career, one of my biggest critics, who also happened to be one of my biggest supporters, gave me some invaluable advice. I got up to speak between *Minchah* and *Maariv* and attempted to learn with the minyan. I approached the podium, quietly looking over the material, and bumbled my way through the brief interlude of learning. After the services, this individual put his arm around my shoulder, looked me square in the eye and said, "If you are not prepared to speak, then don't."

That was one of the best pieces of advice I have ever received in my life; I understood that his input was meant to be constructive and it came from his heart. Since that time, I have been consistently careful to follow his sage words. Nevertheless, a different kind of challenge arises from time to time when teaching.

Generally speaking, I encourage and even ask if anyone has any questions. Occasionally, someone asks a question that is directly on the topic and I can handle the question. But there are times when I am caught off guard, finding myself without a clear answer. My slipup is trying to give an answer without properly researching the material. Sometimes I do give the correct answer on the spot, but there were other times when I should simply have stated, "I'm not sure about this. I'll get back to you." There is a human tendency toward *gaavah* (haughtiness). Offering answers without total knowledge of the material is a good example. Sure enough, a few weeks ago I fell into this trap, only this time I really thought I knew the correct answer. Actually, part of me is still convinced that I was right, even though I was wrong, as is clearly stated in halachah. Someone asked a question related to the material I had prepared to teach, and I gave an answer. Someone in the crowd—a noted Torah scholar—respectfully and humbly quoted the opposite of what I had just said. I responded, reiterating my position, emphatically stating that I was correct. During *Maariv*, the gentleman showed me the halachah, explaining that my response to the question was dead wrong on the halachic side, but perhaps correct within the spirit of the law. In the end, however, I was wrong. And I felt defeated!

When it comes to *Toras emes*, the truth of Torah, there is no defeat (maybe some agony, but certainly no defeat). In the realm of Torah and halachah, we seek out the truth even though it may injure our pride. Immediately after *Maariv*—I was afraid that by the next day some of the attendees might not be present to hear the clarification—I got everyone's attention before they dispersed and said, "I stand corrected. I was wrong," and proceeded to acknowledge the correct course of action for that halachah and thanked the person for pointing it out. After the fact, my pride was not hurt. To the contrary, I was proud to admit the mistake and have clarity in the Torah.

In today's day and age, this is a sticking point that leads to *machlokes*, disputes and arguments, that can lead to an undercurrent of hatred among our people. We should challenge ourselves to face the reality of the statement: "How can it be that everyone is right, and no one is wrong?" Even when two people are arguing, and one clearly has a stronger argument, it is difficult for the person with the weaker argument to step down and admit defeat. Our egos cloud our judgment, making it difficult to analyze an alternative viewpoint with clarity. Nevertheless, it is understandable why a person may believe he is right and the other individual is wrong. The message is a bit deeper than thinking, "I am right, and he is wrong." The greatest challenge to our ego is when we are ultimately arguing within our own head. The internal struggle of "I am right, and I can do this or that" while my alter ego challenges and argues, professing, "No! You are wrong and the correct thing to do is the exact opposite of what you are thinking!" The two-sided battle over who is right and who is wrong is classic when the only person in this battle is you. This comes out when we say one thing, but we think and know that the opposite is true. Do we own up to our mistaken analysis of the situation, or are we not strong enough to do so—maintaining that what we said or thought initially is acceptable?

The Torah states in *Bamidbar* (30:3): "איש כי ידר נדר לה' או השבע שבעה לאסר אסר על נפשו לא יחל דברו ככל היצא מפיו יעשה—If a man makes a vow to God or makes an oath to obligate himself, he must not break his word. He must do all that he expressed verbally." If someone says he is going to do something and he does not do it, or says he is not going to do something and he does it, he is breaking his word. The word *yachel* loosely translated means "break," but it has greater significance; it also means to turn it into the mundane. Our mouths are holy and the words that come out of our mouths are holy. When we do not hold ourselves up to that, we are desecrating our words.

The *Shelah HaKadosh* says that angels are created from our words: good words create good angels, and the opposite is also true. The *Chasam Sofer* writes that not only someone who vows with his mouth is responsible to follow through; even the thought of doing something obligates us to fulfill it, despite our claiming that we never *said* we would do such and such.

Every individual needs to be honest with himself. By committing to something, we must follow through, but if subsequently it turns out that we were mistaken, we need to stand up and correct the situation right away. If we make a statement or even think of one and then realize it is wrong, we should stand up to our error and correct it even when it may be uncomfortable. As we commit to thinking before we speak, we will be training ourselves to be careful about how and what we say in general. An example is *lashon hara*. This will create the impetus to be careful of how we speak about others. Let us strive to "stand corrected" so the Beis Hamikdash will also "stand corrected" speedily in our time.

In every area of life there is more, less, and average. Whether we are talking about a person's temperament, character traits, weight, height, looks, intelligence, finances, religiosity, etc., there is a level we call "average." Even though there are always those people who display extreme levels, they are factored in to what is registered as the mean average. Some people do things quickly, while others do them slowly. Several years ago, I wrote about the law, which clearly states that it is not only forbidden to drive above the speed limit, it is also forbidden to drive too slowly. There is one additional area I would like to critique concerning those who find themselves doing things the wrong way, despite being asked not to do so.

There are some individuals who speak very quickly, so quickly that the listener cannot understand what they are saying. There are differing opinions as to why some people speak quickly, including their ability to visualize the words in their minds, a condition known as "cluttering." Two examples come to mind, one in a religious context, the other regarding our everyday lives.

- On days when the Torah is read (particularly on Mondays and Thursdays) there is a custom to make a *Mi Shebeirach*, a prayer for the sick. After a list of names is mentioned, some attendees will add a name that is not on the list. They orally say the name to the *gabbai*. Typically, the person rattles off the name of the ill person, and the mother's name along with it, at lightning speed. The *gabbai* may never have heard this name before and is unable to catch the name, not once or twice but even three times to fully grasp the name being called out. If the person would only say the name slowly the very first time (which is what happens anyway by the third or fourth repetition), it would save people time, effort, and sometimes embarrassment. Please, just slow down when giving over a name.

- The second scenario involves leaving a phone number on a voice mail or answering machine. I cannot tell you how many times it has been necessary to replay the message over again to catch a phone number someone left for me to call back on. In some cases, it can take me nine times, repeatedly listening to the message because it was given so quickly. On occasion I have no choice but to give up because it is impossible to decipher the number. Some recorded messages give specific instructions to avoid this issue by stating, "Please speak slowly and repeat the number." Occasionally, this works, but unfortunately, not too often.

One should think about these and similar situations when asking another person to do something for them. Simply say it slowly. Whether asking them to return a call or mention a name for a speedy recovery, you want to avoid making it difficult. When someone speaks quickly, and the listener is unable to accurately hear what you are saying, the listener is placed in the awkward position of asking the speaker to repeat themselves or to say, "What?"—sometimes over and over again. The onus should be on the speaker, not the listener, to convey a message or a thought properly.

We might all agree that the responsibility of clarity is on the speaker, but we cannot control the way a person speaks, and we therefore need to prepare for the inevitable. We need to take measures to listen more carefully and figure out ways to understand the speaker despite their babble. If the speaker will not change the way they speak, *we* need to change the way we listen.

We learn a great lesson in listening from Moshe Rabbeinu. It is telling that it was Moshe—who himself suffered from a speech impediment—who consistently recognized the need for patience when listening to others.

The Torah states in *Vayikra* (10:20): "וישמע משה וייטב בעיניו"—When Moshe heard this, he approved." *Rashi*, on this verse, quotes the *Toras Kohanim*, which says that Moshe admitted and was not embarrassed and did not use the excuse, "I did not hear." The Gemara (*Zevachim* 101b) adds to the *Toras Kohanim*, saying, "I did not hear that," but to the contrary, he said, "I heard it and I forgot it," which is a greater disgrace than just saying I did not hear. The *Talmud Yerushalmi* (*Chagigah* 1:8) writes: "I sent you a great person, and what is his greatness? That he was never embarrassed to say, 'I did not hear.'" This means that saying one did not hear something, despite the disgrace it entails, reveals a greatness in that person.

The commentary *Tzion V'Yerushalayim* goes on to elaborate this point. It is one thing to understand that the rabbis and scholars of the Talmud, the disseminators of the oral laws, might be more humiliated to admit, "I did not hear that." But consider Moshe Rabbeinu—the prize student of the Almighty Himself, who learned one-on-one with Hashem and was the first ever to learn Torah and teach Torah, Wouldn't he feel the greatest mortification by admitting, "I heard but I forgot"? It takes a great man to stand up and state the truth despite discomfiture and the desire to protect his pride.

The *Netziv*, Rav Naftali Tzvi Yehudah Berlin, brings a midrash that Moshe made a public announcement stating, "I, Moshe, made a mistake, and Aharon, my brother, came and taught it to me." Why did Moshe do that? Moshe wanted to teach Klal Yisrael this *middah* of admitting a mistake. He taught the people that there is nothing wrong with admitting a mistake, and even he, Moshe Rabbeinu, was capable of making a mistake. By admitting a mistake, we come to correct the falsehood and bring truth to the surface. In addition, by admitting a mistake, we admit that we, too, are human and can learn and grow from our errors.

Therefore, we see the importance of listening with care in order to hear things properly. The utmost honor is given to someone who can recognize and admit his mistake and not hide behind some other excuse. Listen, pay close attention to the few short words Moshe said so openly and clearly. Ultimately, this admission will be viewed with goodness in Hashem's eyes as well.

One need not look far for inspiration; sometimes it is right there in front of us. There are some amazing people we see every day. We think we need to hear great stories and share incredible moments to be inspired by people and the things they do. Take the time to look around. You may notice a neighbor, a coworker, or a relative who has done something awesome—and they do it every day. A clear example is how awestruck we feel when someone donates a kidney. Lo and behold, I have a cousin whose own son gave him a kidney. One might say, "Oh, for a relative this is not so impressive; who wouldn't do that?" Well, let me tell you, from my perspective it is a very big deal.

Closer to home, I have come to not only respect but also be impressed by a man who lives in the shul apartments. Mr. Timothy King, who prefers to be called Tim, is African American (I obtained his permission to write about him) and has been living here for about three years. Whenever I see him, I say hello and we chat for a few minutes, usually about the current sports of the day. Unfortunately, he still smokes and needs to light up off shul grounds, so I usually catch him in the parking lot either on the way toward the gate or back to his apartment. One day, he was struggling up a tiny incline in the parking lot. I immediately went over and asked him if he needed some help. "No, no," he said, "I'm OK. I just need to get a little exercise." You see, Tim was born with some deformities: no legs, one healthy arm, and the other only a stump. I always see him in his motorized wheelchair, but that day he was using an ordinary wheelchair. He was wheeling and pushing himself with his one healthy arm, but it was a gruesome struggle. I asked him if he needed help being pushed, and if something had happened to his motorized chair. He answered in the negative to both questions. His motorized chair was working, and he did not need help (although he appreciated the offer) because this is the way he is able to exercise. Being very limited in his capacity to exercise, wheeling himself gets his heart pumping and his blood flowing. He needed to push, and it wasn't easy for him, nor was it easy for me to watch. The sheer determination and resolve to do it on his own was humbling. There is no question that strength of character and mind is what gives him the will to literally push forward. He is always on the move and is driven by his purpose. Tim knows the only way for him to survive is to continue to work hard, to push forward, and not allow anything stop him from living.

The challenges, walls, and barriers that Hashem places in front of people are the daily tests we must face and go through in life. The success or failure, more often than not, lies in our determination and resolve to push on and tackle the encounters as they come. This is clearly seen in the Torah as the Jewish People, finally set free by Pharaoh, look behind them and see Pharaoh's army chasing them. Staring in front of them is the Yam Suf. With no place to go, the Jews question Moshe by saying, "Weren't there enough graves in Egypt? Why did we need to come here to die? Moshe replies, "Don't worry. God will rescue you today." And so, what did they do? Read on...

The Torah states in *Shemos* (14:15): "ויאמר ה' אל משה מה תצעק אלי דבר אל בני ישראל ויסעו—God said to Moshe, 'Why are you crying out to Me? Speak to the Children of Israel and let them start moving.'" Apparently, as Moshe lifted his staff in order to split the sea, all the people froze in place except Nachshon ben Aminadav. The time was now. Already in the water up to his neck at the split second when Moshe was getting ready to split the sea, Nachshon Ben Aminadav continued to move forward as the sea split. What was it that actually made the Yam Suf split? Was it Moshe and his staff or Nachshon's determination, *emunah*, and *bitachon* in Hashem that something would happen, allowing him and the people to follow to safety? The Gemara (*Sotah* 37a) tells us that each tribe was unwilling to enter the water first. One tribe said, "I will not be the first to descend into the sea," while another tribe declared, "I will not be the first to descend." At that point Nachshon ben Aminadav, the prince of the tribe of Yehudah, leaped forward, descending first into the sea. The *Midrash Rabbah* (*Bamidbar* 13:7) explains: "Why was he called Nachshon? Because he was the first to go down into the surf (*nachshol*) of the Yam Suf. Therefore, God told Moshe, 'He who sanctified My Name in the sea will be the first to bring his offering in the dedication of the Altar.'"

At that precise moment, while Moshe was praying at length. Hashem said to him, "My dear ones are drowning in the sea while you linger in prayer with me?" Moshe said before God: "Master of the Universe, but what is it in my power to do?" God responded: "Speak to the Children of Israel and let them journey forth."

Reviewing this story, we see it was Nachshon's initiative that started the process and forced Moshe to daven to Hashem and get the people behind to follow. Nachshon was able to lead because he dared to go into a place where men do not usually go. What was it that gave Nachshon the fortitude to do what he did? It was his *emunah* and *bitachon*—his faith and security in the Almighty that this was the path on which he had to proceed.

It is easy for me to say I have *emunah* (faith) and *bitachon* (trust), but it is something totally different to live and act with complete *emunah* and bitachon, especially when the pressure is on. Having *emunah* and *bitachon* is not something we are just born with; it develops over time by learning and reading about it, by listening to and reading stories of great people who live and breathe entirely through faith and security from God. By doing so, we strengthen ourselves, and provide ourselves with the fortitude to take the lead and go places that we would otherwise never go. Let us all learn from Nachshon ben Aminadav to always push forward. It is sometimes hard, but it is always worth it. Think of Tim King.

Not too long ago, I was in the checkout line at the supermarket, kibitzing with the cashier. I happen to know most of the older cashiers, having shopped there for many years. Many service people wear name tags, and at that moment the cashier was looking for hers. As she was looking, I thought to myself, *Who knows if these are even their real names; maybe they just wear fake names?* The cashier explained that she was looking for her spare name tag, explaining that they usually have a few of them. I said to her, "Why don't you just take someone else's name tag? Will the customers know the difference?" She then replied, "I don't want to be anybody else; I want to be me!"

I found her response to be extraordinarily deep on many levels:

- In society, and particularly with regard to children, there is an emphasis through Hollywood and sports to become someone we are not. Children grow up idolizing others and this can be harmful if they don't grow out of it by the teenage years. It is critical for parents to encourage their children to be themselves. People do better in life when things are real, not fake.

- Putting religion aside, living a life we do not believe in can be very painful and distressing. More importantly, this applies when a person is capable of reaching their potential in life yet chooses not to.

When we look at great, successful or righteous people we tend to reason that they reached their potential because they had it within them to do so, while the wicked villains of history did not. The fact is that every evil leader, tyrant, or wicked ruler had the potential to use their strengths for good but chose not to. We see this with two great leaders from the Torah, specifically two men who really had the same potential: Yaakov and his twin brother Eisav.

In *Bereishis* (33:4), the Torah states: "וירץ עשו לקראתו ויחבקהו ויפל על צואריו וישקהו ויבכו—And Eisav ran to greet Yaakov and he hugged him, and he fell on his neck and he kissed him, and they cried." Most commentators give explanations on the unique dots placed over the word "and he kissed him." Last week, I heard Rabbi Asher Brander quoting the *Netziv* in his commentary *Ha'amek Davar*. The *Netziv* explains the implication of why both Eisav *and* Yaakov cried. That both cried comes to teach us that not only was Eisav excited about meeting with Yaakov, but Yaakov was excited to meet Eisav. Not only was Eisav trying to show a love for Yaakov, but Yaakov also cried out of love for his brother Eisav. The love that Yaakov cried over was for the emotion of fraternal love he had for his twin brother. More importantly, Yaakov cried for an emotional and intellectual reason: the potential of his brother. There is no question that Yaakov and Eisav, despite being twins, had stark differences between them:

- Yaakov sat and learned, while Eisav hunted.
- Yaakov used his mind for intellectual pursuits, while Eisav chose to use his body for physical pursuits.
- Yaakov used his intellectual capacity to do good, while Eisav used his physical capacity to do evil.

Yaakov cried because Eisav had the potential to have used his physical ability to do good. Perhaps Eisav himself recognized and appreciated Yaakov for what he represented but could not live that lifestyle. But he chose to be someone else, to use his strengths for evil and not for good. He, too, cried over his own potential, bemoaning the fact he did not develop properly, using his body and not his mind.

The *Netziv* continues, using this as a springboard for all future generations. When the descendants of Eisav will have a pure, spiritual awakening to recognize the greatness of the Jewish People, we, the Jewish People, will in turn have strong brotherly feelings toward Eisav, because he is our brother. The great Rabbi Yehudah HaNasi demonstrated this love toward Antoninus (a Roman leader descended from Eisav) because he acknowledged the greatness of Hashem and the Jewish People. Ironically, at the end of Eisav's life, in a remarkable turn of events, he demonstrated that the way he lived his life should have been through the intellect—through knowledge of Hashem and Torah. Fast-forward to the end of *Bereishis*: After Yaakov dies, he is brought to the *Me'aras HaMachpeilah* for burial. Eisav shows up and claims that Yaakov buried Leah there and used up his spot, and the remaining grave should therefore belong to him, Eisav. An argument ensues between Yaakov's children and Eisav, requiring Naftali (who was swift) to go quickly back to Egypt to retrieve the deed and proof of purchase to enable Yaakov to have the remaining spot. Chushim, the son of Dan, who was deaf, did not understand what the commotion was about and concluded that Eisav was holding up the burial of his grandfather. At that, Chushim pulled out a sword and cut off Eisav's head, and it rolled into the cave, coming to rest at Yaakov's feet.

Yaakov and Eisav were reunited, born as twins and buried close to each other. But in the end, it was only the intellectual part of Eisav, his head, that merited being buried there. We can understand this amazing occurrence as a revelation of Eisav's regret for having lived a life of futility, and having come to the realization, though late, that this is where his head wanted to be. That is why Yaakov cried for him.

Let us recognize who we are today—so that we become someone that we ultimately want to be and not regret later on becoming someone that we do *not* want to be.

No two eyes are alike, and no two people literally see eye to eye. There may be understandings of concepts, philosophies, and laws that people generally agree upon. However, you will not see everything exactly the way I do. I think we can all agree that the way adults view a situation differs greatly than that of a child. This differentiation usually narrows as the child ages in years and matures in his thinking. But until that time comes, there will be many frustrating, exhausting, and upsetting battles between parent and child, teacher and student, and for that matter, between the growing adolescent and anyone in an authoritative position. Looking back over time, I would suggest that the teenage years were by far the most challenging as my kids developed their critical thinking skills, learning on-the-job skills of how to argue and rationalize through every minute detail of life.

Without going into all the details, I remember an incident when one of my children was clearly in the wrong but fought me emphatically over an issue they saw with completely different eyes. It was an issue of principle, contrary to the many trivial things we had "lively discussions" about. Due to the importance of the subject, I sought out guidance from my *rebbi*. I carefully laid out the two sides of the dispute my wife and I had with our teenaged child. I was sure that my *rebbi*, knowing we were in the right, would give me some advice and a clever strategy for dealing with the circumstances at hand. To our great surprise and initial disappointment, not only did he not give us any strategy or even basic advice, in his unique way, he sided with our child! My *rebbi*'s words were clear: "We need to look at the situation through the child's eyes." He used phrases such as "in his mind," "from his perspective," and "where the child is coming from."

This was truly an eye-opener for my wife and me. Why do we, as parents, need to look at the story or situation from the kid's perspective? At first, my wife and I looked at each other bewildered. You know, like, aren't the parents always right? And what about the notion that children should listen to what the parents say, regardless of where the child is coming from? Our puzzled looks then gave way to a look of "uh-huh, maybe my *rebbi* is right" (he always is). We were then able to look at things from a different perspective using a more objective manner, and bringing our child's input into the discussion.

We are all influenced by our peers, surroundings, and the information we read and hear about. Nothing influences our ideas and beliefs more than actually *seeing* something; as the old saying goes: "Seeing is believing." The Jewish People have historically made decisions—both good and bad—based upon circumstances we thought were very clear. One instance that caused catastrophic damage was the image the Satan drew for the people, showing them that Moshe Rabbeinu was dead after the Jews miscalculated the timing of his expected return down from Har Sinai. Yet, there is another "vision" that appears in the Torah, which helped the Jewish People traverse the dangers of the desert. Throughout my years of learning, I always thought the Jewish People traveled in the desert by following the *Mishkan*. When the *Mishkan* traveled, we walked, and when it stopped, we camped. The navigation system was the Cloud of Glory during the daytime, while a Pillar of Fire would light up the path during the night. Looking over the verses a little closer reveals something different.

In *Bamidbar* (9:15), the Torah states: "וביום הקים את המשכן כסה הענן את המשכן לאהל העדת ובערב יהיה על המשכן כמראה אש עד בקר—On the day the Tabernacle was erected, the cloud covered the Tabernacle, the Tent of Testimony. Then, in the evening, there was something that appeared to be like fire on the Tabernacle, remaining there until morning." The narration continues (ibid., 9:16): "כן יהיה תמיד הענן יכסנו ומראה אש לילה—From then on it remained that way. There was a cloud covering it [by day], and a fire-like partition by night." *Targum Yonasan Ben Uziel* remarks that it is possible that the cloud remained and was also there at night. The *Midrash Rabbah* asks rhetorically, "What does 'appeared to be like fire' mean?" The wording teaches us that if the cloud was whitish, then the people knew that the sun was rising. When the cloud was reddish, they knew the sun was setting.

The *Malbim* explains that the cloud that led the Jews out during *yetzias Mitzrayim* had one pillar of cloud and one of actual fire. One was used to lead them during the day and the other at night. Thus, in the desert there was only one cloud that served both during the day and night, similar to the words of the midrash. This cloud in the *midbar* was there leading the Jews at night, but it appeared as fire. There was a perception among the people that this nighttime pillar was a fire, but in reality, it was the same cloud. The cloud appeared at night as a fire, as depicted at the end of *Sefer Shemos*: "The cloud of Hashem was over the *Mishkan* during the day, and fire in it at night"—referring to the cloud itself. The essence of where the Shechinah rested was within the cloud rather than the fire. Therefore, from this point onward, there was always a cloud over the *Mishkan*, 24/7.

Initially, we thought the fire was necessary at night to light up the road when they traveled. However, the *Shach* (*Sifsei Kohen*) states that the appearance of the cloud as fire remained even when B'nei Yisrael camped and were stationary. How did the Jews benefit from perceiving the cloud as a fire rather than the same cloud as the daytime? The cloud that looked like a fire was seen even at night because nighttime is filled with fear and worry. At night, a person thinks of his sins and is nervous. The vision of a fire served as a protection for the Jews at night, because it brought to mind the fires of Gehinnom, therefore reminding them to do *teshuvah*. These fires served as a preventive measure from sinning, and would ward off evil spirits and any bad thoughts of sin that might come to mind during the night.

The mind is a powerful tool that perceives things that may or may not be there:

- When it comes to business and secular things in life, a person may be open to hearing and listening to another's perspective and *see* that person's perception of the situation.
- In spiritual matters, when a person already sees himself in a certain way, he should not leave things to his or her own perception but rather get guidance from an objective viewpoint.

Let us grow up and not act like the child who can only see things his way. Let us rather be open enough to ask what the proper way of seeing and doing something is. When it comes to children, we should consider their perception and empower them, but ultimately use that perception and empowerment to lead them forward.

There is an old cliché: "Oh, remember the days of yesteryear," recalling, either with fondness or yearning, a former period of our lives. I remember thinking, as a child growing up, that I would never make my children do the things my parents made me do. Alternatively, I'd tell myself I would never treat my children the way my parents treated me; when I become a parent I'd let my children do what my parents chose not to allow me to do. My *rebbi*, Rabbi Wein, would always mention what a good sense of humor God has. One of those humorous quips was that God punishes children by making them parents! Now, as a parent, I somehow view events differently than I did growing up. Now that the shoe is on the other foot, I seem to have forgotten all those promises I made to myself when I was younger.

Many are familiar with the term "sandwich" generation," referring to those who, in addition to being parents of children and grandchildren, are also children to their own aging parents. It is common to find one-self at this later stage in life saying the same things about one's now-aging parents they thought when they were children: *when I get older, I won't do things the same way my parents are doing now while they are growing older.*

As parents age, there tends to be a denial of some sort in recog-nizing or accepting their growing fragility and ability to take care of themselves. At times, there is a struggle between the senior parents and their middle-aged children regarding what is in the best interest of the parents and family. Aging parents often cannot be objective about their long-term care if they have entered a compromised situation. Obviously, there is a big difference between the reaction of a young child versus that of an adult child to their parents' decision-making. The young child does not see the big picture and is oblivious to the responsibilities of life, but at the other extreme, the aging parents may also unfortunately lack the ability to take in the big picture. It is the adult parent/child who is now in the middle. On the one hand, they realize that their parents were correct in the way they brought them up, but on the other hand, they are also in a position to learn from and prepare for the stage their aging parents are going through, and develop a healthy, flexible mentality toward the eventual time when they will be the ones requiring care.

It is always easy to be the critic, the all-knowing one, the one who would have done it differently, when we are not actually the ones calling the shots at that time. It is easy to criticize the coach, the teacher, the parent, and even the prime minister, when we are not in that position at that time.

One of the greatest challenges we face in life is balance. As children grow up, we nurture and facilitate our own children's growing maturity, encouraging them to make decisions on their own. Hopefully, by the time they are mature, they will understand why a parent made certain decisions and choices for them when they were too young to have the final say themselves. On the other side of life, we hope that a senior parent will recognize when it is time to accept help and follow the opinion of others, especially their children, in making choices for them.

The critical points are to know when to begin making the correct choices and—equally important but far more difficult—to know when it is time to let go of making those choices.

In *Michah* (chapters 5–6), the *Navi* recalls how Hashem protected the Jewish People as they traveled through the desert. Michah mentions how Balak hired the evil Bilaam to curse the Jews. After failing to curse Am Yisrael, Bilaam suggests to Balak that he lure the Jews, particularly the men, into idolatry through acts of lewdness. Rabbi Avraham Sofer brings a Mishnah from *Pirkei Avos* (3:3): "רבי שמעון אומר שלושה שאכלו על שולחן אחד ולא אמרו עליו דברי תורה כאלו אכלו מזבחי מתים—If three people ate at the same table and did not speak words of Torah upon it, it is as if they ate from offerings of the dead." Why is this as though they ate from offerings of the dead? The reason is based upon a verse in *Yeshayahu* (28:8): "כי כל שלחנות מלאו קיא צאה בלי מקום—For all tables are full of vomit and filth without the Omnipresent." The vomit and filth (literally dung or excrement) was the actual service of idolatry for Baal Pe'or. In *Tehillim* (106:28), David HaMelech says: "ויצמדו לבעל פעור ויאכלו זבחי מתים—And the Jewish People attached themselves to the idol of Baal Pe'or, and they ate offerings of the dead."

Notice the difference:

- The Torah emphasizes that due to the Jews eating sacrifices intended for idolatry, they became attached to the idol Baal Pe'or itself.
- In *Tehillim*, David HaMelech seems to indicate that they first got close to Baal Pe'or and then they ate of the sacrifices.

What was the actual order?

The *Chasam Sofer* suggests that once the Jewish People failed with Baal Pe'or, this sin remained within the Jewish world until this very day. While the sin of idolatry is not extant among the Jewish People as it was then, the drive and the attraction to idolatry still exists today. In fact, the Torah in *Devarim* states clearly that anyone who gets close to Baal Pe'or will be destroyed. In *Yehoshua*, it states that the Jews never cleansed themselves completely from the sin of Baal Pe'or idolatry. Even though the idol of Baal Pe'or was destroyed and no longer exists, the sin still lingers. The sin is represented by offerings to the idols—the breads, the oils, the wines—all of which cause us to mingle with the non-Jews, which can lead to intermarriage and further idolatry, ultimately moving us away from God.

Baruch Hashem, we no longer actually serve idols, but unfortunately, we still find ourselves eating of the sacrifices of the dead, the nonexistent idol of Baal Pe'or. This, to our misfortune, has plagued us for many, many generations.

We as a people continue to sin in ways that separate us from Hashem, not necessarily through idolatry itself but through the act of doing things that lead us in that direction. We need to clearly sever not only the idol worship but the *calculations* and *bad decisions* that are the very fringes of idol worship. We have choices, and we often do not lean on those who are best suited to guide us in those decisions. Spiritual dangers abound in this world, and our rabbis are the ones to turn to evaluate what is acceptable or not. From this we learn that it is vital to make the clear distinction between the times in life that we must take responsibility for our own decisions, and when it is time to let others make them for us.

I am on a collision course with myself as my metabolism slows down and my appetite increases. In fact, I am currently having a midlife crisis—not the kind of crisis that focuses on changing careers and such. I have a crisis regarding my health as I now navigate through the middle years of my life. In trying to figure out different ways to motivate me to exercise more and eat healthier, my wife bought me a 'Fitbit." What is a Fitbit? Fitbit is an American company known for its products of the same name, all of which are activity trackers and nasty scales that keep a log of your BMI (body mass index), body/fat index, and every single ounce gained or lost. Fitbit also makes wireless-enabled wearable technology devices that measure data such as the number of steps walked, heart rate, quality of sleep, steps climbed, and other personal metrics. It does not help the user lose weight, but it sure makes a person aware of how few steps have been taken and that the need to walk more for that particular day.

A few weeks ago, while I was learning with someone during our Skype session, he noticed something on my wrist. He remarked, "Is that a Fitbit? When I asked you for your opinion on getting a Fitbit, you told me I shouldn't get one. You said it was a device that starts to control you and people get obsessed with things like that."

I was shocked and taken aback for two reasons. First, I don't remember saying that, and second, whatever I may have said in the past, now I really do think it is a good thing. After thinking about it for a few minutes I started to kind of remember. Maybe I *was* against wearing a Fitbit, but I came to realize that although I believe some of these tech gadgets do run your life, some can be controlled and there may be benefit (no pun intended) to using them.

Another area where I may have changed my mind that recently surfaced is in regard to halachic guidance. Over the years, questions arise and, later on, are asked again. At one time, perhaps I said something was to be done in a certain way, and now, many years later, I may say something different. Please do not misunderstand that last statement. I am not changing the halachah; I am rather presenting a change in understanding the law and its application. Changing one's mind after

receiving new information is an acceptable method of thinking, growing, and maturing. Technology is ever-changing, and that impacts the
way halachah determines certain laws regarding Shabbos, *kashrus*,
and so forth.

People, by nature, change their minds and may even alternate their
viewpoints, bending from one point of view to another and back again
over time. In most cases the changes are not significant enough to
notice or to make a big deal about; nevertheless, changes do occur.
Teshuvah (repentance) is a changing of the mindset. The challenge in
life is to make sure we change for the better, to do the right thing. It is
equally important to make the change while there is time. The *Netziv*
and others delicately point out how some people change their minds in
the nick of time and others do so when time has already run out; when
it's too late.

Korach and his followers were swallowed up by the earth, but his sons
were saved. In *Bamidbar* (chapter 16), the showdown between Moshe
and Korach takes place. Moshe announces that if these men die in the
same manner as all other men, it shows that Hashem did not send him.
The Torah states (ibid., 16:30–32): "But if God creates something entirely new, making the earth open its mouth and swallow them and all
that is theirs, so that they descend to the depths alive, then it is these
men who ae provoking God. Moshe hardly finished speaking when the
ground under [Dasan and Aviram] split. The earth opened its mouth,
and swallowed them and their houses, along with all the men who were
with Korach." The *Netziv* explains that when the earth split open, the
people did not immediately fall in. Rather, the earth began to shake and
tremble, creating more fear and panic among the rebels prior to just
being swallowed up in one quick swoop. At first, the earth opened up,
becoming "a mouth," which then started to swallow. At that very moment, Korach and his followers had the chance to change their minds
and realize their mistake, but they did not do so. Therefore, the mouth
then began to swallow with the power of gravity, pulling and sucking,
one by one, those who were "fit" to be swallowed up. "Fit" in this instance means that they were fit for this punishment because they could
have still repented—they could still have changed their minds—but

they did not do so. As each individual passed up that opportunity, he followed the fate of the previous man.

Regarding the words, *"v'yardu chaim she'olah*—so that they descend to the depths alive," a question is asked: Was Moshe such a cruel person, *chas v'shalom*, that he would ask for such a horrific death? Rabbi Reuvein Margolies, in the name of the Belzer Rebbe, explains to the contrary; that Moshe did a *chessed* for Korach. He specifically requested that they go down alive to give them time to repent and not die immediately. If they would die immediately without repenting, their souls would be lost forever. Moshe's request was that they should still have that opportunity. This answer is seen in the Gemara (*Sanhedrin* 108a): "Rabbi Eliezer says that the ground had covered them up." Shmuel HaNavi proclaimed, *"Hashem meimis u'mechayeh, morid she'ol va'yaal*—God puts to death and revives. He lowers them to *She'ol* and He brings them back up" (*Shmuel I* 2:6), presumably if they do *teshuvah*. Even Korach and his followers had a chance for a portion in the World to Come, as we see from Korach's sons. Even if there is only a little bit of life left, *teshuvah* is still possible. *Teshuvah* must be confessed and recited with one's mouth. Korach and his followers sinned with their mouths by speaking *lashon hara*. They were therefore punished measure for measure, with the earth itself opening its mouth.

It is interesting to note that when the Torah mentions Dasan and Aviram, their "homes" refers to their future offspring, who were also wiped out. This is in contrast to Korach's own family whose children survived, hanging on to the lip of the mouth that opened up (*Sanhedrin* 110a). They survived because they did change their minds when they looked down and saw *She'ol*, which is one of the seven levels of Gehinnom below.

For some people, circumstances in their lives are changing for the worse, but they remain so stubborn that they will not change even if it means throwing away everything special and holy they have worked so hard to accumulate. On the other hand, some people manage to change their minds, even at the cusp of disaster, thereby sparing the fate of their future generations. We should be *zocheh* to revisit situations in order to make the correct changes for ourselves, our immediate family, and for all future generations.

Sometimes a relationship, whether business, marriage, friendship, or even landlord/tenant, comes to an end. Some relationships can end abruptly, others end in a systematic string of events—usually influenced by one or both of the parties involved. In some instances, the decision is made by one person or entity; in other cases, a mutual parting of ways is agreed upon. In many situations, the end of a relationship can be catastrophic for one side while creating a sense of freedom and opportunity in the other. No matter the cause for the breakup, both sides know that life will never be the same as it was during the relationship.

Throughout my rabbinic career, one of the more difficult tasks has always been giving consolation and comfort to people who have lost a relative. All relationships are affected deeply by a death, but the impact on a person who loses their spouse after a long marriage is truly profound. The most common challenge is when the bereaved tells me, "My life will never be the same." I have learned to reply, "That is true. Life will never and can never be the same, but it does not mean you cannot have a good and productive life going forward." Two aspects of change are difficult: the first is going from the status quo to something new, and the second difficulty is learning to adapt to new changes as we grow older.

An important realization is that change is constantly taking place within our lives. Because the changes are small and incremental in relation to our lives overall, we tend not to give these small changes a second thought. Nevertheless, change is occurring as we speak—even as you read these very words. We tend to adapt to the subtle changes, which thereby gives us the innate ability to change and adapt for the larger and greater changes in life.

Life tends to bring staleness without change. As we remove some of the staleness of our lives, we see how we can rejuvenate our lives. On an individual level, the soul of a Jew requires us to each work to peel off some of the baggage we have been carrying for many years in order to gain new perspective on our purpose in life, reorganizing and rethinking our approach to serving Hashem. On a communal level, there is much we can do!

Keep in mind that nothing happens overnight. A relationship over many years requires time to adapt and to make the appropriate improvements. It takes time to make those changes and to put them to use. On the other hand, when it comes to *teshuvah*, repentance, HaKadosh Baruch Hu has the ability to turn our sins into mitzvos instantaneously. The art of change can happen quickly without turmoil and difficulty. Let us all take on new and improved change and dedication to Hashem and to our fellow Jew.

There are two components to man's development: education and practice. There are some who learn about doing something but never end up doing it, and then there are those who do something without really learning how to do it. One of the failings of Jewish life and education is giving emphasis to study/learning while giving too little emphasis to practical and personally meaningful applications. The *baalei mussar*, the rabbis who write and speak about self-development, practiced what they preached. For me, and many others, it is easier to learn *mussar*, self-improvement, but it is difficult to put these lessons addressing self-improvement into practice. The following two analogies are poignant examples of how we need to transform the learning into practice and the theoretical into the practical:

- We all live within a certain type of "box" that has little to do with how we grew up or even how outgoing or overtly friendly we may tend to be by nature. Going outside that box is challenging for each and every one of us. If you were to ask anyone if they are welcoming to newcomers, I believe everyone would say, of course they are. Yet, so often, people visiting different locations are left out. It behooves everyone, myself included, to go over to any person who is visiting and make sure he or she is not left alone even for one minute. We should all feel the need and importance of the situation and personally consider how a visitor may feel and what impressions he is forming about the community. In life, every person needs to give an extra push to overcome a difficult situation, even if it is not so comfortable at first.

- A situation occurred recently at our shul with a tourist who had an obligation to lead the services. We maintain a certain pace for our davening, and this man davened extremely fast—at a much faster pace than we are accustomed to. As much as I explained, begged, and pleaded with him to slow his pace, my requests apparently fell on deaf ears; he barely slowed down. After a while, I realized that he was really not doing it on purpose or intentionally to get under my skin; this was simply the way he is used to davening in his shul at home. After a few days of being here—and continuing to lead the davening—and his hearing my constant pleas to slow him down, it actually made a difference. By the time he left, he was saying words out loud and his davening was taking a little longer. I know this was a great challenge for him, but over time and with extra effort he was able to alter his pace and slow down.

Both examples require a strong effort to change on a very personal and individual level. The first stage is knowing that change is required, and second is understanding that effort is necessary, requiring a willingness to extend that effort.

The verse in *Yeshayahu* (54:2) states: "הרחיבי מקום אהלך ויריעות משכנותיך יטו אל תחשכי האריכי מיתריך ויתדתיך חזקי—Widen the place of your tent and let them stretch forth the curtains of your habitations. Do not spare; lengthen your cords and strengthen your stakes." The *Chasam Sofer* writes that a *talmid chacham*, a Torah scholar, is referred to in this world as a *Mishkan*, a Tabernacle. The letters of the word *Mishkan* in Hebrew are the beginning letters of *mitah*, a bed; *shulchan*, a table; *kisei*, a chair; and *neiros*, candles. These four items were provided by the Shunamite woman for Elisha HaNavi. The items mentioned in the house represent the bare essentials a person needs in this world, illustrating what little importance it is to worry and work for other things in this world, the world of earthly pleasures. The Jewish man's achievements are measured by his devotion to learning in the tent of Torah, not by the quantity of material possessions.

The *Navi* alludes to the need to expanding his tent in order to encompass more of the Jewish People who otherwise might find themselves excluded, therefore feeling left out of the beauty of a Jewish life. This expansion is twofold:

- Expanding the tent to include more people
- Expanding the learning of Torah and the fulfillment of mitzvos by the tent owners, so they will have the resources to give and teach outsiders who are brought in

Having one kind of growth or expansion without the other defeats the purpose.

The personal box each person is in—our daily lives—should be viewed by each of us as our own tent. We should use the words of the *Navi* to expand our horizons and consciously make the effort to step out of our comfort zone, even if just a little bit. We all need to give a ten percent push to improve, to push a little harder.

Push yourself a little more in your own devotion to God. The areas of Torah learning, mitzvah observance, and *chessed* activity must be increased beyond our comfort zone. In tandem with our personal growth, we all need to step up and use this new growth to reach out and affect another Jew's life by becoming an outreach ambassador to Klal Yisrael.

Most school yearbooks have a page dedicated to predicting how a student will turn out. Sometimes the students will try to project where they think their friends will be in ten, twenty, and thirty years down the road. Based upon their interests as a child, they will determine what line of work the person will end up doing—for better or worse. Every class has an overachiever and an underachiever. I think when one goes back to compare where the student was projected to be (at the time of graduation) and where the student is (in the present), about ninety percent of the time that guess will have been wrong. To be honest, I do not have any data to support this claim, but that's my gut feeling.

I find it fascinating when I hear about the individuals who, despite all odds against them, made it big, while others who had everything going for them in grade or high school failed miserably. I am not sure which scenario I am more surprised at: the one who did not end up being successful, or the one least likely to succeed making it big. Regardless of the outcome, I realize today that no one should be surprised when things turn out differently than anticipated early in life. I can easily attribute the "not being surprised situation" to the fact that we are guessing the future of someone who has really not yet fully matured and is not yet developed emotionally or physically. So when it comes to foretelling the future we could easily be far off in our guessing.

There is another area of life change that when I was younger would surprise and disappoint me. This applies to someone who, in his or her adult years, was already established religiously, financially, and emotionally but took a turn for the worse. Hearing and reading about men and women in positions of power and influence who are taken down by their own misjudgments was always surprising to me. On the other side of the spectrum, a man who was not successful at times turns around his life spiritually by doing *teshuvah* and becoming a *baal teshuvah*. It is impressive to see a person who lived a nonobservant life, enjoying the pleasures of the world without constraint and then literally change their entire life. I used to be surprised at the changes a person can undergo in either direction…but I am no longer surprised. When you live long enough, you get to see everything in life from the good to the bad and from the believable to the unbelievable. I have witnessed people who were very religious become nonobservant and the nonobservant become very observant, even during the twilight years of their lives.

I have seen educators and rabbis do things that are the antithesis of true Jewish education. How can a yeshiva that claims to be the place to deal with the troubled child turn around without cause and not accept such a child into their school? I see now through years of experience that these yeshivos and *menahalim* are not doing justice to these children and are not fulfilling their true mission and purpose. I will not go on the record with my theories of why I think this is true. Rather than focusing on the negative side of people and situations, I would like to glean a positive lesson from an unsung hero of the Jewish People.

In *Shoftim*, the *Navi* describes the meteoric rise of someone who was an unlikely choice to become a leader. The verse (*Shoftim* 11:1) states: "ויפתח הגלעדי היה גבור חיל והוא בן אשה זונה ויולד גלעד את יפתח—Now Yiftach the

Giladite was a mighty man of valor, and he was the son of a woman harlot, and Gilad begot Yiftach." How is it that Yiftach, with his shady past,
would rise to be the savior of the Jewish People? The *Midrash Rabbah*
(*Bamidbar* 19) states that Yiftach was not a great Torah scholar but had
many hidden, good *middos*. The *Baal Haturim* comments on the verse in
Bereishis (48:20): "ויברכם ביום ההוא לאמר בך יברך ישראל לאמר ישמך אלקים
כאפרים וכמנשה—On that day [Yaakov] blessed them. He said, '[In time to
come] Israel will use you as a blessing. They will say: May God make you
like Ephraim and Menasheh.'" Yaakov Avinu is revealing to us that the
berachah of Ephraim and Menasheh will be used for Jewish children in
the future. The *Baal Haturim* writes that the word *leimor* is spelled "full"
with an extra *vav* (with the numerical value of six) corresponding to the
six righteous judges who will stand from within them. One of those six
was none other than Yiftach, who descended from Menasheh.

The very last verse of the previous chapter speaks of the Jews of Gilad
as they want to repent. They ask Hashem, "Who is the man that is fit
to fight the Ammonites?" Immediately, God informs them it is Yiftach,
a man of might. *Pirkei Avos* states: "Who is the strong man? Someone
who is able to conquer his evil inclination." Even though Yiftach is
described as having a harlot for a mother (which the commentaries
deflect, demonstrating a different meaning) and is treated as a second-
class citizen by his brothers and peers, he is described by Hashem as
a *gibor*—one who is strong enough to overcome his inclination—and
will be the one to lead.

Yiftach appears to be the kind of individual who is capable of turning
around his life from being viewed as the underdog to being looked up
to as the champion. The man who can overcome adversity and change
is a candidate to lead the Jewish People. He does not necessarily have
to be the greatest Torah scholar and sage in the world to lead the Jews,
but rather a person who can change himself to become a better person.

Everybody goes through changes in their lifetime—some up and
some down. Let us focus on the strong individuals, those inwardly
directed mighty ones who can lead, upgrade, and change their lives
through their good *middos* and character. Ultimately, nothing should
surprise you anymore, even if that great change occurs within *you*!

There are few Jewish communities the size of San Diego that boast a late *Maariv* minyan. Most shuls daven *Minchah* and *Maariv* back-to-back around sunset. Our success rate with the late *Maariv* is approximately ninety percent, which, of course, leaves a ten percent chance that there will not be a minyan. One of the unwritten rules is that we wait until a certain time before we call off the minyan for that night if we did not get ten men. The exception to the waiting rule is when there is a need for someone to say Kaddish for a loved one, specifically a mother or father. We try to make extra calls to gather a minyan so that a person in need of a minyan to daven can fulfill his obligation, but we do not always succeed.

Recently, we had this situation occur twice, and it was resolved one time but not the other. We needed a minyan the last night our summer grill was open, and a family from LA was finishing up their dinner. I mentioned to them that we were going to start soon, but they said they needed to get going back to Los Angeles. Just about the time we would usually call the game, I went outside, and they were still lingering around, I asked again, and they replied, "How many do you need?" I said we needed three and without pause, they said they were coming. We made the minyan, and two people were able to recite Kaddish.

A week earlier, we weren't so lucky. It was the night I'd just flown back from New York, and we only had four people for the late *Maariv*. An attempt was made to get a minyan by calling some people, but to no avail. I felt terrible because there was a young man who had come to rely on this late *Maariv* to say Kaddish for his father, and I was embarrassed to face him. I sheepishly walked over to him, apologized, and said that hopefully we'd have a minyan the following night, and we proceeded to pray individually. As I was walking home, this young man's car pulled up beside me. I thought to myself, *Oh, now he is upset.* Instead, I received an incredible lesson. Just as I was going to apologize a second time, he blurted out, "*Maariv* was really special tonight." I was thinking to myself, *Really? We didn't get a minyan and you couldn't say Kaddish!* He said, "This was the first time I was able to say the entire *Amidah* in Hebrew. You see, my Hebrew reading is not up to par and I need to say some parts of the *Amidah* in English so I can finish with the group in order to say Kaddish." I was totally blown away by this conversation. He'd taken a bad situation and created a great opportunity for himself. I stepped back from that two-minute conversation feeling as if I had just finished learning from a *mussar sefer*. Imagine a world where everyone took bad and disappointing situations and created positive circumstances from them. If we take a moment to look within ourselves, we would perceive how our personal lives could be so much better if we each try to take the bad situations that come our way and focus consciously on creating something positive from them.

This sounds incredible, and in our day and age it unfortunately is. In today's world, the typical response to a bad situation is to exploit it even further, giving no attempt to look for the possible good that could occur as a result. But that is not the way we are supposed to react. To the contrary, the Torah teaches us to counter a difficult and challenging situation with something positive and good. The Torah states in *Devarim* (30:15): "ראה נתתי לפניך היום את החיים ואת הטוב ואת המות ואת הרע"—You can therefore see that today I have set before you [a free choice] between life and good [on one side] and death and evil [on the other]." The *Midrash Tanchuma* (*Parashas Pekudei*, *siman* 3) writes that Hashem decrees upon each person before they are even born what characteristics they will carry. Until recently, people thought this was strictly a metaphor. Now, with the discovery of DNA, we are coming to know this concept in a new light. Hashem creates each person with his own "DNA," and thus we see that it is predetermined whether a person will be weak or strong, poor or rich, short or tall, ugly or handsome, thick or thin, ruddy or smooth, and the final decree of all that will happen to them in their lifetime. But whether a person is a *tzaddik* or a *rasha* is strictly determined by the person himself. He is not predisposed to either characteristic; he chooses which path—righteous or the evil—to take. The verse states: "Behold, I am placing in front of you *life and the good* and *death and the evil*." Later (ibid., 30:19), the Torah states: "ובחרת בחיים למען תחיה"—And you must choose life so that you shall live."

The Torah (God) is telling us that the choice is ours; the decision lies within ourselves. If a person chooses to lean toward and then follow a certain course—whether toward the road to life or the road to death—they are free to do so. The choice is entirely theirs. Therefore, a person will receive punishment for the bad they do (that they chose to do) and others will receive a hefty reward for the good and straight path they chose.

In my humble opinion, the *pshat* (simple understanding) of this life-and-death choice is not so much the issue of either doing the mitzvos or not. Rather, the choosing here is emphasizing the attitude. There is so much to life that is determined by one's own attitude. It is the attitude and approach to life that literally can be the difference between life and death in this world:

- A person who always sees and interprets things in the negative will lead a less enjoyable and possibly a physically shorter life.
- A person who takes everything in stride, determined to figure out a way to take difficult circumstances and make each challenge work for their benefit is a person who chooses life. That person will adapt to any situation and come up with a way to shape it to his advantage.

A mourner goes through many hoops to make sure he has a minyan to say Kaddish. It can be demoralizing when the needed number for the minyan falls short. If we focus on the failure, we choose to feel bad—toward death. If we attempt to take that situation and come up with something positive, then we are choosing good—which ultimately gives us life.

Let each of us focus on making the best of bad situations so that we will all have lives full of goodness and happiness.

Rare is the person who does not have an opinion about a fellow human being. Those opinions are often shaped and formulated by presumptions that may have little or nothing to do with the person being evaluated. Truth be told, we all know that no person has the right to pass judgment on another, and no one has the right to sum up or to assess another person's life. Chazal were emphatic that we have neither the full picture nor the facts to really know or judge another individual; that must be left up to Hashem, not man.

Nevertheless, we all find ourselves performing such evaluations and calculations. In Talmudic discourse, the Rabbis often set up analyses of situations through a process of arguing about different choices. In our case, which is addressing the personalities or traits of individuals, I would like to share four scenarios of human dispositions:

- Those who have nothing going well for them in life and are clearly downtrodden
- Those who seem to have everything yet are unhappy and disappointed
- Those who have everything and are very happy and content
- Those who have had to struggle, who have very little materially, and yet radiate an inner happiness and appreciation for being among the most blessed of all in the world. This is the essence of one who has attained the highest level of all.

The feeling each person conveys to others through outward appearances and actions creates a direct effect regarding the way others view that individual. As important as it is for everyone to formulate a positive opinion of others, it is equally important for each and every one of us to portray ourselves in a manner that demonstrates that life is good—and precious—no matter what kind of *pekaleh* (burden) we may each be schlepping. We can change the way people view us if we maintain an upbeat, positive outlook toward life. We see these scenarios around us day in and day out. We marvel at someone who is struggling with health or livelihood or who has suffered the loss of a loved one yet, despite all that, makes the effort to give comfort to others. They display inner strength and belief in Hashem, demonstrating that it is all for the best and that they can overcome and survive. It gives strength and renewed hope to all who are privileged to be around such a person.

The personalities throughout *Tanach* show and teach us how to accept the hand Hashem has dealt us and how to make the best of it. I believe each person in *Tanach* represents certain dimensions and personalities that we all share. Even the prophets who foretold doom and gloom were only doing the job Hashem had given them, fulfilling the mission they were sent out to accomplish. Yirmiyahu and Yeshayahu epitomize this. The *Yalkut Hamachiri* contrasts the words of Yirmiyahu to Yeshayahu—one reflecting upon the destruction of the Beis Hamikdash and the exile of the Jews from their land, and the other predicting the hope and the future of Klal Yisrael, the rebuilding of the Beis Hamikdash, and the reclaiming of our land.

In *Yeshayahu* (61:10) the *Navi* states: "שוש אשיש בה׳ תגל נפשי באלקי כי הלבישני בגדי ישע מעיל צדקה יעטני כחתן יכהן פאר וככלה תעדה כליה—I will rejoice with the Lord; my soul shall exult with my God, for He has attired me with garments of salvation, with a robe of righteousness He has enwrapped me; like a bridegroom, who, priest-like, dons garments of glory, and like a bride who adorns herself with her jewelry." The midrash says there was no curse that Yirmiyahu predicted that Yeshayahu did not come to heal. Here is a list of Yeshayahu's replies to Yirmiyahu:

- Yirmiyahu says, "Woe to this nation that sins," and Yeshayahu answers, "Here comes the righteous nation."
- Yirmiyahu says, "Seeds that produce bad things," and Yeshayahu answers, "Sons that do not lie."
- Yirmiyahu says, "They were like widows," and Yeshayahu answers, "We will rejoice with the bride and groom."
- Yirmiyahu says, "She has become a tributary," and Yeshayahu answers, "A nation that will not know of renting."
- Yirmiyahu says, "They cried greatly at night," and Yeshayahu answers, "Hashem will wipe away tears from faces."
- Yirmiyahu says, "The way of Zion is mourning," and Yeshayahu answers, "Pass through the gates and turn to the ways of Hashem."
- Yirmiyahu says, "I will turn them away from the sound of joy," and Yeshayahu says, "I will rejoice with Hashem in this world and my soul shall exalt Hashem in the world to come."

It was Yirmiyahu's lot in life to be known throughout the ages as "the prophet of doom," for he was God's main spokesman in the generation of the destruction of Jerusalem's First Beis Hamikdash. The role of Yeshayahu was to transmit warnings from God to His nation, to be the conscience of the Jewish People; however, his message was also one of comfort. There is the joy and the hope of a look ahead to the perfect world of the Messianic Era.

Nothing and no one in life is perfect, but we have a choice: to pick the gloom and doom or to choose the joy of hope. How do we want people to view us, with hope and happiness or with sadness and desperation? Every year we look forward to making changes, pledging commitments to changing our behavior. The key to change is not the actual mitzvos and service to Hashem; it is focusing on what lies behind all our actions, and that is attitude.

For better or for worse, we do characterize and encapsulate people. There is not any person in the world who does not possess something good within them. Our challenge is to focus on the good, redeeming quality we find in every person and not dwell on the negative side of a person. When we look at our fellow Jews, we must view each of them literally as brothers and sisters whom we love and accept despite their shortcomings. Whether it is the lack of observance of mitzvos or the lack of commitment to Torah Judaism, we should not marginalize anyone. Rather than viewing them with doom and gloom, let us use the loftiness of Yeshayahu to see the hope and aspirations of every Jew. Indeed, let us reach out and recognize the purity and inner beauty of every Jew.

God treats us measure for measure. We are all far from perfect and we ask Hashem to look away from our shortcomings, focusing instead on our good qualities. So, too, we need to focus in on the good qualities of our fellow Jews.

There is a certain thrill one gets when learning Torah with others. The different levels of excitement or appreciation come from the person with whom one is learning. The Gemara in *Taanis* relates that in general there are three kinds of people we learn from: a teacher, a colleague, and a student.

Personally, I get the most out of my Torah learning when a student reaches a level to ask and derive questions from other things we have learned previously. It displays a genuine depth of understanding and grasping of material, revealing measurable signs of growth.

Last week, one of my study partners asked the following question: Hashem gave Moshe three signs by which to convince the Egyptians and the Jews that he, Moshe, was a messenger from God (*Shemos* 4:3,6,9). These were the three signs:

- Moshe's staff turned into a snake and back again to a rod.
- Moshe's hand developed leprosy when inserted in his shirt and, after repeating the process, it came out healthy again.
- Moshe took some water and turned it into blood as a sign that this would be the first of the ten plagues.

My *chavrusa* asked: If later, Hashem was not going to allow Moshe to smite the Nile, as we see in *Parashas Va'eira*, why did Hashem bother doing the miracle of the water with him? Didn't Hashem know that Moshe would not be able to hit the Nile because he had to show *hakaras hatov*, gratitude, toward the water that had "saved him" when he was a baby?

I went through a few stages of thinking about this excellent question:

- My initial thought was that God does not take decisions out of our hands; rather He places the challenge or situation in front of us to make the decision on our own. Hashem wanted Moshe to come to the realization that he needed to have gratitude to the Nile for protecting him.
- After reviewing further, I realized that the initial test in *Shemos* commands Moshe to take some water out from the Nile and turn it into blood, in contrast to turning the entire river red. This answer removes the question completely.
- Upon further and deeper review, however, I discovered another answer in an obscure *sefer*, which I will elaborate on below.

If we step back to analyze this, we might reach a different conclusion regarding the reason Moshe should not have been the one to perform the first three *makkos* (plagues). The water and the sand did not really *do* anything to protect him. The protection came from his sister Miriam, when she placed him in the basket. The water was just helping Miriam. Thus, in reality, the water by itself did not deserve any particular mention or reward. Therefore, even if Moshe would have hit the Nile, he still would not have violated the principle of *hakaras hatov*. We should not apply the principle of "denying the good" vis-à-vis the river. Furthermore, we could argue that the river was just doing its job exactly as God had intended.

Also, the river did fulfill the will of Hashem, therefore elevating its level of holiness. The fact that the river turned into blood proves that it followed the will of its Creator and raised its level of sanctity. We should not view the river turning into blood as a punishment. So, why do all the commentaries—led by *Rashi*—explain that Moshe had to have a sensitivity and gratitude to the river and therefore needed to have Aharon begin the plague?

Rav Alexander Yehoshua Levinson of Har Nof, Yerushalayim, in his *sefer K'Ayal Taarog*, formalized this approach and answers in the following manner: There are two approaches or paths when it comes to the fulfillment of mitzvos between man and his fellow man:

- The obvious one is the benefit that the recipient of the kindness receives from the giving of his friend.
- The benefit to the giver. At the same moment that he is giving or doing the kindness, he is refining his good character qualities. When a person does *chessed*, acts of kindness, they become a *baal chessed*, a master of kindness. The act of *chessed* they perform transforms the person's *middos* and refines them a notch higher. The act of *chessed* converts into the *middah* itself and strengthens it.

This notion is now all the more emphatic: doing a chessed *causes* the person to develop into a kinder individual.

The perspective of "the letter of the law"—the concern that Moshe should not hit the Nile or the sand that protected him is now easily understood. But we must realize it was not because Moshe was under any obligation. To the contrary, he could have performed the *makkah* because his only true gratitude was toward Miriam, who hid him, and also toward Basya, the daughter of Pharaoh, who drew him out of the Nile. Still, he did not hit the Nile himself because the *middah* of *hakaras hatov* would have been weakened within him had he done so. He strengthened the character trait of gratitude by overcoming and withdrawing from doing so a little more each time. That is why Hashem told Moshe to let Aharon to perform the *makkah*—to sensitize Moshe to a greater degree, improve his *middos* that much more, and fine-tune his overall character as the leader of His people.

Rabbi Dessler compares a person's *middos* to a ladder. Each one of us is on a certain rung. All the *middos* that are beneath that rung have been conquered by that person, having been victorious over each previous challenge. The evil inclination no longer has the upper hand over those, so it gives up on that point. Any *middos* that are above the rung are those we still strive to perfect. When we fulfill a mitzvah, not only do we receive reward, but we put another notch into the ladder we are climbing of that trait. Through this process, a person begins to change, conquering the trait and making it part of his essence.

Rabbi Yosef Dov Soloveitchik, in his *sefer Al Hateshuvah*, explains the difference between atonement and purity. A sin causes two negative outcomes for a person:

- The person receives a punishment.
- The person becomes a sinner. He defiles himself, lowering himself from what a human being should be.

Teshuvah comes to fix these two corrupt outcomes: it atones for the punishment and purifies the sinner from the impurity of the sin.

CONCLUSION
The End Is Actually the Beginning

WHEN I was a *bachur*, a friend and colleague of mine, Rabbi Daniel Wasserman, asked me to help lead davening on Rosh Hashanah and Yom Kippur in a shul in Jersey City, New Jersey. At the time, I was not fully acquainted with the *nusach* (tunes or proper liturgy) of *Yamim Noraim*. It was recommended that I ask Cantor Jack Rosenbaum, *a"h*, to teach me the *nusach*. With trepidation I called him, and he invited me over to his home to discuss the matter. At the time, I had no extra money to pay for the lessons. By paying for them, I would essentially have been using the money I would earn from the davening, and not really come out ahead. Cantor Rosenbaum asked me how much I could pay, but before I was able to respond, he said, "I'll make you a deal." If I agreed to commit to a yearlong cycle of *shnayim mikra v'echad targum* (reading the Torah portion twice and the commentary of *Onkelos* once), he would give me the lessons at no charge. I immediately agreed and not only learned how to daven for the High Holidays, which was a skill set I would use later in my career, I also learned through the Torah that year.

The Kabbalists were awestruck at the veracity and enormity that is accomplished through reviewing *SHM"T* (*shnayim mikra v'echad targum*). The *sefer Yesod V'Shoresh Ha'Avodah* and the *Chasam Sofer* in his *chiddushim* to *Chullin* says that by reading *SHM"T*, a person removes the small shell fragments that stuck on the Torah when Moshe smashed the *Luchos* (Tablets). The shell fragments are an impediment to fully grasping the depth and understanding of the Torah due to the negative influence of the smashing of the *Luchos*. Reviewing the *parashah* in this fashion removes that barrier. It is amazing how the simple reading of the verses has such force, allowing us to open up the deeper meaning of the Torah. The *Shelah HaKadosh* (*Maseches Shabbos*), the *Megaleh Amukos* (*Parashas Kedoshim*), and the *Kaf Hachaim* (285:32), all relate in the name of the Kabbalists that through the reading of *SHM"T*, a person merits and prepares himself for the *neshamah yeseirah*, the extra soul we are given for Shabbos. That second *neshamah* is called "*Adam*," which is a praise and crowning of all the names of mankind. Some other names, such as "*Ish*" or "*Enosh*," are the simpler names, but the name *Adam* is the most notable. A hint to this is found in the verse in *Bereishis* (2:10): "ויקרא האדם שמות לכל הבהמה ולעוף השמים ולכל חית השדה ולאדם לא מצא עזר כנגדו—And he called them [all the animals] by their names." Adam was given the task and charge to name every creature by knowing its essence. Adam had special wisdom that gave him the ability to name the animals based upon their inner nature and essence. I would suggest that it was through the *neshamah yeseirah* before Shabbos that Adam had extra wisdom through which he was able to name the animals. We often hear that the essence of a person comes from his *neshamah*, his soul. Therefore, Adam was able to use his *neshamah* to identify the other *neshamos* of the animals (referring here to the essence of the animal). Every Shabbos, we receive an additional soul in its raw state. We decide if, how, and when we will use it for something positive or negative; whether we will use it to give us more strength, wisdom, and courage to make proper decisions for that coming week, or choose to do nothing with it. Week in and week out, we take on the role of Adam HaRishon and can identify the essence of beings, situations, and life experiences.

The very last *parashah* of the Torah, "וזאת הברכה—And this is the blessing [that Moshe gave to the Children of Israel]," is the ability to take something from its end and start again. The *Chasam Sofer* writes that the last three words of the Torah (*Devarim* 34:12), "לעיני כל ישראל—in front of all the eyes of the Jewish People" are connected to "בראשית ברא אלוקים—In the beginning God created the world." The Gemara (*Sotah* 14a) quotes Rav Simlai that "the Torah begins with *chessed* and ends with *chessed*." In *Bereishis*, after Adam and Chavah ate from the forbidden tree, they had knowledge of their nakedness. With kindness, God fashioned leather clothing and dressed them to spare them from embarrassment. The Torah (*Devarim* 34:6) ends with *chessed*—God took care of Moshe after he died and buried him. Rabbi Yerucham Levovitz, the *mashgiach* of the Mirrer Yeshiva, said that from here we see that the essence of the entire Torah is *chessed*, and caring for others is exemplified by Hashem Himself in the beginning and in the end.

As the Torah begins with the Six Days of Creation, it was not until the seventh day that Shabbos, the day of rest, was created. Why do we have another *neshamah* on a day of rest? The simple answer is that Shabbos entails resting after the week and preparing for the new week. Shabbos by itself is "resting" from the six days of work, while the *neshamah yeseirah* prepares us for the upcoming week. Shabbos is the actual last day of the week, but it prepares us for the coming week. So too, at the end of the year, we immediately look forward to the new year and what we will accomplish. Many people grow during the seven-week period of feeding and nourishing our souls from Rosh Chodesh Elul through Simchas Torah. *Baruch Hashem*, I see many in our *kehillah* who take the old or last part of the year and use it to continue nourishing the new year and new winter season, taking the spirituality of the *neshamos yeseiros* and applying them to nurture and continue the growth that was embedded in them in the previous two months. I truly hope and pray that we do not look at the concluding of Elul, Rosh Hashanah, Yom Kippur, Sukkos, Chol Hamoed, Hoshana Rabbah, Shemini Atzeres, and

Simchas Torah as the end, but rather take all of this beauty that has nourished our souls to lead us into the new beginning of a prosperous year, both physically and spiritually.

As you reach the end of this *sefer*, I hope you take the lessons from here and use them to "raise your community, your family, and yourself"!

Index of Torah Personalities

Short biographies of Torah personalities quoted

ALSHICH

Moshe Alshich (1508–1593), known as the Alshich Hakadosh (the holy), was a prominent rabbi, preacher, and Biblical commentator in the latter part of the sixteenth century. The Alshich was born in the Ottoman Empire and died in Tzfas. He was the son of Chaim Alshich. He later moved to Tzfas where he became a student of Rav Yoseph Karo. His students included Rabbi Chaim Vital and Rabbi Yom Tov Tzahalon.

ARIZAL

Yitzchak ben Shlomo Luria Ashkenazi (1531–1572), known as Ha'Ari (the lion) or Arizal. He was a leading rabbi and Jewish mystic in Tzfas in the Galilee region of Ottoman Syria, now Israel. He is considered the father of contemporary Kabbalah. The Ari HaKadosh Shul is located in Tzfas and was built in his memory during the late sixteenth century. He is buried in the Old Jewish Cemetery in Tzfas.

BAAL SHEM TOV

Yisrael ben Eliezer (1698–1760), known as the Baal Shem Tov or the Besht. He is regarded as the founder of the Chassidic movement of Orthodox Judaism. *Besht* is the acronym for *baal shem tov*, which means "master of the good name" or "one with a good reputation." Yisrael was born to his poor parents, Eliezer and Sarah, in a settlement near Okopy, a newly built fortress close to Kaminetz in West Ukraine. He died in Medzhybizh, which was part of Poland and today is situated in the Ukraine.

BE'ER HEITEV

Yehudah ben Shimon Ashkenazi (1730–1770) was born in Frankfurt and served as a *dayan* on the rabbinical court in Tykocin, Poland. He is best known as the author of a portion of the *Be'er Heitev*, a major commentary on the *Shulchan Aruch* sections *Orach Chaim* and *Even Ha'ezer*.

BEIS YOSEF

Yosef ben Ephraim Karo (1488–1575) is the author of the last great codification of Jewish law, the *Shulchan Aruch*, which is still authoritative for all Jews pertaining to their respective communities. To this end, he is often referred to as HaMechaber (the author) and as Maran. In 1492, aged four years old, he was forced to flee Spain with his family and the rest of Spanish Jewry as a result of the Alhambra Decree and subsequently settled in the Kingdom of Portugal.

BRISKER RAV

Yitzchak Zev HaLevi Soloveitchik (1886–1959), known as Velvel Soloveitchik (the word *zev* means "wolf" in Hebrew, and the word *velvel* is the diminutive of "wolf" in Yiddish) or the Brisker Rav. Commonly referred to as the Gry"z (an acronym for Gaon Rabbi Yitzchak Zev), he was a scion of the Soloveitchik rabbinical dynasty and was the *rosh yeshiva* of the Brisk yeshiva in Jerusalem, Israel.

CHAFETZ CHAIM

Yisrael Meir HaKohen Kagan (1838–1933), known as the Chafetz Chaim, the name of his famous work on guarding one's tongue. He was born in Grodno, today Belarus. The Chafetz Chaim published twenty-one books. His first work, *sefer Chafetz Chaim* (1873), is the first attempt to organize and clarify the laws regarding *lashon hara*. Other notable works include the *sefer Shemiras Halashon*, an ethical work on the importance of guarding one's tongue, and the *Mishnah Berurah* (printed between 1894–1907), which is a commentary on *Orach Chaim*, the first section of the *Shulchan Aruch*, and has been accepted universally as an authoritative source of halachah.

CHASAM SOFER

Moses Schreiber (1762–1839), known to his own community and Jewish posterity in the Hebrew translation as Moshe Sofer, and also known by his main work, *Chasam Sofer*, was one of the leading Orthodox rabbis of European Jewry in the first half of the nineteenth century. He was a teacher to thousands and a powerful opponent of the Reform movement in Judaism, which was attracting many people from the Jewish communities in the Austrian Empire and beyond. As Rav of the city of Pressburg, he maintained a strong Orthodox Jewish perspective through communal life, first-class education, and uncompromising opposition to the Reform movement and radical change.

CHIDA

Chaim Yosef David Azulai ben Yitzhak Zerachia (1724–1806), known as the Chida. He was born in Jerusalem, where he received his education from some local prominent scholars. He was the scion of a prominent rabbinic family, the great-great-grandson of Moroccan Rabbi Abraham Azulai. The Yosef part of his name came from his mother's father, Rabbi Yosef Bialer, a German scholar. His main teachers were the *Yishuv Ha'yashan* rabbis Yitzchok HaKohen Rapaport, Shalom Sharabi, and Chaim ben Attar (the Ohr HaChaim).

CHIDDUSHEI HARIM

Yitzchak Meir Rotenberg-Alter (1799–1866) was the first *rebbe* of the Ger Chasidic dynasty, which he founded in the town of Góra Kalwaria (known as "Gur" in Yiddish), Poland. He headed the Kupas Rabbi Meir Baal Haness Kollel in Poland. He was also known as the Chiddushei HaRim for his Torah writings and became known as a Talmudic *gaon*. He was sometimes fondly called Reb Itche Meir (Yiddish) by his followers. Rabbi Alter and the Kotzker Rebbe became brothers-in-law, when the latter married Chaya Lipszyc, the sister of Rabbi Alter's wife, Feigele.

CHOVOS HALEVAVOS/RABBEINU BACHYA

Bachya ben Asher ibn Chalawa (1255–1340) was a rabbi and scholar of Judaism. He was a commentator on the Torah. He was one of two people now known as Rabbeinu Bachya, the other being philosopher Bachya ibn Paquda. He is considered by Jewish scholars to be one of the most distinguished of the Biblical exegetes of Spain. He was a pupil of Rabbi Shlomo ibn Aderet (the Rashba.)

HAKESAV V'HAKABALAH

Yaakov Tzvi Mecklenburg (1785–1865) was a German rabbi and scholar of the nineteenth century, best known as author of the Torah commentary *HaKesav V'HaKabbalah*. He was born in Lissa in the province of Posen, Germany, into the family of Rabbi Gamliel. At the time, Lissa was a famous center of Torah studies, and Rav Mecklenburg began studying Torah as a student of the local *rav*, Rabbi Zechariah Mendel, a friend and correspondent of Rabbi Akiva Eiger. Thereafter, Rav Mecklenburg went into business. In 1831, at the age of forty-six, following commercial difficulties, he decided to quit business and was offered the rabbinical position in the city of Königsberg, East Prussia. At that time, Königsberg Jews were under the increasing influence of the Haskalah, a reform movement, which Rabbi Yaakov Tzvi Mecklenburg strongly opposed. Together with the Malbim, he publicly opposed Reform Judaism's 1844 Braunschweig convention.

IBN EZRA

Abraham ben Meir Ibn Ezra (1089–1167) was one of the most distinguished Jewish Biblical commentators and philosophers of the Middle Ages. He was born in Tudela in northern Spain, one of the oldest and most important Jewish communities in the present-day Spanish province of Navarre. Ibn Ezra was a close friend of Rabbi Yehudah Halevi, who was some fourteen years older, and the two became close friends.

KAF HACHAIM

Yaakov Chaim Sofer (1870–1939) was a Sephardi rabbi, Kabbalist, Talmudist and *posek*. He is the author of *Kaf Hachaim*, a work of halachah for which he came to be known. Rav Sofer was born in Baghdad,

Ottoman Iraq. He studied Torah under Rabbi Abdallah Somech and the Ben Ish Chai. In 1904, he journeyed to Ottoman Palestine and after visiting Jerusalem, he decided to settle there permanently. He studied in the Bet El yeshiva in the Old City of Jerusalem, which was well-known for the study of kabbalah.

KANFEI NESHARIM
Avraham Lichtenstein was an eighteenth-century rabbi of Prassnysz, in the region of Plotzk, Poland, and author of *Kanfei Nesharim*.

KAV HAYASHAR
Tzvi Hirsch Kaidanover (1648–1712), authored the *Kav Hayashar* (lit., the Just Measure.) It is one of the most popular works of *mussar* literature of the last three hundred years. First published in 1705 in Frankfurt am Main, it has appeared in over eighty editions, in nearly every country around the world. The work was famous for uplifting the spirits of Jewish communities in Europe after the Chmelnitzki Massacres of 1648–1649.

KESAV SOFER
Avraham Shmuel Binyamin Sofer (1815–1871), known by his main work, *Kesav Sofer*, was one of the leading rabbis of Hungarian Jewry in the second half of the nineteenth century and *rosh yeshiva* of the famed Pressburg Yeshiva. His official German name was Samuel Wolf Schreiber. His father, the famed Chasam Sofer, rabbi of Pressburg, was the leader of Hungarian Jewry and one of the leading Rabbis of European Jewry. His mother, Serel (1790–1832), was the daughter of Rabbi Akiva Eiger, rabbi of Posen, one of the greatest Talmudic scholars of his time.

When he was six years old, his family fell ill and among them little Shmuel Volf, as he was called. The doctors had already given up on him. As a *segulah*, they added Avraham to his name, but to no avail. The Chasam Sofer went to a corner where all his manuscripts were and said a short prayer. Shmuel Binyamin's condition took a turn for the better. The students of the Chasam Sofer later testified that the Chasam Sofer said at the time that "for one Jubilee, I begged him out," as Shmuel

Binyamin lived for another fifty years and died at age fifty-six. The *Kesav Sofer* died in Bratislava, and the mantle as rabbi of Pressburg passed to his son, Rabbi Simcha Bunim Sofer, known as the *Shevet Sofer*.

KLI YAKAR

Shlomo Ephraim ben Aharon Luntschitz (1550–1619) was a rabbi and Torah commentator, best known for his Torah commentary *Kli Yakar*. He was born in Łęczyca (also known as Luntschitz) and studied under Rabbi Shlomo Luria in Lublin, and subsequently served as *rosh yeshiva* in Lvov (Lemberg). In 1604, he was appointed rabbi of Prague, a position he filled until his death. In the introduction of his *Kli Yakar*, he relates that the name Shlomo was added to his name during a life-threatening illness, a common practice in Judaism.

KOZHNITZER REBBE

Yisroel Hopstein (1737–1814), known as the Maggid of Kozhnitz, was the founder of Kozhnitz Chassidism, and a noted Chassidic leader in Poland during the late eighteenth and early nineteenth century. As a young child, he was recognized as an *illui* (prodigy). He studied under the tutelage of Rabbi Shmelke of Nikolsburg, who eventually convinced Hopstein to learn with Rav Dov Ber, the Maggid of Mezritch. After the passing of Rav Dov Ber, he went to learn with Rav Elimelech of Lizhensk. He wrote many books on Chassidus and Kabbalah.

KOZHNITZER REBBE II

Moshe Elyakim Hopstein, son of the Avodas Yisrael.

LEV ARYEH

Aryeh Leib Grossnass studied in Kaminetz under Rav Baruch Ber. He was one of the founding figures of the Gateshead Kollel, later on becoming a leading member of the London Beis Din. A highly regarded *dayan* and *talmid chacham*, he was well respected by many of the giants of his time. One finds *teshuvos* written to him by the *Minchas Yitzchak*, *Igros Moshe*, and *Har Tzvi*.

LUBAVITCHER REBBE

Menachem Mendel Schneerson (1902-1994), known to many as the Lubavitcher Rebbe or simply as the Rebbe. Rabbi Schneerson's published teachings fill more than three hundred volumes, and he is noted for his contributions to Jewish continuity and religious thought, as well as his wide-ranging contributions to traditional Torah scholarship. He went on to receive separate rabbinical ordinations from the Rogatchover Gaon, Rabbi Yosef Rosen, and Rabbi Yechiel Yaakov Weinberg, author of *Seridei Aish*.

MAHARSHA

Shmuel Eliezer HaLevi Eidels (1555–1631) was a renowned rabbi and Talmudist famous for his commentary on the Talmud, *Chiddushei Halachos*. Rabbi Eidels is also known as Maharsha, a Hebrew acronym for "our teacher, the rabbi, Shmuel Eidels."

The Maharsha was born in Kraków, Poland. His father, Yehuda, was a Talmudist and both parents were descendants of rabbinic families—his mother, Gittel, was a cousin of Rabbi Yehuda Loew, the Maharal of Prague, and his father was a direct descendant of Rabbi Yehuda HaChassid.

MAHARSHAM/TECHEILES MORDECHAI

Shalom Mordechai Schwadron (1835–1911), known by his acronym Maharsham, was a rabbi and foremost halachic authority. His main works, *Sh'eilos U'teshuvos Maharsham* and *Daas Torah*, are widely studied sources of practical Jewish law. Among his prominent works are *Mishpat Shalom* on *Choshen Mishpat*. He was well-known as a very lenient rabbi. He also authored *Techeiles Mordechai*, a three-volume commentary of the Torah. It is known that after each *din Torah* (case in a rabbinical court), he would explain to the loser the reason he lost until he understood clearly. If the person was unable to understand, he would tell him: "You must have a good friend or family member that is a Torah scholar. Send him to me and I will explain it to him so you will feel that you were done justice." His grandson, Rabbi Shalom Schwadron, was known as the "Maggid of Jerusalem."

ME'AM LO'EZ

Initiated by Rabbi Yaakov Culi in 1730, *Me'am Lo'ez* is a widely studied commentary on *Tanach* written in Ladino. It is perhaps the best-known publication in that language. While Rabbi Culi died only two years later after completing the Book of Genesis and two thirds of Exodus, due to its mass popularity—and the extensive notes already written by Rabbi Culi—a decision was made to complete the commentaries by a cadre of *rabbanim*. The *Me'am Lo'ez* quickly became extremely popular in the Jewish communities of Turkey, Spain, Morocco, and Egypt. In 1967, a Hebrew translation, *Yalkut Me'am Lo'ez*, was produced by Rabbi Shmuel Kravitzer. The first English translation, the *Torah Anthology*, was written (primarily) by Rabbi Aryeh Kaplan. The resulting work introduced *Me'am Lo'ez* to the broader Ashkenazi world.

MEGALEH AMUKOS

Nosson Nata Shapira (1585–1633) was a Polish rabbi and Kabbalist, who served as Chief Rabbi of Kraków. A student of Rabbi Meir Lublin, Rabbi Shapira played an important role in spreading Rabbi Yitzchak Luria's teachings throughout Poland. Rabbi Shapira was the author of a number of works, most notably the *Megaleh Amukos*.

MEI SHILOACH

Mordechai Yosef Leiner of Izbica (1801–1854) was a rabbinic Chassidic thinker, founder of the Izhbitza-Radzyn dynasty of Chassidus, and author of *Mei Shiloach*. Rabbi Mordechai Yosef was born in Tomashov. He became a disciple of Rav Simcha Bunim of Peshischa, where he joined Rabbi Menachem Mendel of Kotzk and Rabbi Yosef of Yartshev; both were also born in Tomashov. His leading disciple was Rabbi Yehuda Leib Eiger (1816–1888), grandson of Rabbi Akiva Eiger. His students included Rav Tzadok HaKohen of Lublin (1823–1900), his son, Rabbi Yaakov Leiner (1828–1878), and his grandson, Rabbi Gershon Henoch Leiner of Radzyn. Rav Mordechai Yosef Leiner is buried in the Jewish cemetery in Izbica.

MINCHAS MARCHESHES

Pinchas Shlomo Pollak (1917–2005).

MISHNAS CHASSIDIM

Refael Emmanuel Chai ben Avraham Rikki (1688–1743) was born in Ferrara, Italy.

His *sefarim*, in the order in which they were written, are (1) *Ma'aseh Choshev* (Venice, 1716), a commentary on the building of the *Mishkan*, built in the desert; (2) *Choshev Machashavos* (Amsterdam, 1727), on the technical halachic issues which bear no Biblical textual source, known as *halachah l'Moshe miSinai*, like the size of a *mikveh* or some specifics of the tefillin; (3) *Hon Ashir* (Amsterdam, 1731), a commentary on the six orders of the Mishnah; (4) *Mishnas Chassidim* (Amsterdam, 1727), a book modeled on the six orders of the Mishnah, with each order divided into tractates.

NETZIV

Naftali Tzvi Yehuda Berlin (1816–1893), known by the acronym Netziv, was born in Warsaw, Poland and was the *rosh yeshiva* of Volozhin. His first wife was the daughter of Rabbi Yitzchak of Volozhin, the son of Rabbi Chaim Volozhin. His second wife was his niece, a daughter of Rabbi Yechiel Michel Epstein, the author of the *Aruch Hashulchan*. A son from his first marriage, Chaim Berlin, became the rabbi of Moscow, a daughter married Rabbi Rephael Shapiro, and his son from his second marriage was Rabbi Meir Berlin.

OHR HACHAIM (HAKADOSH)

Chaim ibn Attar (1696–1743), also known as the *Ohr Hachaim* after his popular commentary on the Torah, was a Talmudist and Kabbalist. He is arguably considered to be one of the most prominent rabbis of Morocco. Before permanently settling in the Land of Israel, he went to Algiers where he recruited students for a yeshiva he was planning on opening in the Land of Israel. He soon arrived at the Acre port in the Land of Israel with his two wives and thirty students. However, he could not immediately proceed to Jerusalem, due to an epidemic. In the middle of 1742, he arrived in Jerusalem, where he founded Yeshivas Knesset Yisrael. One of his greatest disciples there was Rav Chaim Yosef David Azulai. He is buried on Har Hazeisim in Yerushalayim.

PIASECZNA REBBE

Kalonymus Kalman Shapira (1889–1943), the Grand Rabbi of Piaseczna, Poland, authored a number of works and was murdered by the Nazis during the Holocaust along with his wife and two children. He was named after his maternal great-grandfather, the renowned Maor Va'Shemesh, and was a scion of a distinguished family, which included Rabbi Elimelech of Lizhensk, the Chozeh of Lublin, and the Maggid of Kozhnitz. At the age of three, he was orphaned by the death of his father. In 1905, he married Rachel Chaya Miriam, daughter of his nephew Grand Rabbi Yerachmiel Moshe of Kozhnitz. In 1909, he was appointed rabbi of Piaseczna, near Warsaw, and subsequently attracted many Chassidim. He was deeply focused on the education of children and young men, establishing the yeshiva Da'as Moshe in 1923, which became one of the largest Chassidic yeshivas in Warsaw between the wars.

PILTZER REBBE/SIFSEI TZADDIK

Pinchas Menachem Elazar Yustman (1848–1920) was known as the Piltzer Rebbe, also known by the title of his main work, *Sifsei Tzaddik*. In his early years, he was known as Rav Mendel of Ger, and was a Chassidic rabbi who, after the passing of his brother-in-law Rabbi Yehudah Aryeh Leib Alter, became a *rebbe* for some Gerrer Chassidim, in Pilica, Poland. He was born in Góra Kalwaria, to Rabbi Binyamin Leizer Yustman and Tzina Pesa (née Alter), daughter of the Chiddushei HaRim, the first Gerrer Rebbe. His mother died when he was young. Orphaned of his mother, he was brought up by his grandparents, Rabbi Yitzchak Meir Alter (the Chiddushei HaRim) and his wife. When he was about nine years old, his grandfather took him to visit the Kotzker Rebbe, an event which left a lifelong impression on him. He married Hendel Lea, daughter of his uncle Rav Avraham Mordechai Alter, in 1864.

RA'AVAN

Eliezer ben Nosson of Mainz (1090–1170) was a halachist and liturgical poet. As an early Rishon, he was a contemporary of the Rashbam and Rabbeinu Tam, and one of the earliest of the Tosafists. He was the son-in-law of Rabbi Eliakim ben Yoseph of Mainz, a fellow student of

Rashi. Through his four daughters, Eliezer became the ancestor of several learned families which exerted a great influence upon religious life in the subsequent centuries. One of his great-grandsons was Rav Asher ben Yechiel (the Rosh), father of Rav Yaakov ben Asher, author of the *Tur*. The work mentions the year 1152 and must therefore have been completed after that date. The year 1247, which appears on two copies, may be credited to later transcribers. In the subsequent centuries, Rav Eliezer came to be regarded as a great authority, but his work was little known. Not until its importance had been specially urged by the most influential rabbis of Poland—Rav Mordechai Yaffa, the Maharsha, and Rav Luntschitz (the Kli Yakar), among others.

RABBI AHARON LEIB SHTEINMAN

Aharon Yehuda Leib Shteinman (1914–2017) was born in Kaminetz and raised in Brisk. In Brisk, he attended *shiurim* given by Rabbi Yitzchak Zev Soloveitchik, the Brisker Rav. He also studied in Kletzk under Rabbi Aharon Kotler. He was widely regarded as the *Gadol Ha'dor* (leader of the generation) in the last few years of his life. He, along with several other rabbis, is credited with reviving and expanding the appeal of European-style yeshivas in Israel. Rav Shteinman was known for his extremely modest lifestyle. His apartment, on Chazon Ish Street 5, was sparsely furnished and had not been painted in many years. Until 2014, he slept on the same thin mattress that he had received from the Jewish Agency upon his arrival in Israel in the early 1950s.

RABBI AKIVA EIGER

Akiva Eiger (1761–1837) was an outstanding Talmudic scholar, influential halachic decisor, and foremost leader of European Jewry during the early nineteenth century. He was also a *mohel*. He was the rabbi of Märkisch Friedland, West Prussia, from 1791 until 1815, and for the last twenty-two years of his life, he was the rabbi of the city of Posen. He was a rigorous casuist of the old school, and his chief works were legal notes and responsa on the Talmud and the *Shulchan Aruch*. He was a determined foe of the Reform movement, which had begun to make itself felt in his time.

RABBI BEREL WEIN

Berel Wein (b. 1934) is an American-born Orthodox rabbi, *rosh ye-shiva*, lecturer, and writer. He authored several books concerning Jewish history and popularized the subject through more than a thousand audio tapes, newspaper articles, and international lectures. He was born in Chicago to a family descended from Lithuanian rabbis. His father, Rav Zev Wein, emigrated to the United States and served as a rabbi in Chicago until the 1970s. In 1955, he married Yocheved (Jackie) Levin. Rabbi Wein received *semichah* from Hebrew Theological College, which was founded by his maternal grandfather, Rabbi Chaim Tzvi Rubinstein. His main teacher was Rabbi Chaim Kreiswirth, and his personal mentors there included Rabbis Mordechai Rogow and Yisrael Mendel Kaplan. He was a student of the late Rabbi Oscar Z. Fasman in Chicago. He received a bachelor's degree from Roosevelt University in Chicago and earned a law degree from DePaul University. After passing the Illinois Bar, he practiced as an attorney in Chicago for a number of years. In 1964, Rabbi Wein accepted the pulpit of Beth Israel Congregation in Miami Beach, Florida, where he remained until 1972. He moved to New York City when he was appointed as executive vice-president of the Union of Orthodox Organizations of America (OU). Within that organization, he served as rabbinic administrator of the *kashrus* supervision division until 1977. At the same time, he founded Congregation Bais Torah in Suffern, New York, and served as its rabbi for the next twenty-four years. Rabbi Wein also founded Yeshiva Shaarei Torah of Rockland, with a large high school and a post-high school division in 1977. The yeshiva subsequently moved onto the grounds of his synagogue and he served as *rosh yeshiva* (dean) until his move to Israel in 1997. He and his wife settled in the Rechavia neighborhood of Jerusalem, where they became the *rav* and *rebbetzin* at Bet Knesset Hanassi. He is presently a senior faculty member of Ohr Somayach Yeshiva in Jerusalem, where he lectures to the mostly English-speaking student body. He also lectures extensively in Israel and abroad and writes a regular weekly column for *The Jerusalem Post*.

RABBI CHANOCH OF ALEXANDER

Chanoch Henoch HaKohen Levin (1798–1870) of Alexander served as the *rebbe* of a community of thousands of Chassidim during the "interregnum" between the Chiddushei HaRim of Ger and the Sfas Emes. Rav Levin was one of the leading students of the *rebbe* Reb Simcha Bunim of Peshischa. After the latter's death, he became one of the most prominent followers of Rebbe Menachem Mendel of Kotzk and the senior disciple of Chiddushei HaRim. Following the death of the Chiddushei HaRim in 1866, the bulk of his numerous Chassidim chose Rabbi Chanoch Henoch as the next *rebbe*.

RABBI EIZEL CHARIF

Yehoshua Isaac Shapiro (1801–1873), known as Rav Eizel Charif, was born in Glubki, near Vilna, and his first teacher was his father, Rav Yechiel. Rav Eizel was a child prodigy whose genius was recognized by the age of seven, and he was soon nicknamed, "The Iron Head" (presumably because he never forgot what he learned). He later earned the nickname Charif (the sharp one), although he claimed, in his humility, that it was only an acronym of Chatan Rav Yitzchak Fein (son-in-law of Rav Yitzchak Fein). In 1853, Rav Eizel was appointed rabbi of Slonim, the town with which he associated for posterity. In every town where he served, Rav Eizel somehow found time, despite his superhuman schedule of learning and writing, to engage in numerous communal and charitable activities. In addition, many *dinei Torah* (legal disputes) were brought to Rav Eizel for resolution, and he was one of the three judges appointed to rule on the dispute involving the leadership of the Volozhin Yeshiva.

Rav Eizel's nickname, Charif, alludes in part to his sharp sense of humor, which he readily used to humble those who he felt needed humbling and to criticize those whose scholarship was not up to par with the standard that he expected of Torah leaders. In particular, Rav Eizel was adept at making puns or plays on the words of verses and Talmudic statements. He authored eleven works including *Emek Yehoshua*, *Nachalas Yehoshua*, and a commentary on the Jerusalem Talmud, *Noam Yerushalmi*.

RABBI ELIEZER PAPO

Eliezer Papo (1785–1828) was the rabbi of the community of Silistra. He authored the *Pele Yoetz*, his most famous work, as well as *Elef Hamagen*, *Oros Eilim*, *Chesed La'Alafim* (on *Orach Chaim*), *Yaalzu Chassidim* (on *Sefer Chassidim*), and *Chodesh HaAviv*. One of his noted works is *Beis Tefillah*, which is filled with many different prayers for specific situations, including one for the welfare of the Jewish people. A Ladino edition was published in the 1860s, and a Hebrew version was printed in Jerusalem in 1968.

RABBI ELIYAHU ELIEZER DESSLER

Eliyahu Eliezer Dessler (1892–1953) was a rabbi, Talmudic scholar, and Jewish philosopher of the twentieth century. He was the *mashgiach ruchani* (spiritual counselor) of the Ponevezh yeshiva in Israel. Rabbi Dessler was a disciple of one of the main leaders of the Mussar Movement, Rabbi Simcha Zissel Ziv, best known as the Alter (Elder) of Kelm. His students edited his collected correspondence and ethical writings posthumously in the six-volume *Michtav Me'Eliyahu* (letter from Eliyahu), which alludes to the letter that the prophet Eliyahu sent to the King of Yehudah that arrived after Eliyahu ascended to Heaven in a chariot of fire, later translated into English and published as *Strive for Truth*. In Kelm, Eliyahu was a diligent student and received *semichah* (Rabbinic ordination) from his uncle, Rabbi Chaim Ozer Grodzinski, who was the spiritual leader of Orthodox Lithuanian Jewry until his death in 1939, and who rarely granted ordinations.

RABBI ELIYAHU KITOV

See above, *Sefer HaParshios*.

RABBI JOSEPH BER SOLOVEITCHIK

Joseph Ber Soloveitchik (1903–1993), Yosef Dov HaLevi, was an American Orthodox rabbi, Talmudist, and modern Jewish philosopher. As a *rosh yeshiva* of Rabbi Isaac Elchanan Theological Seminary at Yeshiva University in New York City, the Rav, as he came to be known (alternatively referred to as Rav Yoshe Ber by other rabbinic figures), ordained close to two thousand rabbis over the course of almost half a century. He came from a rabbinical dynasty dating back some two hundred years: his paternal grandfather was Rav Chaim Soloveitchik, and his great-grandfather and namesake was Rav Yosef Dov Soloveitchik, the Beis HaLevi. His great-great-grandfather was Rav Naftali Tzvi Yehuda Berlin (the Netziv), who, in turn, was a great grandson of Rav Chaim Volozhin. His father, Rav Moshe Soloveitchik, preceded him as head of the RIETS rabbinical school at Yeshiva University. On his maternal line, Rav Soloveitchik was a grandson of Rav Eliyahu Feinstein and his wife, Guta Feinstein, née Davidovitch, who, in turn, was a descendant of a long line of Kapulyan rabbis, and of the Tosafos Yom Tov, the Shelah, the Maharshal, and Rashi.

RABBI LEVI YITZCHAK OF BERDITCHEV

Levi Yitzchak Dervarmdiger (compassionate in Yiddish) (1740–1809), also known as the holy Berditchever and the Kedushas Levi, was a Chassidic master and Jewish leader. He was one of the main disciples of the Maggid of Mezritch, and of his disciple Rabbi Shmelke of Nikolsburg, whom he succeeded as rabbi of Ryczywół. Rav Levi Yitzchak was known as the "defense attorney" for the Jewish people, because he would intercede on their behalf before God. Known for his compassion for every Jew, he was one of the most beloved leaders of Eastern European Jewry. He is considered by some to be the founder of Chassidim in central Poland, and is known for his fiery service of God. Rav Levi Yitzchak was known to have had a very close relationship with Rabbi Schneur Zalman of Liadi, the first Chabad *rebbe*. Rabbi Nachman of Breslov called him the *Pe'er* (glory) of Israel.

RABBI MENACHEM MENDEL OF KOTZK

Menachem Mendel Morgenstern of Kotzk (1787–1859), better known as the Kotzker Rebbe, was a Chassidic rabbi and leader. Born to a non-Chassidic family near Lublin, Poland, he became attracted to Chassidus in his youth. He was known for having acquired impressive Talmudic and Kabbalistic knowledge at an early age. He was a student of Rav Bunim of Peshischa, and upon the latter's death, attracted many of his followers. The Kotzker was well-known for his incisive and down-to-earth philosophies and sharp-witted sayings. He appears to have had little patience for false piety or stupidity. The Kotzker Rebbe never published any works. He wrote many manuscripts, but he had them all burned before his death. Several collections of his sayings have been published, most notably *Emes Ve'Emunah* (truth and faith). One of his major students was Rabbi Mordechai Yosef Leiner of Izbica. From 1839, he lived in seclusion for the last twenty years of his life.

RABBI NOTA GREENBLATT

Nota Greenblatt (b. Elul 1925) was born in Washington, D.C., to Rav Yitzchak and Sarah Rivka (Applebaum), both of Brisk. Rav Nota is the leading and foremost expert in the writing and the laws of *gittin* in America. His family moved to Palestine in 1931 and returned while he was a teenager. Rav Nota learned with Rav Michel Feinstein and Rav Moshe Feinstein in MTJ. In 1946, Rav Nota traveled to Eretz Yisrael to learn, and was the first American-born *bachur* to learn in Israel after the Holocaust. Upon his return to America in 1949, still a single yeshiva student, he went to Memphis, Tennessee, and founded the day school. In 1950, he married a local girl and traveled throughout the United States under sometimes incredible circumstances to ensure a couple received a proper halachic *get*, Jewish bill of divorce.

RABBI REUVEN MARGOLIOS

Reuven Margolios (1889–1971) was an Israeli author, Talmudic scholar, and head of the Rambam library. Rabbi Margolios was born in Lemberg (now Lvov), then part of the Austrian-Hungarian Empire and now in Ukraine, and from 1918 to 1940 in Poland. After the passing of his wife, he emigrated to Israel in 1934, settling in Tel-Aviv.

RABBI SHIMSHON RAPHAEL HIRSCH

Shimshon Raphael Hirsch (1808–1888) was a German *rav* best known as the intellectual founder of the *Torah Im Derech Eretz* school of contemporary Orthodox Judaism. Rabbi Hirsch was born in Hamburg, which was then a part of Napoleonic France. His father, Raphael Aryeh Hirsch, though a merchant, devoted much of his time to Torah studies; his grandfather, Mendel Frankfurter, was the founder of the Talmud

Torah schools in Hamburg and the unsalaried assistant rabbi of the neighboring congregation of Altona. Rabbi Hirsch led the secessionist Orthodox community in Frankfurt am Main. He wrote a number of influential books, and for a number of years published the monthly journal *Jeschurun*, in which he outlined his philosophy of Judaism. He was a vocal opponent of Reform Judaism, and similarly opposed early forms of Conservative Judaism.

RABBI SIMCHAH BUNIM OF PESHISCHA

Simcha Bunim Bonhardt of Peshischa (1765–1827), also known as the Rebbe Reb Bunim, was the Second Grand Rabbi of Peshischa as well as one of the key leaders of Chassidus in Poland. Born in Vodislav, Poland, to a wealthy German Orthodox Jewish family, Simcha Bunim's childhood was defined by traditional Jewish values juxtaposed with the secular German cultural orbit. He is considered by some to have been an *illui* (child prodigy).

RABBI YAAKOV LORBERBAUM/NACHALAS YAAKOV

Yaakov ben Yaakov Moshe Lorberbaum of Lissa (1760–1832) was a rabbi and *posek*. He is most commonly known as the Ba'al HaChavas Da'as or Ba'al HaNesivos for his most well-known works, or as the Lissa Rav for the city in which he was Chief Rabbi. Rabbi Lorberbaum was the great-grandson of the Chacham Tzvi, Rabbi Tzvi Ashkenazi; he was therefore related to Rav Yaakov Emden (who was the Chacham Tzvi's son). According to one tradition, his father, Rabbi Yaakov Moshe, died before he was born, and his relative Rabbi Yosef Teomim, the rabbi of Bursztyn, brought him up. This accounts for the common name that both father and son share. Along with Rabbi Akiva Eiger and Rabbi Eiger's son-in-law, the Chasam Sofer, Rabbi Lorberbaum vehemently fought against the *maskilim*, the reformers of the Jewish Enlightenment.

RABBI YEHUDAH ROSANES/PARASHAS DERACHIM

Yehudah ben Shmuel Rosanes (1657–1727) was rabbi of Constantinople and son-in-law of Rav Avraham Rosanes. He took a very active part in condemning and denouncing the Shabbethaians, and he was one of the signers of an appeal to the German communities to oppose the movement. His major works were *Parashas Derachim* (Constantinople, 1727), a work containing twenty-six homiletic treatises on various subjects; a pamphlet entitled *Derech Mitzvosecha,* a treatise on the 613 commandments, based on the treatises on the same subject by Maimonides and others; and *Mishneh La'Melech* (1731), glosses and comments on Maimonides' *Mishneh Torah* which was later printed together with the *Mishneh Torah.*

RABBI YERUCHAM LEVOVITZ

Yerucham Levovitz (1873–1936), also known by his hundreds of students simply as the Mashgiach, was a famous *mashgiach ruchani* and *baal mussar* (master of Jewish ethics) at the Mir yeshiva in Belarus. Rav Yerucham was born in Lyuban, near Slutsk, to Avraham and Chasya Levovitz. He received his education in the yeshivas of Slobodka and Kelm. He was a disciple of Rav Nosson Tzvi Finkel and Rav Simcha Zissel Ziv of Kelm. Some of his better known disciples include Rav Shlomo Wolbe, Rav Chaim Shmuelevitz, Rav Aryeh Leib Malin, Rav Dovid Povarsky, Rav Abba Berman, Rav Zelig Epstein, and Rav Shimon Schwab.

RABBI YISRAEL SALANTER

Yisrael ben Ze'ev Wolf Lipkin (1809–1883), also known as Rav Yisrael Salanter was the father of the Mussar Movement in Orthodox Judaism, and a famed *rosh yeshiva* and Talmudist. The epithet "Salanter" was added to his name since most of his schooling took place in Salant, where he came under the influence of Rabbi Yosef Zundel of Salant. He was the father of mathematician Yom Tov Lipman Lipkin. At Lipkin's suggestion, the *mussar* writings of Rav Moshe Chaim Luzzatto, Rav Shlomo ibn Gabirol, and Rav Menachem Mendel Lefin were reprinted and popularized in Vilna.

RABBI YITZCHAK MEIR ROTENBERG/GERRER REBBE

See Chiddushei HaRim above.

RABBI YITZCHAK OF VOLOZHIN

Yitzchak Itzkowitz (1780–1849), known as Rav Itzele of Volozhin, was the son of Rav Chaim of Volozhin. Rav Yitzchak took over the leadership of the yeshiva upon his father's death in 1821. One of Rav Yitzchak's daughters married Rav Naftali Tzvi Yehuda Berlin, who headed the Volozhin Yeshiva after Rav Yitzchak's death in 1849. The dispute over Rav Naftali's eventual successor aroused concern among Russian authorities that the yeshiva could turn into a hotbed of revolutionary activity, and they ordered the closing of the institution in 1892, citing noncompliance with demands for secular studies as an excuse. The Volozhin yeshiva reopened a few years later but never recovered its preeminence.

RABBI YOSEF SHLOMO KAHANEMAN

Yosef Shlomo Kahaneman (1886–1969), known also as the Ponevezher Rav, was *rosh yeshiva* of the Ponevezh Yeshiva. He was a renowned Talmudic scholar, and a distinguished member of the Council of Torah Sages of Agudath Israel. Rabbi Kahaneman was born in Kovno, Lithuania, a small town of three hundred, of which about a third were Jews. At the age of fourteen, he went to study at the Telshe yeshiva, where he studied Torah until he was twenty, under the tutelage of Rabbi Eliezer Gordon and Rabbi Shimon Shkop. He then spent a half year in the Novardok yeshiva, after which he spent three years in the Raduń yeshiva, studying under the Chafetz Chaim and Rabbi Naftali Tropp.

RABBI YOSEF YOIZEL HOROWITZ/MADREIGAS HA'ADAM

Yosef Yozel Horowitz (1847–1919), known as the Alter of Novardok, was a student of Rabbi Yisrael Salanter, the founder of the Mussar Movement. Rav Horowitz was also a student of Rabbis Yitzchak Blazer and Rabbi Simcha Zissel Ziv, and he spent some time in Brisk, learning from Rabbi Chaim Soloveitchik. He established the Novardok yeshiva in the city of Navahrudak. Additionally, he established a network of yeshivas in Dvinsk, Minsk, Warsaw, Berditchev, Lida, and Zetl. Some of his discourses were recorded in the book *Madreigas Ha'adam* (stature of man). The most basic and important theme in his book is *bitachon* (trust in God).

RABBI YOSEF ZUNDEL OF SALANT

Yosef Zundel of Salant (1786–1866) was an Ashkenazic rabbi and the primary teacher of Rabbi Yisrael Salanter. As a young man, Zundel studied in the Volozhin yeshiva under Rabbi Chaim of Volozhin. Following Rav Chaim's death in 1821, Zundel would make trips to study with Rabbi Akiva Eiger. Rabbi Yosef Zundel of Salant died due to a plague and was buried on the Mount of Olives. Among the many instructions that Rabbi Zundel mentioned in his will were that no eulogies be held for him and no titles should be added to his name on the tombstone.

RABBI ZALMAN SOROTZKIN/AZNAYIM LATORAH

Zalman Sorotzkin (1881–1966), also known as the Lutsker Rav, served as the rabbi of Lutsk, Ukraine. He was a son-in-law of the Telzer Rav and *rosh yeshiva*, Rabbi Eliezer Gordon. In 1953, Chinuch Atzmai was formed and Rabbi Sorotzkin was chosen to head it. He was survived by five sons: Rabbis Elchanan Sorotzkin, author of *Leman Achai VeRe'ai* and leader of the Chinuch Atzmai; Baruch Sorotzkin, *rosh yeshiva* of the Telz yeshiva in Cleveland, Ohio; Eliezer Sorotzkin, founder of Kiryat Telz-Stone in Israel; Yisrael Sorotzkin, *rosh yeshiva* in Lomza and *Av Beis Din* in Petach Tikvah; and Benzion Sorotzkin, leader of Chinuch Atzmai. By the end of his life, he was noted for his leadership of the Moetzes Gedolei HaTorah (Council of Torah Sages, Agudath Yisrael). The main street in Jerusalem's Kiryat Itri neighborhood, Rechov Sorotzkin, is named after him.

RADAK

David Kimchi (1160–1235) was a medieval rabbi, Biblical commentator, philosopher, and grammarian. Rav Kimchi was born in Narbonne, Provence, the youngest son of Rabbi Yoseph Kimchi and the brother of Rabbi Moshe Kimchi, both also Biblical commentators and grammarians. His father died while he was still a child, and Kimchi was raised by his brother Moshe.

RADVAZ

David ben Shlomo ibn Avi Zimra (1479–1573), also called Radvaz after the initials of his name, Rabbi David ibn Zimra, was an early Acharon of the fifteenth and sixteenth centuries who was a leading *posek*, *rosh yeshiva*, chief rabbi, and author of more than three thousand *responsa* (halachic decisions), as well as several scholarly works. The Radvaz was born in Spain, and he was thirteen years old when his parents, like all Spanish Jews, were banished from Spain and settled in Tzfas. In 1517, the Radvaz moved to Cairo, where he was appointed Chief Rabbi of Egypt, a title he held for forty years. He was highly revered for his vast knowledge, integrity of character, and extensive philanthropy. Independently wealthy, the Radvaz was a successful merchant with business connections in other countries. The yeshiva which he founded and supported attracted many distinguished students, among them Rav Betzalel Ashkenazi and Rav Yitzchak Luria.

RAMBAM

Moshe ben Maimon (1138–1204), acronym for "**R**abbeinu **M**oshe **b**en **M**aimon" (our rabbi/teacher, Moses, son of Maimon). A preeminent medieval Sephardic Jewish philosopher and astronomer, he became one of the most prolific and influential Torah scholars of the Middle Ages, as well as a renowned physician. He was born in Córdoba, Spain, and died in Egypt, from where his body was taken to the lower Galilee and buried in Tiberias. His fourteen-volume *Mishneh Torah* carries significant authority as a codification of Talmudic law. Maimonides studied Torah under his father, who had in turn studied under Rabbi Yoseph ibn Migash, a student of Rabbi Yitzchak Alfasi.

RAMBAN

Moshe ben Nachman (1194–1270), commonly known as Nachmanides, was a leading medieval Jewish scholar, Sephardic rabbi, philosopher, physician, Kabbalist, and Biblical commentator. He was raised, studied, and lived for most of his life in Girona, Catalonia. He is also considered to be an important figure in the re-establishment of the Jewish community in Jerusalem following its destruction by the Crusaders in 1099.

RASHI

Shlomo Yitzchaki (1040–1105), today generally known by the acronym Rashi, was a medieval French rabbi and author of a comprehensive commentary on the Talmud and on the *Tanach*. Rashi was an only child, born in Troyes, Champagne, in northern France. Rashi has been claimed to be a direct descendant of David HaMelech. Rashi appeals to both learned scholars and beginner students, and his works remain a centerpiece of contemporary Jewish study. His commentary covers most of the Talmud and all of *Tanach*. Rashi's surname, Yitzchaki, derives from his father's name, Yitzchak. The acronym is sometimes fancifully expanded as **R**abban **Sh**el **Yi**srael, which means the "rabbi of Israel."

ROSH

Asher ben Yechiel (1259–1327), known as the Rosh, was an eminent rabbi and Talmudist, best known for his abstract of Talmudic law. He is often referred to as Rabbeinu Asher. The Rosh was born in Cologne and died in Toledo. His family was prominent for learning and piety; his father Rav Yechiel was a Talmudist, and one of his ancestors was Rabbi Eliezer ben Nathan (the Raavan). Rav Asher had eight sons, the most prominent of whom were Rav Yaakov (author of the *Arba'ah Turim*) and Rav Yehuda. The great teacher of the Rosh was Rabbi Meir of Rothenburg, who was captured and imprisoned. The Rosh raised a ransom for his release, but Rabbi Meir refused it, for fear of encouraging the imprisonment of other rabbis. Thereafter, the Rosh assumed Rabbi Meir's position in Worms.

SEFAS EMES

Yehudah Aryeh Leib Alter (1847–1905), also known by the title of his main work, the *Sefas Emes*, was a Chassidic rabbi who succeeded his grandfather, Rabbi Yitzchak Meir Alter, as the *av beis din* (head of the rabbinical court) and *rav* of Góra Kalwaria, Poland (known in Yiddish as the town of Ger). He succeeded the *rebbe* Rav Henach of Alexander as *rebbe* of the Gerrer Chassidim.

SEFER CHASSIDIM

Sefer Chassidim (Book of the Pious) is a text by Rabbi Yehuda ben Shmuel of Regensburg, a foundational work of the teachings of the *Chassidei Ashkenaz* (the pious ones of Germany). It offers an account of the day-to-day religious life of Jews in medieval Germany, and their customs, beliefs, and traditions. There is some debate as to who the author was. Some say *Sefer Chassidim* is not the product of one author, although it is greatly attributed to Rav Yehuda. It has been said that Rav Shmuel HaChassid is the author of the first twenty-six sections. In its present form, according to the historian Güdemann, the book contains three revisions of the same original work, of which Rav Yehuda is undoubtedly the author; and both the contents and language of the book indicate that it originated in Germany. Important additions were made also by Rav Yehuda's pupil Rav Elazer Rokeach, for which reason the authorship of the whole work has sometimes been ascribed to him.

SEFER HAPARSHIOS AND SEFER HATODAAH

Avraham Eliyahu Mokotow (1912–1976), better known as Eliyahu Kitov, was a rabbi, educator, and community activist. One of his works, *Sefer Haparshiyos* (1961–1976), is a rich, comprehensive set on the weekly Torah portions. Although it is mainly based on midrash and Talmud, early Biblical commentaries, and Chassidic texts, the imprint of the author is noticeable, and many of his own insights are blended into the text.

SHACH

Shabsi ben Meir HaKohen (1621–1662) was a noted seventeenth-century Talmudist and halachist. He became known as the Shach, which is an abbreviation of his most important work, *Sifsei Kohen* (lips of the priest), on the *Shulchan Aruch Yoreh Deah*. He married the daughter of the wealthy Shimon Wolf, a great-grandson of Rav Moshe Isserles (the Rama), and shortly after was appointed to the *beis din* as one of the assistants of Rav Moshe ben Yitzchok Yehuda Lima, author of the *Chelkas Mechokek*. He published his magnum opus, the *Sifsei Kohen,* in Cracow in 1646. Rav Shabsi HaKohen was born in Vilna, Lithuania, and died in Holleschau, Moravia.

SHELAH HAKADOSH

Yeshayahu ben Avraham Horowitz (1555–1630) was born in Prague, a disciple of Rav Moshe Isserles (the Rama). His most important work, *Shnei Luchos HaBris* (two tablets of the Covenant, abbreviated *Shelah*), is an encyclopedic compilation of rituals, ethics, and mysticism. The work has had a profound influence on Jewish life—notably, on the early Chassidic movement, including the Baal Shem Tov. Rav Horowitz also wrote the *Sha'ar HaShamayim* siddur (prayer book), which had an influence on the later Ashkenazic *nusach*. Rabbi Horowitz wrote that the eve of the first day of the month of Sivan is the most auspicious time to pray for the physical and spiritual welfare of one's children and grandchildren, since Sivan was the month that the Torah was given to the Jewish people. He composed a special prayer to be said on this day, known as the *Tefillas HaShelah* (the *Shelah*'s prayer).

SHULCHAN ARUCH

Yosef ben Ephraim Karo (1488–1575) authored the *Shulchan Aruch*, sometimes dubbed in English as the Code of Jewish Law, in Tzfas in 1563. It is the most widely consulted of the various legal codes in Judaism. Together with its commentaries, it is the most widely accepted compilation of Jewish law ever written. The *Shulchan Aruch* and its forerunner, the *Beis Yosef*, follow the same structure as the *Arba'ah Turim* by Rabbi Yaakov ben Asher. There are four volumes, each subdivided into many chapters and paragraphs: (1) *Orach Chayim*—laws of prayer and synagogue, Sabbath, holidays; (2) *Yoreh De'ah*—laws of *kashrus*, religious conversion, mourning, laws pertaining to Israel, and laws of family purity; (3) *Even Ha'ezer*—laws of marriage, divorce and related issues; and (4) *Choshen Mishpat*—laws of finance, financial responsibility, damages (personal and financial), and the rules of the *Bet Din*, as well as the laws of witnesses.

SOCHOTCHOVER REBBE

Avrohom Borenstein (1838–1910) was a leading *posek* in late-nineteenth-century Europe and founder and first *rebbe* of the Sochatchover Chassidic dynasty. He is known as the *Avnei Nezer* (stones of the crown) after the title of his posthumously published set of Torah responsa, which is widely acknowledged as a halachic classic. His only son, Rav Shmuel, author of *Shem Mishmuel,* succeeded him as *rebbe.* In his teens, he became a close *talmid* of the Kotzker Rebbe, who chose him as his son-in-law. He married the *rebbe's* daughter, Sara Tzina, in 1853. He and his wife resided in Kotzk for seven years, until the Kotzker Rebbe's death in 1859. During that time, he was known to sleep only two hours each day and dedicated the rest of his waking hours to Torah learning. His son, Rav Shmuel, was born in Kotzk in 1857. Rav Borenstein's other works include *Eglei Tal* on the thirty-nine *melachos* of Shabbos, unpublished *sifrei Chassidus,* and many writings in manuscript form, including *chiddushim* on the Rambam. Many of his Torah sayings to his Chassidim appear in his son's work, *Shem Mishmuel.*

TARGUM YONASAN BEN UZIEL

Yonasan ben Uziel is known as the author of *Targum Yonasan.* He is also said to have written a book of Kabbalah, known as *Migdanim.* He was one of the eighty Tanna'im who studied under Hillel the Elder. Yonasan ben Uziel's tomb is in Amuka, Galilee, near Tzfas, Israel. Traditionally, those who are unmarried visit this location seeking to be granted blessings, and in his merit, hope to find a marriage partner.

TUR

Yaakov ben Asher (1269–1343), also known as the Ba'al HaTurim as well as Rabbi Yaakov ben HaRosh (Rabbeinu Asher), was an influential Medieval rabbinic authority. He was born in Cologne and died in Toledo. He was the third son of the Rabbi Asher ben Yechiel (known as the Rosh), a rabbi of the Holy Roman Empire who moved to Castile due to increasing persecution of Jews in his native Germany.

TZROR HAMOR

Abraham Saba (1440–1508) was a *darshan* in Castile who became a pupil of Yitzchak de Leon. At the time of the expulsion of the Jews from Spain, he took refuge in Portugal, where he met with further misfortune. He fled to Lisbon, but before reaching there was told of a new order of the king decreeing the death of any Jew with whom a Hebrew book or tefillin were found. He hid his manuscripts and tefillin under an olive-tree and entered the city. His works include *Eshkol HaKofer*, *Tzror HaChaim*, *Tzror HaKesef*, and *Tzror HaMor*. *Tzror HaMor* is a commentary on the Torah, containing interpretations according to both the ordinary sense and the mystical method of the *Zohar*.

YADVANA RAV/SHAAR BAS RABIM

Chaim Aryeh Leib ben Yosef Fenster of Edvabno or Yadvana authored the *Shaar Bas Rabim*, was printed in Warsaw, 1911. He gathered over five hundred different sources and compiled a five-volume homiletical discourse on Chumash. He then published a work on the *haftarahs* and *megillahs* in 1914.

YALKUT SHIMONI

There is a debate as to who authored the *Yalkut Shimoni*. Most claim it was written by Rav Shimon Kara, who lived in southern Germany at that period, and the title HaDarshan was bestowed upon him. The *Yalkut Shimoni*, or simply *Yalkut*, is an Aggadic compilation on the books of *Tanach*. It is a compilation of older interpretations and explanations of Biblical passages, arranged according to the sequence of those portions of the Torah to which they referred.

About the Author

Rabbi Avraham Bogopulsky has been the rabbi of Beth Jacob Congregation in San Diego for twenty-five years. Born and raised in New York, he received his bachelor's degree in psychology from St. Thomas Aquinas and his *semichah* from Rabbi Berel Wein at Yeshiva Shaarei Torah. He continues to maintain a close *rebbi/talmid* relationship with Rabbi Leibel Reznick.

Rabbi Bogopulsky is involved with every part of the Jewish community in San Diego. He teaches at the local yeshiva high schools for both girls and boys. He maintains the current *eruv* in San Diego and administers the *kashrus* agency of the local Vaad. In addition, he provides pastoral care and leads the life-cycle events of his shul and community.

Rabbi Bogopulsky and his wife, Leah, raised five children in warm and sunny San Diego, who have since grown up, married, and moved to various communities in the United States and Israel.

לעילוי נשמת

ר׳ יהודה לייב בן יהושע העשל
ואסתר רחל בת נחום
בוגופולסקי

Dedicated by

THE BOGOPULSKY
AND MASLIANSKY FAMILIES

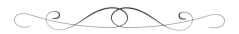

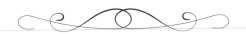

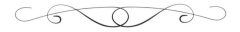

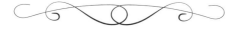

MORE BY THE SAME AUTHOR

Our time spent in yeshiva and seminary is fundamental to our lives, but our growth can't end in our youth.

HOW DO WE, SLOWLY BUT SURELY,
CHANGE OURSELVES?

HOW DO WE LIVE IN THE MODERN WORLD,
WORK AND RAISE CHILDREN,
AND GET CLOSER TO G-D?

HOW CAN EACH OF US DEVELOP
A TORAH PERSONALITY?

MOSAICA PRESS

BOOK PUBLISHERS

Elegant, Meaningful & Bold

info@MosaicaPress.com
www.MosaicaPress.com

The Mosaica Press team of
acclaimed editors and designers
is attracting some of the most
compelling thinkers and teachers
in the Jewish community today.
Our books are available around
the world.

HARAV YAACOV HABER
RABBI DORON KORNBLUTH